CANADIAN CURRICULUM STUDIES

CANADIAN CURRICULUM STUDIES

A Métissage of Inspiration/Imagination/Interconnection

Edited by Erika Hasebe-Ludt and Carl Leggo

CANADIAN
SCHOLARS

Toronto | Vancouver

Canadian Curriculum Studies: A Métissage of Inspiration/Imagination/Interconnection
Edited by Erika Hasebe-Ludt and Carl Leggo

First published in 2018 by
Canadian Scholars, an imprint of CSP Books Inc.
425 Adelaide Street West, Suite 200
Toronto, Ontario
M5V 3C1

www.canadianscholars.ca

Library and Archives Canada Cataloguing in Publication

Canadian curriculum studies (2018)
      Canadian curriculum studies : a métissage of inspiration/imagination/interconnection / edited by Erika Hasebe-Ludt and Carl Leggo.

Includes bibliographical references and index.
Issued in print and electronic formats.
ISBN 978-1-77338-055-1 (softcover).--ISBN 978-1-77338-056-8 (PDF).--
ISBN 978-1-77338-057-5 (EPUB)

      1. Education--Curricula--Canada. I. Hasebe-Ludt, Erika, 1951-, editor II. Leggo, Carl, 1953-, editor III. Title.

LB1564.C3C345 2018   375.000971   C2018-901300-1
                                                                 C2018-901301-X

Text design by Elisabeth Springate
Typesetting by Brad Horning
Cover design by Gordon Robertson
Cover image: *Encounters with Causal Earth*, by Darlene St. Georges

18   19   20   21   22   5   4   3   2   1

Printed and bound in Canada by Webcom

MIX
Paper from
responsible sources
FSC® C004071

Dedication

For Ted Tetsuo Aoki
the exemplary educator
who teaches us to sing
with playful purpose
in the midst of lingering
with curricular hope
for learning to live
with wellness and wisdom

Table of Contents

Acknowledgements   *xii*

About the Cover Art   *xiii*

Foreword: Revealing Interrelationality, Unearthing Histories, William F. Pinar   *xv*

Foreword: Walking in a Good Way With All Our Relations, Vicki Kelly   *xvi*

Editors' Ruminations: Opening to a Métissage of Curricular Provocations   *xviii*

Landscape Invocations, *Rita L. Irwin*   xxxi

MÉTISSAGE A: INSPIRATION: TOPOS/LANGUAGE/SOUND

A1.   As Long as the Grass Grows: Walking, Writing, and Singing Treaty Education, *Sheena Koops*   *2*

A2.   The Practicality of Poetry: A Meditation in 10 Tankas, 3 Sonnets, 2 Free Verses, and a Jazz Coda, *Anna Mendoza*   *11*

Provoking Understanding through Community Mapping Curriculum Inquiry, *Diane Conrad, Dwayne Donald, and Mandy Krahn*   18

A3.   Understanding Teacher Identity with(in) the Music Curriculum, *Katie Tremblay-Beaton*   *20*

Curriculum-as-Living-Experience, *Rebecca Lloyd*   26

A4.   Listening to the Earth, *Diana B. Ihnatovych*   *27*

Rumination on Pedagogical Rhythm, *Claudia Eppert*   34

A5.   Artful Portable Library Spaces: Increasing Community Agency and Shared Knowledge, *Amélie Lemieux and Mitchell McLarnon*   *35*

A6.   The Spacing of the Hegemonic *Chora* in the Curriculum of First-Language Attrition, *Wisam Kh. Abdul-Jabbar*   *47*

Old Mournings, New Days, *Robert C. Nellis*   **55**

A7.   Navigating a Curriculum of Travel through Geneva: Museums, Gardens, and Governance, *Rita Forte*   *56*

A8.   A Quantumeracy Reading List, *Kyle Stooshnov*   *66*

Reading the Water for the Wind: On the Remnants of Curriculum, *Lisa Farley and RM Kennedy*   *77*

A9.   The Character of Contemporary Curriculum Studies in Canada: A Rumination on the Ecological and Metaphorical Nature of Language, *Kelly Young*   *78*

Siren's Ghost Net, *Pauline Sameshima and Sean Wiebe*   *85*

MÉTISSAGE B: IMAGINATION: IDENTITY/ETHOS/SPIRIT

B1.   Provoking the Intimate Dialogue: A Path of Love, *Samira Thomas*   *88*

Three Invocations That Provoke: Strangler Figs, Madness, and Earthquakes, *Peter P. Grimmett*   *96*

B2.   Eros, Aesthetics, and Education: Intersections of Life and Learning, *Boyd White*   *98*

B3.   The Question Holds the Lantern, *Margaret Louise Dobson*   *108*

Curriculum Grammar for the Anthropocene, *Jackie Seidel*   *113*

B4.   Learning about Curriculum through My Self, *Shauna Rak*   *114*

B5.   A Response to *Still Dancing: My Bubby's Story*, *Bruce G. Hill*   *123*

Dear Canadian Curriculum Studies Colleagues, *John J. Guiney Yallop*   *130*

B6.   Rumi and Rhizome: The Making of a Transformative Imaginal
Curriculum, *Soudeh Oladi*   *131*

To Enchanted Lands, *David Lewkowich*   *140*

B7.   Theorizing as Poetic Dwelling: An Intellectual Link between Ted
Aoki and Martin Heidegger, *Patricia Liu Baergen*   *141*

Lane Muses, *Kent den Heyer*   *151*

B8.   Transitional Spaces and Displaced Truths of the Early-Years
Teacher, *Sandra Chang-Kredl*   *152*

B9.   Be/long/ing and Be/com/ing in the Hy-phens,
Veena Balsawer   *159*

Space for "Thinging" about Ineffable Things, *Wanda Hurren*   *164*

B10.   Religion, Curriculum, and Ideology: A Duoethnographic
Dialogue, *Saeed Nazari and Joel Heng Hartse*   *165*

Living with Generosity: A Rumination, *Anita Sinner*   *174*

B11.   Agency and the Social Contract: Algorithms as an Interpretive
Key to Modernity, *Sean Wiebe*   *175*

Nocturne, Curriculum, and Building a Bench, *Hans Smits*   *183*

MÉTISSAGE C: INTERCONNECTION: RELATIONS/HEALING/ PATHOS

C1.   "What Happened Here?": Composing a Place for Playfulness
and Vulnerability in Research, *Cindy Clarke and
Derek Hutchinson*   *186*

Viscera, *Celeste Snowber and Tamar Haytayan*   *199*

C2.   Conversations in a Curriculum of Tension, *Stephanie J. Bartlett and Erin L. Quinn*   *200*

C3.   Dwelling in Poiesis, *Shirley Turner*   *207*

"To Know the World, We Have to Love It," *David W. Jardine*   *224*

C4.   Provoking "Difficult Knowledge": A Pedagogical Memoir, *Mary J. Harrison*   *226*

C5.   Kizuna: Life as Art, *Yoriko Gillard*   *233*

Detention, *Elizabeth Yeoman*   *249*

C6.   Haunted by Real Life: Art, Fashion, and the Hungering Body, *Alyson Hoy*   *250*

C7.   Dadaab Refugee Camp and the Story of School, *Karen Meyer, Cynthia Nicol, Muhammad Hassan, Ahmed Hussein, Mohamed Bulle, Ali Hussein, Samson Nashon, Abdikhafar Hirsi Ali, Mohamud Olow, and Siyad Maalim*   *257*

Re-memoring Residential Schools through Multimodal Texts, *Ingrid Johnston*   *266*

C8.   The Melody of My Breathing: Toward the Poetics of Being, *Anar Rajabali*   *268*

C9.   Passing from Darkness into Light: A Daughter's Journey in Mourning, *Sandra Filippelli*   *280*

A Narrative Template for Making Room and Vitalizing English-Speaking Quebec, *Paul Zanazanian*   *290*

C10.   Provoking the (Not So?) Hidden Curriculum of Busy with a
            Feminist Ethic of Joy, *Sarah Bonsor Kurki, Lindsay Herriot, and
            Meghan French-Smith*   *292*

leaf spinning, *Susan Walsh*   *301*

Contributors   *302*
Index   *313*

Acknowledgements

We acknowledge the contributions and support of the following colleagues:

William F. Pinar
Professor and Canada Research Chair, University of British Columbia

Vicki Kelly
Associate Professor, Simon Fraser University

Natalie Garriga
Editorial/Production Manager, Canadian Scholars/Women's Press

Nicholas Ng-A-Fook
President, Canadian Society for the Study of Education (CSSE)

Tim Howard
Director of Administration, Canadian Society for the Study of Education (CSSE)

Robert Nellis
Co-President, Canadian Association for Curriculum Studies (CACS)

Margaret McKeon
Doctoral Candidate, University of British Columbia

About the Cover Art

Encounters with Causal Earth
Darlene St. Georges

Incipient oracle of the causal Earth
borderless and coherent
enchanting
generous
deserving
capable
compelling
lucid
laying claim on my grasp of love
stirring up impressions of
tranquility
solitude
unfolding my gaze
in/between dreams
with melodies of blooming hues
creation stories of
life
sacrifice
death
echoed by sparrows
in their misty playgrounds
lingering among shadows
transmuting through time
imprecise encounters
that leave you breathless
transfixed
vast

As a Métis artist, poet, researcher, and teacher I endeavour to explore, through an evolving ontological process, my deepening connection with All My Relations. A practice of contemplation is at the heart of my creative work, facilitated through encounters and experiences I have while photographing Earth's intricate places and spaces. Here, I am submerged in a multiplicity of colour, form, shadow and light, rememberings, sensations, epiphanies, dreams, and visions. My artwork invites the viewer in, to engage in these multi-textural dialogues in order to discover the realms of our delicate and complex interrelationship with Earth's creations.

Foreword

REVEALING INTERRELATIONALITY, UNEARTHING HISTORIES

William F. Pinar

It was a memorable and energizing event, the 7th Provoking Curriculum Studies Conference. Among the superb presentations—a number of which are published here, now complemented by "invocations"—was an event honouring the Elders. It was deeply moving, including in a literal way: Antoinette Oberg and her husband, Daniel, performed a dance dedicated to Bill Doll. It was moving symbolically, as the event recalled the first Provoking Curriculum Studies Conference, held in 2003 on the UBC campus (as Erika and Carl note). Ted Aoki was very much present at that meeting, asking (after my paper praising him): "Who is this Ted Aoki? I'd like to meet him." The spirit of provoking curriculum is conveyed in Ted's humour, serious and subtle, resisting (I thought) his repositioning into my view of him (however praising that view was), humbly acknowledging what I'd said while affirming the right to his own self-characterization. At least as early as the World War II relocation, Aoki knew that representation risked objectification. "Meeting" someone—as when Ted asked to meet the person I'd described—can perforate the abstractedness of objectification: subjective presence can show singularity. "Rapprochement" and "empathetic inquiry"—as Carl and Erika describe the mission of *métissage*—preserve the alterity that meeting both reveals and conceals, histories of violence submerged in the flesh, buried in the land, personified in the person. Braiding preserves particularity while at the same time encouraging the crafting of patterns that interweave singularities, revealing interrelationships and unearthing histories. My congratulations to Erika and Carl for conceiving a collection so congruent with the conference itself, documenting as it demonstrates provoking curriculum. Congratulations to the contributors: your individual threads shine brightly in the quilt to which you have contributed. If one draws near, one sees the individual threads—and the patterns they produce—in motion, disclosing their origins, imagining their destinations, positioning us as partners dancing to celebrate those in our midst, honour those no longer present, and welcome those who are yet to come.

Foreword

WALKING IN A GOOD WAY WITH ALL OUR RELATIONS

Vicki Kelly

Me: Why do I use a drum?
Old Woman: To touch the Earth.
Me: Then why do I sing with it?
Old Woman: To allow the earth to touch you.
Me: What am I singing for?
Old Woman: So that someday you might sing the one note that joins your heartbeat
  and the earth's heartbeat to the heartbeat of everything.
Me: You're saying drumming and singing, anything that leads me inward and then
  outward, are just like praying and meditating.
Old Woman: You are getting wiser, my boy.
(Wagamese, 2016, p. 93)

Boozhoo, Aaniin,
  It is indeed an honour to be asked to contribute a foreword to this important gathering of scholarship to represent the current fullness of our field in Canadian Curriculum Studies. What is a foreword, if not a portal through which a pathway flows on its way to accessing the spaces within. When I first encountered the manuscript, I was awed at the significance and complexity of its various interlocking texts. Thus, there is no one way into the heart of this work. Nor is there a single theme with variations, but an elegant and eloquent tapestry of texts interwoven through which one experiences a polyphonic chorus of urgent voices singing, ringing, reverberating through the gathering spaces found within the ecological landscape of the manuscript. There are a few things that have rung true for me in my reading. One is that this gathering of scholarship exemplifies what I have come to hold dearly, our field *is* our family, and our family *is founded* on friendship, respectful relations between deeply divergent scholars who understand their role as an honourable one. The editors acknowledge what I know to be true, that I am called to witness the earnest work of Education for Reconciliation, or Reconciliation through Educational Inquiry and Practice, at a time of great urgency and complexity within the country we now call Canada.

The second truth is that I am not alone in my witnessing. I am always aware that just behind me stand the Elders and Ancestors, watching and waiting to see if we will take up our work in the spirit of the ancient ones honouring the teachings of all our relations toward our essential work of being human. And also there, just in front of me, are the children to come, the next generations, also waiting and watching to see if our vision of our work, as curriculum scholars, is indeed clear and courageous enough to answer the call for healing and making whole of what has become dislocated, wounded, and injured though our actions.

The third truth is concerning what American curriculum scholar Maxine Greene (1978) acknowledges: that praxis is the radical participation in the transformation of the world. For this work of profound change we need *Spirited Inspiration* and *Visionary Imagination* that honour our *Sacred Interconnections*. The Truth and Reconciliation Commission of Canada (2015) acknowledged what many other countries around the world have had to acknowledge, that much harm has been done through education and it is now the time to make education a place for healing and transformation. The Calls to Action sound strong and clear, asking for shared action to transform our institutional spaces so they celebrate the vibrant diversity of our human community, and give agency to the call for attending to our reciprocal relations with the land so that we become wholehearted, walk in a good way, and are wisely aware of all our relations, as Blackfoot Elder Narcisse Blood often reminded us.

> There are periods when you exist beyond the context of time and fact and reality. Moments when memory carries you buoyant beyond all things and life exists as fragments and shards of being, when you see yourself as you were and will be again—sacred, whole and shining. (Wagamese, 2016, p. 98)

REFERENCES

Greene, M. (1978). *Landscapes of learning*. New York, NY: Teachers College Press.

Truth and Reconciliation Commission of Canada. (2015). *Honouring the truth, reconciling for the future. Summary of the final report of the Truth and Reconciliation Commission of Canada*. www.trc.ca.

Wagamese, R. (2016). *Embers: One Ojibway's meditations*. Madeira Park, BC: Douglas & McIntyre.

Editors' Ruminations: Opening to a Métissage of Curricular Provocations

Break out! Break from all safe
comprehensive arrangements
never completely comprehended by
controllers or controlled.
         (Margaret Avison, 2002, p. 79)

In February 2015 the 7th Biennial Provoking Curriculum Studies Conference was held at the University of British Columbia (UBC) in Vancouver. The first Provoking Curriculum Conference was organized at UBC in 2003 when conference participants examined a wide range of issues related to curriculum studies from personal, postmodern, postcolonial, political, performative, pedagogical, and poetic perspectives. The 7th Provoking Curriculum Studies Conference presented a unique opportunity almost 12 years later for scholars and educators to continue engaging creatively and critically with diverse conceptions, disciplines, goals, and understandings of curriculum studies. As conference co-chairs, together with a local and national organizing committee, we were especially keen to engage with provoking curriculum studies at this time and to recall Cynthia Chambers' (1999) four challenges for Canadian curriculum theory:

> to create curriculum languages and genres that name the sociopolitical, geophysical, and imaginative landscape in which Canadians live now, as well as the landscapes of the past and the future; to turn to Canadian scholars, indigenous languages, and traditions for that language and those genres; to seek new interpretive tools for understanding what it means to be Canadian and what Canadians might become in the 21st century; and, finally, to create curriculum theory that is written at home but works on behalf of everyone. (p. 137)

Into the second decade of the 21st century, the topographic landscape of our field has never been both more vibrant, verdant, and yet also threatened and compromised in the context of social, cultural, political, linguistic, and economic movements worldwide. The definitions of *provoke* include: to arouse, elicit, excite, generate, goad, induce, inflame, infuriate, instigate, kindle, madden, prick, prod, ruffle, stimulate, sting, and stir. The primary motivation behind the Provoking Curriculum Studies conferences is that curriculum scholars should always be provoking (and convoking, evoking, invoking, and revoking). This involves a movement toward a curriculum of *métissage* (Hasebe-Ludt, Chambers, & Leggo, 2009), one that seeks a rapprochement between divergent identities and histories (Donald, 2012), speaks and writes truthful stories as a form of empathetic inquiry (Chambers, Hasebe-Ludt, Leggo, & Sinner, 2012), and works toward retribution and reconciliation between these identities and histories, especially indigenous and non-indigenous traditions on this Canadian *topos* (Blood, Chambers, Donald, Hasebe-Ludt, & Big Head, 2012).

The first Provoking Curriculum Conference celebrated the teaching and scholarship of Ted Tetsuo Aoki (1993b/2005), who was always devoted to "provoking a discursively live moment" (p. 281) by investigating "the language of the lived curriculum, the more poetic, phenomenological and hermeneutic discourse in which life is embodied in the very stories and languages people speak and live" (1993a/2005, p. 207). Aoki described the "curricular landscape" as "a multiplicity of betweens" (p. 207) where "a multiplicity of lines moving from between to between, is ever open, knowing no beginning and no end, resisting enframing" (p. 207). Aoki's understanding of curriculum studies that resist enframing continues to represent the spirit of *Canadian Curriculum Studies: A Métissage of Inspiration/Imagination/ Interconnection*, which includes writing by scholars from across Canada, scholars who accepted our invitation to arouse, excite, kindle, and stir our individual and collective convictions, imaginations, practices, and stories. Aoki noted how curriculum theorists were opening "themselves to the realm of language, linguistics, discourse and narratives to understand their own field" (1992/2005, p. 264) in order "to consider language as the ground that makes possible the revelation of the life experiences of humans" (1987/1991/2005, p. 235). Aoki encouraged curriculum scholars to attend to the urgent task of recovering "the fullness of language" (p. 238). In this book the authors continue to take up Aoki's questions and convictions in diverse ways that honour curriculum studies as an ongoing complex and creative engagement with human being and well-being.

In addition to Aoki, the vision of curriculum studies represented in this book is inspired by a strong group of scholars who have held leadership positions in the Canadian Association for Curriculum Studies (CACS) and in our curricular community with Aokian poetic and pedagogical poise. The influence of these significant scholars continues to inform Canadian curriculum studies. They are all committed to innovative and creative approaches to understanding curriculum studies. Nevertheless, this book does not seek to emulate their scholarship as a model of exemplary scholarship that must simply continue to be promoted. Instead,

Canadian Curriculum Studies seeks to be inspired by the kind of radical, activist, artful, and innovative scholarship that they all represent while asking both old and new questions. Like William F. Pinar (2011), we understand curriculum as a "'complicated conversation,' an expansive definition of curriculum that includes dialogue and recognition, as well as incommunicability and misrecognition, each accenting ongoing subjective and social reconstruction" (p. 73). This concept of curriculum reminds us that the conversation is always ongoing, never conclusive, always interrogative. So, this collection of 30 essays examines and provokes the idea of curriculum studies as an interdisciplinary field across transnational contexts, with particular emphasis on Canadian educators' work. Both established and new scholars are included in the collection, illustrating the wide range of contemporary and leading-edge writing in the field. Curriculum studies are always personal, pedagogical, political, prophetic, plural, and polyphonic, and so the scholars who have contributed to this book are all theorizing, researching, and teaching curriculum studies in diverse voices that, on the one hand, resonate with one another but, on the other hand, sustain their singular originality.

The book is organized in three thematic sections. Each section is a métissage where related themes and topics are braided or woven together. These themes and topics open up affinities as well as juxtapositions within each braid and across the braids. The intention of weaving the writings in these ways is not to be exclusive or definitive but rather to offer an example of how métissage presents an expansive and creative tool for working organically with braiding diverse threads of text for writers, editors, and artists.

In addition, in the spirit of continuing the creative and critical dialogue of the 7th Biennial Provoking Curriculum Studies Conference and further highlighting the imaginative conversations that are abundant in our curriculum communities, we invited "invocations" into the métissage braids. We asked well-known curriculum scholars from Canadian universities to write succinctly about their ideas and hopes for provoking Canadian curriculum studies and evoking an inspiriting and imaginative call for reconnection, repair, reconciliation, and rapprochement of our land and people in this time. We received 21 invocations, including ruminations, letters, stories, vignettes, poems, postcards, images, and visual artifacts. We have mixed and juxtaposed these brief invocations throughout the book as further threads in between the métissage braids, to create an intricate and multi-textured weaving that we anticipate will raise many questions, memories, responses, and connections.

We see these luminous threads of wisdom as warps woven into the longer texts, as invitations to consider the potential of métissage to create affinities and a new kind of rapprochement across cultures and callings. In this spirit, true to the words of Margaret Avison in the epigraph to these ruminations, we encourage a non-linear reading and viewing of this book. Although we have assigned letters and numbers to the three main métissage sections and the braids within them for ease of locating the individual pieces for readers, this is not meant as a linear or controlled arrangement. Following the braiding from beginning to end is only one way of accessing the texts. We also invite readers and viewers to choose different entry points into the métissage sections, so that the braids can be worked in multiple ways, each time unfolding new ways of braiding and creating relationships between the writing and the images. Mindful of Chambers' (1999) challenges, this is also the way we see curriculum—as an organic, relational text that resists numerical or linear ordering and instead invites us to seek multiple meanings in between the textured languages and places present here.

This book is firmly situated within Canadian curriculum studies, a field we have both been associated with, published in, and served as executive members of CACS for many years. The title *Canadian Curriculum Studies: A Métissage of Inspiration/Imagination/Interconnection* reflects important genealogical and historical traditions as well as current trends in the field. While we do not claim to be representative of this entire vast field, we are confident that the collection will accomplish the goal of "provoking curriculum studies" in timely and substantive ways. Our selections of texts in this book have been made with a view toward respectful relations and dialogues between diverse scholarly backgrounds, including indigenous perspectives. This is indeed one of the most urgent tasks, not only for Canadian researchers but for educators across the globe. The conceptualization from a "métissage" perspective is uniquely Canadian in this context. The idea of métissage is to bring together indigenous and non-indigenous scholarship of diverse kinds, and it is finding a growing resonance across the field here and abroad (see Blood et al., 2012; Hasebe-Ludt et al., 2009; Ng-A-Fook, 2014).

The etymological origin of *métissage* comes from the Latin *mixticius*, meaning the weaving of a cloth from different fibres. In Greek mythology Metis was an ancient Titaness, the primordial figure of wisdom, descended from Gaia and Uranus, and married to Zeus. She was a figure of skill and craft, and a trickster goddess with powers of transformation who resisted notions of purity by weaving and blurring textiles. Métissage, derived from these origins, is thus an artful craft and practice, an active literary and pedagogical act of negotiating different texts, ones that are often conflicting or dichotomous. It is a political praxis of seeking to reconcile value systems and rediscover the wisdom of lost or forgotten origins. It is a way through which researchers and writers can reformulate understandings of self and other in ways that are a movement toward a rapprochement that is meaningful and appropriate for our times (Donald, 2012; Lionnet, 1989, 2001). In curricular and pedagogical contexts, métissage encourages genuine exchange, sustained engagement, and the tracing of mixed and multiple identities in "the complex and often 'messy' threads of relatedness and belonging" (Hasebe-Ludt et al., 2009, p. 1). Our use of métissage is an integral part of our ongoing scholarship, and this focus is respectfully represented in the book. Like the mythical Metis, métissage works against notions of purity by seeking affinities and resonances between text/iles without eliminating or disregarding the original individual threads (Chambers et al., 2008).

We understand that there are many approaches to Canadian curriculum studies, and we are actively involved in theorizing, promoting, and supporting those many approaches by provoking Canadian curriculum studies. Our own scholarship and the scholarship of the contributing authors are firmly situated within current and innovative approaches and connected with respective knowledge dissemination networks across Canada and beyond.

Based on our own work in the field and our knowledge of publications by many new, mid-career, and established scholars, we know that métissage and arts-based and performative-inquiry approaches represent many of the most current approaches to Canadian curriculum studies, along with strong and uniquely Canadian reconceptualist and post-reconceptualist orientations. The authors who have submitted articles for the book represent a wide range of curriculum scholars located in universities across Canada. They are pursuing research in many different areas that include traditional curriculum disciplines (such as science, social studies, music, and languages) as well as emergent and innovative disciplines (such as digital literacies, indigenous education, museum education, environmental education, and embodied education).

"To pursue life's passions, puzzles, and possibilities," muses Ronald J. Pelias (2004), "writers and readers benefit from a close association with a scholarship that is evocative, multifaceted, reflexive, empathic, and useful" (p. 12). These are the kinds of modifiers that characterize the approaches to curriculum studies in this book. For Pelias, "Evocative scholarship has language doing its hardest work, finding its most telling voice, and revealing its deepest secrets" (p. 12). Also, "multifaceted scholarship turns and twists, stands to all sides, considers; it looks under and over, searches from top to bottom, ponders; it walks around, digs into, and tunnels through before it acknowledges that it can never see it all," while "reflexive scholarship comes back around, points to itself in order to say this is where it stands, at least at this moment, with these qualifiers and with these questions" (p. 12). In turn, "empathic scholarship connects person to person in the belief in a shared and complex world" and "useful scholarship reaches toward an audience. It cares" (p. 12).

Our intent is not to include every subject area or issue that curriculum studies might address. Most authors in the book are subject specialists and their writing is informed by their disciplinary knowledge, but we are particularly excited that many new scholars are taking up curricular traditions and subjects in innovative ways, writing with a critical yet hopeful stance of theorizing from their multiple backgrounds while respectfully honouring those traditions that need to be remembered as important signposts in the topography of the field.

Our main goal in editing this book is to help contextualize Canadian curriculum studies in contemporary and cosmopolitan times. While no single book can address every topic that is connected to Canadian curriculum studies, this book provokes a lively and ongoing conversation about curriculum studies while addressing the wide-ranging issues that comprise the field. While some issues are addressed more specifically than others, *Canadian Curriculum Studies* aims to open up the themes and questions that characterize Canadian curriculum studies in national and transnational contexts. We are inspired by David G. Smith's (2006) conviction that "if the recovery of personal truth is a necessity in the age of globalization, so too is its possibility recoverable only in the context of relations" (p. 31).

As a way of honouring our relations to many other scholars, we offer *Canadian Curriculum Studies* into a conversation that includes many valuable publications in curricular and pedagogical scholarship with a focus on delineating the field of curriculum studies, such as W. F. Pinar's *What Is Curriculum Theory?* (2nd ed., 2012) and *International Handbook of Curriculum Research* (2nd ed., 2014); Darren Stanley & Kelly Young's *Contemporary Studies in Canadian Curriculum* (2011); Erik Malewski's *Curriculum Studies Handbook: The Next Moment* (2009); João Paraskeva & Shirley Steinberg's *Curriculum: Decanonizing the Field* (2016); David Flinders and Stephen Thornton's *The Curriculum Studies Reader* (4th ed., 2012); Susan Gibson's *Canadian Curriculum Studies: Trends, Issues, Influences* (2012); Nicholas Ng-A-Fook & Jennifer Rottmann's *Reconsidering Canadian Curriculum Studies: Provoking Historical, Present, and Future Perspectives* (2012); and Nicholas Ng-A-Fook, Awad Ibrahim, & Giuliano Reis' *Provoking Curriculum Studies: Strong Poetry and Arts of the Possible in Education* (2016).

Building on curriculum studies' long traditions of provoking, this collection draws attention to new and ongoing conversations in the field in a unique way. It especially highlights the creative, poetic, narrative, ruminative, performative, interactive, and imaginative nature of the field. Following the editors' earlier co-edited anthologies and special issues of curriculum journals (Chambers et al.,

2012; Hasebe-Ludt & Hurren, 2003; Hasebe-Ludt & Jordan, 2010; Hasebe-Ludt & Leggo, 2016; Hasebe-Ludt et al., 2009; Hurren & Hasebe-Ludt, 2014; Prendergast, Leggo, & Sameshima, 2009; Walsh, Bickel, & Leggo, 2015), we once again take up the challenges and potential of "curriculum in a new key" (Pinar & Irwin, 2005) by mapping curriculum and pedagogy in contemporary and cosmopolitan Canada. This book represents the importance of contributions by Canadian scholars to curriculum studies, marking its past, present, and future developments while reaching out to a larger cross-national audience.

With this book we stand on a bridge, and, like Aoki (1996/2005) reminds us, "on this bridge, we are in no hurry to cross over; in fact, such bridges lure us to linger" (p. 316). Provoking curriculum studies invites us to linger. It embraces Pinar's (2011) invitation: "Perhaps we can allow ourselves to go into temporary exile, to undergo estrangement from what is familiar and everyday and enter a third space, neither home nor abroad, but in-between, a liminal or third space" (p. 76).

What we call contemporary Canadian curriculum studies seeks to be at the cutting edge, the threshold of the topography of the field, while acknowledging our liminal connections to many traditions. Writing about reverence in philosophy, Paul Woodruff (2001) notes that "Socrates hides his meanings in inaccessible places" (p. 188). According to Woodruff, if Socrates "knows anything, he rarely admits it." Instead, "he twists and turns away from the role of a teacher, and if he has answers to the questions he asks, he seldom allows them to be unveiled" (p. 188). If curriculum studies were designed on the pedagogical practices of Socrates, what might they look like?

In the current culture of speed, John Tomlinson (2007) calls for "balance-as-control," which "is not about coming to rest." Instead, it is "a process of constant reflexive *re-balancing* in the face of contingency" (p. 158). According to Tomlinson, balance is "taking positive control of life" by being "capably and sensitively attuned to our fast-moving environment" (p. 158). He especially promotes the need to be creatively "flexible, responsive and resilient" (p. 159). This is the understanding of curriculum studies that is represented in *Canadian Curriculum Studies*. Instead of conceptions of curriculum that are devoted to filling teachers with more knowledge of disciplines and psychological development and strategies for classroom management, teachers need opportunities to foster healthy, holistic, and hopeful ways for living in the midst of the countless challenges that characterize the experiences of teaching and learning. We believe that a contemplative pedagogical attunement to "the sounds of pedagogy" (Aoki, 1991/2005) and a respectful reverence for the pedagogy of the land (Chambers, 2006) akin to indigenous and other sacred epistemologies (Latremouille et al., 2016) constitute a viable way of living with these challenges. As the contributors to this collection attest—with their ruminations, poems, essays, invocations, and images of mixed compositions—the call for understanding curriculum differently through new interpretive tools such as métissage, developed and honed here at home, has never been so resonant.

Jonathan Culler (1997) explains that theory is interdisciplinary, analytical, and speculative. He also notes that theory is reflexive—"thinking about thinking," and involves "a critique of common sense, of concepts taken as natural" (p. 15). Culler acknowledges that there is a considerable "hostility to theory" that he claims "no doubt comes from the fact that to admit the importance of theory is to make an open-ended commitment, to leave yourself in a position where there are always important things you don't know" (p. 16). We think that Culler's notions about theory are useful for imagining a hopeful vision for provoking curriculum studies. As Culler observes, the position of agnosticism, of knowing there is a great deal "you don't know," is "the condition of life itself" (p. 16).

So, while we engage in many traditions of curriculum studies, including teaching new teacher candidates how to design and compose engaging lessons and projects for supporting students in learning, we also invite teacher candidates to investigate their understanding of curriculum studies with a creative perspective steeped in imagination and contemplative theorizing and practice (Bai, Cohen, & Park, 2016; Hurren & Hasebe-Ludt, 2014; Walsh et al., 2015). We invite teacher candidates to ask questions, to inquire about issues of identity, representation, meaning, and agency in the processes of becoming teachers and learners. Ernst Bloch (2006) refers to "the terror of the desire to know" (p. 167). He thinks we need to promote more wonder. He is concerned that we do not keep up our "questioning wonder past the first answer" (p. 170). So, we take up Bloch's call to question more and provoke readers to consider the many questions that reside within the many métissage braids of the collection, to employ the book as a useful and creative guide for individual inquiry and collaborative exploration of interrelated issues that live in the curriculum field. As a possible framing for class discussions and other dialogues, the following heuristic may be one possible way to approach the book as a teaching/learning source:

The first strand, entitled "Inspiration: Topos/Language/Sound," addresses questions related to place, voice, rhythm, and text(s), juxtaposed with meditations on poetic and musical landscapes, communities, and ecologies. The authors and artists contemplate and ruminate on the ways in which language(s) and literacies of diverse kinds and modes shape teachers and learners, and vice versa; the ways in which thoughtful pedagogical action and reflection are influencing the topography of curriculum; and how curriculum is taught in a particular place/how it teaches us about place.

In the second strand, "Imagination: Identity/Ethos/Spirit," the authors and artists urge us to ask questions about the empathetic dimension and dialogical nature of curriculum. These questions reside in the inner life of the teacher as a compassionate, caring human being in relation with other beings in the world. These questions permeate the heart of curriculum through both deep contemplation and passionate agency.

The third and final strand of the book, "Interconnection: Relations/Healing/Pathos," addresses questions about the values teachers and their students live with, often in tension and with difficulty. How can curriculum provide a healing space for wounded souls and haunted spirits, through the arts and other transformative, loving acts that open up to true vulnerability, embodied knowing, feminist sensibility, and storied remembering? In all the interwoven braids, in all the multi-textured weavings, and in all the pointed and poignant invocations juxtaposed within the braids, we ask: How is curriculum related to imagination, creativity, and joy? Where is curriculum caring, compassionate, and curious? When is curriculum subversive, transgressive, critical, radical, and reparative?

IN/CONCLUSION

Mary Aswell Doll (2000) writes that "wisdom, not knowledge" is "education's only real concern" (p. xix). Like Donald E. Hall (2004), scholars and educators need to embrace a keen sense of their agency, of their "ability to act with intent and awareness" and "how we conceive of and define responsibility and culpability" (pp. 124–125) in "what is finally a creative act" (p. 130). In her book of poems *Robinson's Crossing*, Jan Zwicky (2004) writes about memory, nostalgia, mystery, landscape, history, and geography, all rendered through the language and perspectives of a poet and philosopher. In the poem "Night Driving," she writes:

> *Our headlights*
> *scoop a tunnel in the dark,*
> *and we drive into it.* (p. 70)

This is an apt analogy for the writing in *Canadian Curriculum Studies*, where the stories, poems, memories, ruminations, invocations, questions, metaphors, and essays are all inviting us to journey, especially in places that are unknown and cannot yet be seen. Audrey J. Whitson (2003) understands how the "illusion of belonging" has held her back in her life:

Wanting to stick with the old course. Afraid I won't find any companions
out in that wilderness beyond fences. Afraid that there are few maps for this
new terrain I've taken on, and what maps there are, I cannot read. (p. 29)

The scholars and educators in *Canadian Curriculum Studies* are eager to journey
"beyond fences." They call out to one another with inspiration, imagination, and
interconnection. By attending to questioning and conversation, we can all continue
to live our experiences as teachers and learners with a commitment to creativity and
inquiry and teaching as transformative and hopeful. The authors of this collection
continue the vibrant tradition of ongoing conversations about curriculum and the
people and places that have shaped the field. They provide a current and expanded
view of the complex field of curriculum studies at a time of unprecedented local and global educational, political, and environmental changes. They address a
Canadian and international readership about issues that matter to educators around
the globe and they point to innovative scholarship emanating from multiple places
in Canada. In their diverse voices, perspectives, orientations, disciplines, and experiences they offer an orientation to curriculum studies that is timely in the context
of our contemporary challenges, the history of the field, and the people who have
shaped it. They particularly acknowledge the importance of intergenerational and
intercultural dialogues at a time of unprecedented loss of wisdom traditions and
an urgent need for social and cultural healing and reparation.

Erika Hasebe-Ludt & Carl Leggo
May 2017

REFERENCES

Aoki, T. T. (1987/1991/2005). The dialectic of mother tongue and second language: A
    curriculum exploration. In W. F. Pinar & R. L. Irwin (Eds.), *Curriculum in a new key:
    The collected works of Ted T. Aoki* (pp. 235–245). Mahwah, NJ: Erlbaum.

Aoki, T. T. (1991/2005). The sound of pedagogy in the silence of the morning calm. In
    W. F. Pinar & R. L. Irwin (Eds.), *Curriculum in a new key: The collected works of Ted T.
    Aoki* (pp. 389–401). Mahwah, NJ: Erlbaum.

Aoki, T. T. (1992/2005). In the midst of slippery theme-words: Living as designers of
    Japanese Canadian curriculum. In W. F. Pinar & R. L. Irwin (Eds.), *Curriculum in a
    new key: The collected works of Ted T. Aoki* (pp. 263–277). Mahwah, NJ: Erlbaum.

Aoki, T. T. (1993a/2005). Legitimizing lived curriculum: Toward a curricular landscape of multiplicity. In W. F. Pinar & R. L. Irwin (Eds.), *Curriculum in a new key: The collected works of Ted T. Aoki* (pp. 199–215). Mahwah, NJ: Erlbaum.

Aoki, T. T. (1993b/2005). The child-centered curriculum: Where is the social in pedocentricism? In W. F. Pinar & R. L. Irwin (Eds.), *Curriculum in a new key: The collected works of Ted T. Aoki* (pp. 279–289). Mahwah, NJ: Erlbaum.

Aoki, T. T. (1996/2005). Imaginaries of "East and West": Slippery curricular signifiers in education. In W. F. Pinar & R. L. Irwin (Eds.), *Curriculum in a new key: The collected works of Ted T. Aoki* (pp. 313–319). Mahwah, NJ: Erlbaum.

Avison, M. (2002). *Concrete and wild carrot*. London, ON: Brick Books.

Bai, H., Cohen, A., & Park, S. (2016). Classroom as dojo: Contemplative teaching and learning as martial art. *The Journal of Contemplative Inquiry, 3*(1), 113–131.

Bloch, E. (2006). *Traces*. (A. A. Nassar, Trans.). Stanford, CA: Stanford University Press.

Blood, N., Chambers, C., Donald, D., Hasebe-Ludt, E., & Big Head, R. (2012). *Aoksisowaato'op*: Place and story as organic curriculum. In N. Ng-A-Fook & J. Rottmann (Eds.), *Reconsidering Canadian curriculum studies: Provoking historical, present, and future perspectives* (pp. 47–82). New York, NY: Palgrave Macmillan.

Chambers, C. (1999). A topography for Canadian curriculum theory. *Canadian Journal of Education, 24*(2), 137–150.

Chambers, C. (2006). "The land is the best teacher I ever had": Places as pedagogy for precarious times. *JCT: Journal of Curriculum Theorizing, 22*(3), 27–37.

Chambers, C., Hasebe-Ludt, E., Donald, D., Hurren, W., Leggo, C., & Oberg, A. (2008). Métissage: A research praxis. In J. G. Knowles & A. L. Cole (Eds.), *Handbook of the arts in qualitative research: Perspectives, methodologies, examples, and issues* (pp. 141–153). Los Angeles, CA: Sage.

Chambers, C. M., Hasebe-Ludt, E., Leggo, C., & Sinner, A. (Eds.). (2012). *A heart of wisdom: Life writing as empathetic inquiry*. New York, NY: Peter Lang.

Culler, J. (1997). *Literary theory: A very short introduction*. Oxford, England: Oxford University Press.

Doll, M. A. (2000). *Like letters in running water: A mythopoetics of curriculum*. Mahwah, NJ: Erlbaum.

Donald, D. (2012). Indigenous métissage: A decolonizing research sensibility. *International Journal of Qualitative Studies in Education, 25*(5), 533–555. doi: 10.1080/09518398.2011.554449

Flinders, D. J., & Thornton, S. J. (Eds.). (2012). *The curriculum studies reader* (4th ed.). New York, NY: Routledge.

Gibson, S. E. (2012). *Canadian curriculum studies: Trends, issues, influences*. Vancouver, BC: Pacific Educational Press.

Hall, D. E. (2004). *Subjectivity*. New York, NY: Routledge.

Hasebe-Ludt, E., Chambers, C. M., & Leggo, C. (2009). *Life writing and literary métissage as an ethos for our times*. New York, NY: Peter Lang.

Hasebe-Ludt, E., & Hurren, W. (Eds.). (2003). *Curriculum intertext: Place/language/pedagogy*. New York, NY: Peter Lang.

Hasebe-Ludt, E., & Jordan, N. (Eds.). (2010). "May we get us a heart of wisdom": Life writing across knowledge traditions [special issue]. *Transnational Curriculum Inquiry, 7*(2), 1–4. Available at: www.ojs.library.ubc.ca/index.php/tci/article/viewFile/2035/2182

Hasebe-Ludt, E., & Leggo, C. (Eds.). (2016). Canadian curriculum studies: A métissage of polyphonic textualities [special issue]. *Journal of the Canadian Association for Curriculum Studies, 14*(1). Available at: jcacs.journals.yorku.ca/index.php/jcacs/issue/view/2276

Hurren, W., & Hasebe-Ludt, E. (Eds.). (2014). *Contemplating curriculum: Genealogies/times/places*. New York, NY: Routledge.

Latremouille, J., Bell, A., Kasamali, Z., Krahn, M., Tait, L., & Donald, D. (2016). kistikwânihk êsko kitêhk: Storying holistic understandings in education. *Journal of the Canadian Association for Curriculum Studies, 14*(1), 8–22.

Lionnet, F. (1989). *Autobiographical voices: Race, gender and self-portraiture*. Ithaca, NY: Cornell University.

Lionnet, F. (2001). A politics of the "we"? Autobiography, race, and nation. *American Literary History, 13*(3), 376–392.

Malewski, E. (Ed.). (2009). *Curriculum studies handbook: The next moment*. New York, NY: Routledge.

Ng-A-Fook, N. (2014). Provoking the very "idea" of Canadian curriculum studies as a counterpointed composition. *Journal of the Canadian Association for Curriculum Studies, 12*(1), 10–69.

Ng-A-Fook, N., Ibrahim, A., & Reis, G. (Eds.). (2016). *Provoking curriculum studies: Strong poetry and arts of the possible in education*. New York, NY: Routledge.

Ng-A-Fook, N., & Rottmann, J. (Eds.). (2012). *Reconsidering Canadian curriculum studies*. New York, NY: Palgrave Macmillan.

Paraskeva, P., & Steinberg, S. (Eds.). (2016). *Curriculum: Decanonizing the field*. New York, NY: Peter Lang.

Pelias, R. J. (2004). *A methodology of the heart: Evoking academic & daily life*. Walnut Creek, CA: AltaMira Press.

Pinar, W. F. (2011). *The character of curriculum studies: Bildung, currere, and the recurring question of the subject*. New York, NY: Palgrave Macmillan.

Pinar, W. F. (2012). *What is curriculum theory?* (2nd ed.). New York, NY: Routledge.

Pinar, W. F. (Ed.). (2014). *International handbook of curriculum research* (2nd ed.). New York, NY: Routledge.

Pinar, W. F., & Irwin, R. L. (Eds.). (2005). *Curriculum in a new key: The collected works of Ted T. Aoki.* Mahwah, NJ: Erlbaum.

Prendergast, M., Leggo, C., & Sameshima, P. (Eds.). (2009). *Poetic inquiry: Vibrant voices in the social sciences.* Rotterdam, The Netherlands: Sense Publishers.

Smith, D. G. (2006). *Trying to teach in a season of great untruth: Globalization, empire and the crises of pedagogy.* Rotterdam, The Netherlands: Sense Publishers.

Stanley, D., & Young, K. (Eds.). (2011). *Contemporary studies in Canadian curriculum: Principles, portraits, and practices.* Calgary, AB: Detselig.

Tomlinson, J. (2007). *The culture of speed: The coming of immediacy.* London, England: Sage.

Walsh, S., Bickel, B., & Leggo, C. (Eds.). (2015). *Arts-based and contemplative practices in research and teaching.* New York, NY: Routledge.

Whitson, A. J. (2003). *Teaching places.* Waterloo, ON: Wilfred Laurier University Press.

Woodruff, P. (2001). *Reverence: Renewing a forgotten virtue.* Oxford, England: Oxford University Press.

Zwicky, J. (2004). *Robinson's Crossing.* London, ON: Brick Books.

INVOCATION

Landscape Invocations

Rita L. Irwin

Rita L. Irwin (2016). *Landscape invocations.* Acrylic painting

Turning the world end over end, upside down, downside up, close up, far away, side by side. An artist's eye sees the world differently, experiences the world in multiple ways, and in a post-human era, embraces the non-human and human, the material and the immaterial, in unexpected ways (Truman & Springgay, 2016). Invoking curriculum is about invoking an artist's eye within the world. Following walks along the Fraser River, I return home to experiment with paint, to think about the paths I have taken and those I have yet to take; the paths taken by animals and animal companions to other humans; the paths erased across time; the paths I should have taken; the paths I am not yet able to see. Invoking curriculum is seeing curriculum differently. Painting allows me to examine my relationship with the land and interrogate my paths with a view to healing my history, reconciling differences, and appreciating the potential of walking seen and unforeseen paths (Triggs, Irwin, & Leggo, 2014). Turning the world end over end, side-by-side, I invoke an invitation to the potential of painting for curriculum invocations.

REFERENCES

Triggs, V., Irwin, R. L., & Leggo, C. (2014). Walking art: Sustaining ourselves as arts educators. *Visual Inquiry: Learning and Teaching Art, 3*(1), 21–34.

Truman, S. E., & Springgay, S. (2016). Propositions for walking research. In P. Burnard, E. Mackinlay, & K. Powell (Eds.), *The Routledge international handbook of intercultural arts research* (pp. 259–267). New York, NY: Routledge.

MÉTISSAGE A

INSPIRATION: TOPOS/LANGUAGE/SOUND

A1

As Long as the Grass Grows: Walking, Writing, and Singing Treaty Education

Sheena Koops

TREATY WALKING AND SONGWRITING

I am sitting on a comfy rose chair in my home, black guitar strapped around my neck. I look onto a hill of aspen, glowing with sunlit snow. Beneath the snow there is green grass, and at the bottom of the coulee, the ice on Mission Lake will melt soon, flowing down the Qu'Appelle Valley in Treaty Four Territory near Fort Qu'Appelle, Saskatchewan, Canada.

It is late January, 2015. In my journal I have written, "As Long as the Grass Grows: A Treaty Song from Saskatchewan." I am preparing my presentation, "Treaty Walks: An Unsettling Journey from Bully to Benevolence and White Back Again," for February's Provoking Curriculum Studies Conference in Vancouver (Koops, 2015). I am a settler-descendant Canadian learning about Treaties.

In July 2011, I had written in my morning pages, "I should get in better shape. I should walk to school for a year. And as I walk, I should meditate on the Treaties." In 2008, the Saskatchewan government mandated Treaty Education; however, I knew nothing about the Treaties. In fact, my master's thesis, *Blue Eyes Remembering Toward Anti-Racist Pedagogy* (Koops, 2007), examined my whiteness, living on and off reserve, but I never mentioned Treaties.

On August 29, 2011, I wrote my first *Treaty Walks* blog post, and the next morning I walked—the first of 200 walks to and from school—through the heart of Treaty Four territory, meditating on the Treaties. The next year I *Treaty-Walked* about 100 times, and since then, Treaty awareness walks with me everywhere, but I seldom take time to blog. I am overwhelmed with Treaty awareness. How can I continue to write for two, three, four hours per day to unpack this growing reality?

Here I sit, with my guitar on my knee, trying to pull my Treaty story together. Trying to say something I've not been able to say for two years now.

The chorus has a simple, minor tune, built on a poetic *hendiatris*, attributed to Lieutenant Governor Morris, the Crown's Treaty negotiator: "As long as the grass grows, as long as the sun shines, as long as the river flows, through this *heart* of mine" (Koops, 2015). Then, in a second sweep of these lines, I replace *heart* with *land*. Just as the phrase "Peace, Order and good Government" (Constitution Act 1867, Section 91) articulates Canada's commitment to justice, this Treaty *hendiatris* is clear; the Treaties are to be honoured forever. I continue into the first verse, establishing the significance of Treaty:

> *They are living documents, First Peoples and the Crown*
> *Building blocks of Canada, to which we are bound*
> *Sacred agreements, the pipe and the pen*
> *Brother to Brother, peace—good order to men.*

I am especially happy with "the pipe and the pen." First Nations peoples have explained the spirituality of the pipe to us, and we, as settler-descendants, hold our signatures sacred, our contracts, our word.

The second verse further quotes Morris in a found poem, recorded in the Office of the Treaty Commissioner (OTC) (2008):

> *My Indian brothers of the plains, I shake hands with you today,*
> *I shake hands in my heart, God has given us a good day.*
> *I trust His eye is upon us, and all that we do,*
> *will be for the benefit of His children, Lieutenant Governor Morris told this to ...* [1]

In verse 3, Chief Ben Pasqua represents the other side of the iconic Treaty medal handshake. Keitha Brass, to whom I dedicated my *Treaty Walks*, is the great-granddaughter of this Treaty signator; she is the second-oldest of his living relatives. I have known Keitha for over 10 years, and she has become a big sister to me. I am learning more about her great-grandfather through the song in Bob Beal's (2007) article "An Indian Chief, an English Tourist, a Doctor, a Reverend, and a Member of Parliament: The Journeys of Pasqua's Pictographs and the Meaning of Treaty Four":

Chief Ben Pasqua, he was there, September 1874
On the Pasqua Pictograph, he documented Treaty Four
Now his great-granddaughter honours me as her friend.
We shake hands in our hearts, wîtaskêwin.

The next two verses, 4 and 5, tell the story that has led to our current Treaty reality:

But the Indian Act came along, Treaty broken across the land
Residential School stole the children, systemic racism played its hand
And the settlers, we closed our eyes, with worries of our own
And the Treaties we've forgotten, as history has shown.

Well, it's time we opened up our eyes, promise breakers be no more.
This land we call Canada, from shore to shore to shore
Is calling us to honour, our word, our law, our truth.
We are the seventh generation.[2] If not us, then who?

Verses 2 to 5 take us from the dream of Treaty to the tragedy of broken Treaty, and leave us with the question of responsibility. I have spent the last four years beginning to decolonize (Donald, 2012), unsettle (Regan, 2010), and indigenize (Pete, Schneider, & O'Reilly, 2013) our shared Canadian past, present, and future.

I end the chorus, "As long as the river flows, through this land of mine." I add an echo, "... of ours."

But the song is not finished. I want to use the three *Nêhiyaw itwêwina* (Cree words of saying, or ways of expressing) from the OTC (2008)—*miyowîcêhtowin, pimâcihowin,* and *wîtaskêwin*—which were present at the Treaty negotiations; these concepts hold hope as we consider our Treaty responsibility.

Getting along with others, miyowîcêhtowin.
Making a living, pimâcihowin.
We are one with the land,[3] wîtaskêwin.
We are the people of Turtle Island, the Treaty makes us kin.

I sing the chorus once more, and the last line does not say "this land of mine" but is fully replaced by "this land of ours." I remember Terence Kasagan, a former student from Treaty Eight territory in Black Lake, who wrote a Facebook reply on October 7, 2013, "The land belongs to no man, we belong to the land," after my post, "Thank you for sharing the land." I have heard Terence's worldview before from Dene Elders.

GO FORTH AND BE AWKWARD

Soon report cards are on, and I am writing new blog posts for the 2015 conference in February. I know Kētē-ayah (Elder) Alma Poitras, a fluent *Nēhiyawak* speaker, and she has invited me to follow protocol with her any time I have a question, to bring a little tobacco to ask for her help in a good way. I should take Kētē-ayah Alma tobacco, I think, but now I am on the plane, heading for Vancouver, with no text or call to Alma. Maybe I will leave out the three *Nēhiyaw-itwēwina* at the conference.

I am singing my Treaty song in Vancouver. I pronounce the three *Nēhiyaw-itwēwina* incorrectly, and afterwards, I confess my mistakes. Julie Vaudrin-Charette from the University of Ottawa raises her hand and thanks me for teaching her the meaning of these indigenous words, and doing my best to pronounce them and situate them in context, as a first step of advocacy for indigenous language to thrive.

Back from the conference, I am cooking at Fort Qu'Appelle's fiddle camp during the Easter break. I get an email from Gord Barnes with Regina's Amnesty International Human Rights Radio with an invitation to be a guest that Friday in Regina.

As I am driving into Regina for the radio show, I cannot bear the thought of not having at least started the conversation around the three *Nēhiyaw-itwēwina*. I pull over on the highway and text a friend, Mike Cook, my daughter's best friend's dad, and I text Kētē-ayah Alma Poitras; both are fluent in their dialects as *Nēhiyawak* speakers.

Within 15 minutes, both have answered my text. I pull over again to talk with Mike; I make phonetic notes; he then calls my phone, leaving a voicemail, enunciating the words so I will have backup on the radio. Alma also calls, and after talking for a bit, she reminds me of protocol and tells me a story about herself rushing through something. "That's when things unravel," she says.

When I am on the radio, I talk about the Treaties and settler-descendant responsibility. Then I sing the song, sing the words wrong, then use the story as an example of my awkwardness, my backwardness in being an ally, and the generosity of our Treaty partners.

The next week Kētē-ayah Alma and I meet for breakfast. Over coffee, I offer Alma tobacco and ask for her help. Alma's soft voice softens even more, and she explains how wonderful it is to follow this protocol and what good things will come.

We order bacon and eggs. Delma, Alma's sister, joins us. The sisters talk *Nēhiyawak*, and I see Alma pat the tobacco with her hand, and Delma says, "Ahh," and nods.

At a lull in the conversation, I pull out the lyrics and ask if I can read through them. The sisters nod and listen. They offer detailed explanations. "Treaties are not only for us, as humans, but also the animals, medicines, and plants, all living elements, all my relations are included in the concept of *miyowîcêhtowin*, in a caring relationship, giving back good things for the future, to even make sacrifices as we are getting along with others" (A. Poitras & D. Poitras, personal communication, April 2015).

The conversation between the sisters is animated as they discuss *pimâcihowin*. "*Pi-ma* means going about," says Alma. "Going about, living, at that time, there were no boundaries. Going from place to place; it must have been when they followed the buffalo. They weren't sedentary people. They made a living from season to season, moving to different areas" (A. Poitras & D. Poitras, personal communication, April 2015).

Soon we are talking about *wîtaskêwin*. I have used the phrase "Living together on the land" from my reading in the OTC (2008), but Kētē-ayah Alma and Delma prefer "We are one with the land." Alma explains, "The elements are most important, then the plant life, animal life, and then human life. We can't live without the elements, plant life, and animal life, but they don't need us to survive, but we are the ones that are doing all the damage" (A. Poitras, personal communication, April 2015).

We are now finished our breakfast.

"Let's go outside and I'll sing the song for you," I say.

These lovely sisters sit on the tailgate of my truck and I sing. The wind is blowing, trucks and cars are driving by on the highway. The women nod as the verses go by and soon join in on the chorus.

I get to the final verse and we stop, mid-song, and workshop the three *Nēhiyaw-itwēwina*. Sitting on the tailgate, singing, we laugh a lot, call ourselves Rock Stars.

As the sisters gain confidence in the rhythm of the song, and as we sing the last verse, "the treaty makes us kin," Alma shouts out in perfect timing, "*wâhkôhtowin*." She tells me that this is the word for kinship, for relationship.

SINGING TREATY EDUCATION

I play the song in my guitar class during circle time, the four *Nēhiyaw-itwēwina* written phonetically on the whiteboard. The kids strum and sing along. The majority of the class is indigenous: Métis, Nēhiyawak, Nahkawē (Saulteaux), and Dakota (Sioux). One boy and I are European settler-descendants. Two students are recent immigrants from Korea. For our final assessment my students and I have organized a coffee house performance, and each of us will choose one song. I choose my Treaty song.

It is the beginning of July and I have been invited to return to Human Rights Radio; Kētē-ayah Alma and two of my students will join us: Yeongkwang, from Korea, and Felicity, whose family comes from Peepeekisis First Nation.

On air, we give tobacco to Kētē-ayah Alma and the interview begins in a good way. Alma explains the importance of *miyowîcêhtowin, pimâcihowin, wîtaskêwin,* and *wâhkôhtowin*. I confess my mispronunciation and protocol breach, but celebrate how far we have come. Then we sing the song.

Alma has invited me to a sweat, a prayer ceremony for her daughter Evelyn Poitras' Treaty Law School at First Nations University of Canada (FNUC) in Regina. We pray for the people, for our good relationships, for our families, and for the Treaties to be honoured. In the third round, in the dark and heat, I am asked to sing my song. I sit up straight. I sing every verse. I hear weeping. I hear "hei hei." I hear "mmm." After I am done with the song, I lie down in the darkness, my face close to the edge of the lodge where the air is one wisp less than smoldering.

"You have done things in a good way, now," says Alma at the end of round three. "Good things will come from that song. It will be different now."

At the Treaty Law School, we sit in a circle in the glass ceremonial tipi at FNUC. Kētē-ayah Alma is leading a pipe ceremony. We hear of reconciliation. We hear of broken families because of broken Treaties. In the afternoon, James Daschuk (2013) shares highlights from his book *Clearing the Plains: Disease, Politics of Starvation, and the Loss of Aboriginal Life*. Alma and I share our song.

Before I know it, I am back in the classroom; I wonder if I can make a YouTube video with the song. I pull up pictures from *Treaty Walks*. Six hours later, I have not moved, but I have made my first video (see Koops, 2015).

The leaves are turning yellow. The Treaty Four Gathering is in town, celebrating the September 15, 1874, signing in Fort Qu'Appelle. I have made arrangements to teach from the grounds all week, a living library, in my new role as Teacher Librarian.

My Native Studies classes are big and diverse. In preparation for the gathering, I give my Grade 10 students copies of the Treaty song lyrics. I tune my guitar. They are not settling down. I wait. When they settle, I start, but the kids are restless. I stop. Tears in my eyes. "I cannot sing this song unless there is respect in the room," I say. I am scolding and it feels wrong. We are all unsettled. I pull up the YouTube video. The kids listen and then write 10 new things they have learned about Treaty Four.

At the Treaty Four Gathering, the trees are turning the hills orange and yellow. Kētē-ayah Alma has brought her small group of students from Ocean Man

First Nation, where she has been teaching for the past year; many Grade 8s flank Alma and me. We sing together. People wander by. Some stop to listen.

The fall turns into blustery winter and I am enjoying the energy that four interns are bringing to our staff. Brooklyn Orban, my husband's intern, tells me that she has made an Arts-Education activity from my song. When I visit the hallway display, I see Grade 9s have used the lyrics to make found poetry.

It is February again, 2016, when Yeongkwang asks me, "Mrs. Koops, are we all Treaty people?" I am surprised to learn that this is a question on the University of Saskatchewan's application. I remind him of the Treaty song from guitar class and we look at the lyrics.

I remember guitar class last spring. We practiced the song at least once a day, but at the coffee house, despite all the extra preparations, when the big performance came, I lost the words and lost my place in the song. I remember saying into the microphone, "Felicity, did I sing verse two yet?"

I remember Kētē-ayah Alma's sweat lodge. As she was making preparations, she occasionally asked her daughters, two of whom are also pipe carriers, if she had remembered the order correctly. "No," she told herself once, "I've done that backwards. But it's okay to make mistakes. This reminds us that we are pitiful people."

Alma's daughter Evelyn told me that Alma is sometimes a backwards person. I remember my mother's counter-intuitive teaching, "If it's worth doing, it's worth doing poorly."[4] At different times in my Treaty story, I have got the protocol backwards, the words incorrect, the delivery tentative, but this has not stopped beautiful things from happening.

As I am learning to be an ally, I often share a benediction, "Go forth and be awkward," because ally work is not begun by perfect or perfectly prepared people. I may even go so far as to say, if you are not aware of your awkwardness, what are you doing wrong? Maybe this is just my backwards self-talk as the grass pokes through the snow again this spring, and I continue walking, writing, and singing Treaty Education.

NOTES

1.   Morris says these words at the 1876 Treaty Six negotiations. They may or may not have been used in Treaty Four, where Chief Ben Pasqua signed; however, there is an understanding that what was said at any of the numbered Treaties applies to all numbered Treaties.

2.   I first heard Beth Cuthand's poem "Four Songs for the Fifth Generation" while taking a creative writing class at the Saskatchewan Indian Federated College (which is now the First Nations University of Canada) with Beth Cuthand and Gail Bowen in 1988. Since then I have heard teaching around the concept of the seventh generation, and that all decisions should be mindful

of seven generations. In Treaty negotiations, they say the women reminded the negotiators to remember the children and their children's children. Also, my friend Mike Cook says that the Seventh Generation is the now-or-never generation, for language retention, especially.

3.   Kētē-ayah Alma thought we should change "Living together on the land" (OTC, 2008) to "We are one with the land."

4.   Mom tells me that she is quoting G. K. Chesterton. A quick internet search tells me that he is credited with saying, "Anything worth doing is worth doing badly."

REFERENCES

Beal, B. (2007). An Indian chief, an English tourist, a doctor, a reverend, and a member of parliament: The journeys of Pasqua's pictographs and the meaning of Treaty Four. *The Canadian Journal of Native Studies*, 27(1), 109–188.

Constitution Acts, 1867 to 1982 (A consolidation of the). Section 91. (2012). Ottawa, ON: Department of Justice Canada. Retrieved February 29, 2016, from: laws-lois. justice.gc.ca/PDF/CONST_E.pdf

Daschuk, J. (2013). *Clearing the plains: Disease, politics of starvation, and the loss of Aboriginal life*. Regina, SK: University of Regina Press.

Donald, D. (2012). Forts, colonial frontier logics, and Aboriginal-Canadian relations: Imagining decolonizing educational philosophies in Canadian contexts. In A. A. Abdi (Ed.), *Decolonizing philosophies of education* (pp. 91–111). Rotterdam, The Netherlands: Sense Publishers.

Koops, S. (2007). *Blue eyes remembering toward anti-racist pedagogy*. (Unpublished master's thesis). University of Regina, Saskatchewan.

Koops, S. (2015, February 20). As long as the grass grows: A Treaty song from Saskatchewan. [YouTube video]. Available at: www.youtube.com/watch?v=CQ2qI2SKzpA

Koops, S. (2016, July 9). Viewing the Pasqua Pictograph with Keitha Brass. Available at: treatywalks.blogspot.ca/2016/07/viewing-pasqua-pictograph-with-keitha.html

Morris, A. (1876). Treaty 6 negotiations. Available at: firstpeoplesofcanada.com/fp_trea-ties/fp_treaties_treaty6.html

Morris, A. (1880/1971). *The Treaties of Canada with the Indians of Manitoba and the North-West Territories*. Toronto, ON: Coles Canadiana Company.

Office of the Treaty Commissioner. (2008). *Treaty essential learnings: We are all Treaty people*. Saskatchewan.

Pasqua, B. (1874). Pictograph housed at the Royal Saskatchewan Museum, Regina, Saskatchewan.

Pete, S., & Cappello, M. (2014). SAFE Conference Keynote Address. University of Regina.

Pete, S., Schneider, B., & O'Reilly, K. (2013). Decolonizing our practice—Indigenizing our teaching. *First Nations Perspectives, 5*(1), 99–115.

Regan, P. (2010). *Unsettling the settler within: Indian residential schools, truth telling, and reconciliation in Canada.* Vancouver, BC: University of British Columbia Press.

A2

The Practicality of Poetry: A Meditation in 10 Tankas, 3 Sonnets, 2 Free Verses, and a Jazz Coda

Anna Mendoza

I.
To make something
practical, practitioners
must consider both
      place *and* historicity.[1]
To be practical, action

must be steeped in
what feeds, clothes, and shelters
us each day, as we
inhabit a given place.
The creation of every

curriculum of place
involves these four dimensions:
first, an expanded
sense of time past the current
lesson plan, unit, semester

or term, longer than
the scope, phase, or budget year
in question. People learn
what's appropriate to do
in a place over centuries.

Second, they become
skilled through actions requisite
to their survival
    and through that process become
themselves. Enskillment *is not*

mere skilling, since
the line dissolves between
dancer and dance,
as Yeats[2] once observed, noting
we teach children "to cipher,

study reading-books ...
cut, sew, be neat in everything
in the best modern way."
These "generalizable" skills
are no longer bound to place.

The third dimension
    entails paying attention—
watching, listening
which build relationships since
these acts mean perceptual

and intellectual
    engagement with who's being
    watched or listened to;
learning to watch and hear those
in this place is enskillment.

The fourth dimension
is wayfinding: becoming
enskilled together,
people find the common ground
necessary to survive.

II.
From 10 to 11, every other day
fifteen undergrads and Professor Briggs
pored over and exchanged their thoughts on page
after page of poetry in two brick-
like anthologies: from Beowulf
in September to "living greats" in May.
Contentedly, we let ourselves be engulfed
in his expressive recital, arranged
in a circle no text message could break.
To say Anne and John were two compass legs
was not to say, "Look there, a metaphor!"
but to empathize with Donne, painfully
standing on the galleon's deck, unsure
he'd see his wife and babes again. It begs

the question why we should analyze things;
is it to learn so many strategies
that writers use, urging ourselves to think
how to construct rich metaphors like these
in advertising, election speeches,
legal suits, grant applications, and all
manner of Argument?—The mode they teach
last in high school, for which you must recall
and apply exposition, description,
narration; logos, ethos, pathos ...
Writing is personal in the early years
since young children have little conception
of any viewpoints other than their own,
but as they grow, they slowly come to see

others' perspectives, and can thus be trained
to convince others through round upon round
of artful rebuttal of statements made
by their opponents, till they've brought around
dissenters to the view authorities
encourage all to espouse. If all roads
lead to Argumentation, hierarchies

are born among textual forms, poems
to the lazy seeming somewhat easy.
A haiku, a free verse, some cheesy rhymes
and congrats on having made a speedy
end of your homework—no need to revise
since teachers don't fail poems. Who can find
a voice, when at last allowed to use "I"?

III.
Teachers: offer no apologies for your expertise! You've been told
by mass media not to lecture, but to focus on teaching students
Life Skills. Who thought up this dichotomy?
Learning about life occurs when one
hears the backstory and historical context behind a particular instance of
enjambment—not just how it has been deployed
"effectively."

Gwendolyn Brooks' "We Real Cool"[3]
is not written like that to create a "catchy" effect
through the syncopated rhythm;
it does not belong in a lesson whose implied outcome is
the learning of how to get one's audience-slash-victims
rocking to one's message. "They are supposedly
dropouts, or at least they're in the poolroom
when they should possibly be in school, since they're probably young enough,
or at least those I saw were when I looked in a poolroom,"
Brooks told George Stavros of Contemporary Literature *in 1969.*
"Let me tell you how that's supposed to be said,
because there's a reason why I set it out as I did.
These are people who are essentially saying,
'... we are.' But they're a little uncertain of the strength of their identity.
The 'We'—you're supposed to stop after the 'We' ...
and of course there's no way for you to tell
whether it should be said softly or not, but I say it rather softly
because I want to represent their basic uncertainty,
which they don't bother to question every day, of course."
Stavros, grasping at stylistic choices
that could define African American poetry, replied with a non-sequitur:

"Are you saying that the form of this poem, then,
was determined by the colloquial rhythm you were trying to catch?"
"No, determined by my feeling about these boys,
these young men," Brooks said.

IV.
In many places, as children grow older,
adults teach them to consider
place and historicity with increased depth and scope.
But this modern curriculum, this Language Arts ladder
is built on a hierarchy of forms—*with argumentation*
arbitrarily occupying top position,[4]
and content an incidental afterthought,
unless intended to be nationalistic (something uniquely Canadian),
apologetic (a token minority piece)
or globalistic ("Let the peoples of the world unite
in the production and consumption of X").

A Piagetian model of cognition suggests
children and teenagers develop as writers
when they write less personally and more formally,
or go from reporting things to making their own arguments.
"Different students pass through stages at different chronological times.
What holds for different people is the order,
regardless of timing," said Moffett & Wagner,
authors of a book that has defined
English curricula since the '70s.[5] *However,*
with a form-focused measuring stick,
it oddly seems to take longer
for the more emotional sex,
racial groups that tend to speak "colloquially"
and cultures that putatively pass on previous knowledge
rather than creating new knowledge
to master the craft of logical, formal, critical argumentation.

V.
When test takers write about their world, markers see it as trite.
When test takers write trite arguments about affairs they can't yet know,

those are viewed in a better light.
At what age can youth claim it has something to teach?
To publicize its knowledge, through rhetoric and narrative
if speech is a right, not undue privilege.

Imparting general skills, or a generalizable education
means giving someone a home, a particular situation
involving reciprocity *and* community,

since you can't grow enskilled if you've never learned
to do so in some previous place—called adaptability,
that most valued skill in our modern world.

Before becoming a teacher, I'd never heard
of Indigenous Studies, had never learned
any non-white poetry from the Norton Anthology,

but what I did know, was how a writing community
could change a reserved undergraduate's identity:
a lesson with tremendous applicability.

And so we might share what we have learned—
that the "I" of poetry, far from merely individual,
is not only generalizable, but better yet, practical.

NOTES

1.   Chambers, 2008.
2.   Yeats, 1928, p. 25.
3.   Brooks, 1960.
4.   DeStigter, 2015.
5.   Newkirk, 1985, p. 594.

REFERENCES

Brooks, G. (1960). We real cool. *The bean eaters*. New York, NY: Harper & Row.
Chambers, C. (2008). Where are we? Finding common ground in a curriculum of place.
     Journal of the Canadian Association for Curriculum Studies, 6(2), 112–128.

DeStigter, T. (2015). On the ascendance of argument: A critique of the assumptions of academe's dominant form. *Research in the Teaching of English, 50*(1), 11–34.

Newkirk, T. (1985). The hedgehog or the fox: The dilemma of writing development. *Language Arts, 62*(6), 593–603.

Stavros, G. (1970). An interview with Gwendolyn Brooks. *Contemporary Literature, 11*(1), 1–20.

Yeats, W. B. (1928). Among school children. *The tower: A facsimile edition*. New York, NY: Simon & Schuster.

INVOCATION

Provoking Understanding through
Community Mapping Curriculum Inquiry

Diane Conrad, Dwayne Donald, and Mandy Krahn

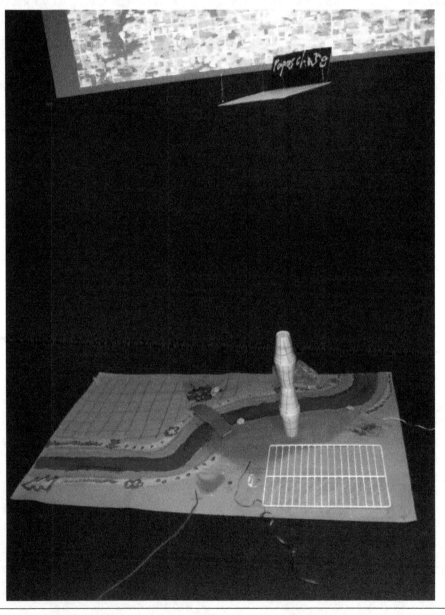

Diane Conrad, Dwayne Donald, & Mandy Krahn (2014). *Edmonton map.* Digital photograph

M aps help us understand the world and where we are in the world (Berry, 2011). Maps that we create ourselves also represent how we see the world. In this way creative, imaginative maps—maps as art—can express our inner and outer worlds. Understanding curriculum as *currere*, the map is an artifact of the autobiographical journey (Donald, 2004).

The image depicts a multi-media map that we created as part of a community-mapping workshop. Our map is a response to colonial cartographic conventions, which include:

- accurate representation of reality
- north at the top
- scale/legend
- boundaries/borders
- roads/key features of landscape
- gridwork/survey
- exploration/ownership

The grid patterns that dominate our urban landscape in Edmonton, Alberta, and constrain us both in our movements through the land and in our imaginations are represented in various ways on our map, including through a projected image in the background. Suspended in mid-air is a layer of our map representing the history of the Papaschase peoples, the original inhabitants of the territory that we today call Edmonton. This layer informs our understandings of and our relationships with our built-up urban environment. If kept ever-present in our relations with this place, this history helps us to respond ethically as we move together into our unknown futures.

REFERENCES

Berry, J. K. (2011). *Personal geographies: Explorations in mixed-media mapmaking*. Fort Collins, CO: North Light Books.

Donald, D. (2004). Edmonton pentimento: Re-reading history in the case of the Papaschase Cree. *Journal of the Canadian Association for Curriculum Studies, 2*(1), 21–54.

A3

Understanding Teacher Identity with(in) the Music Curriculum

Katie Tremblay-Beaton

School performing ensembles in Ontario have historically focused on direct instruction and reductionist thinking, meaning that their successes were measured based on the ability of the students to perform at a high level and of the director to fix musical misconceptions quickly (Elliott & Silverman, 2015; Wasiak, 2013). Critiques of these traditions (Bartel, 2004) aim to inspire change, thus proposing a shift to a more student-centred music education pedagogy (Gould, Countryman, Morton, & Stewart Rose, 2009). Research shows that a student-centred music pedagogy increases student success through problem solving, social constructivism, and schema-building praxis (Elliott & Silverman, 2015; Wiggins, 2001; Yilmaz, 2008). While music teachers are interested in accepting this new paradigm of music education in theory, it can be difficult to enact change in practice. This is why, despite our best intentions, many of our programs are still reflective of the values and interests that we learned through traditional, direct-instruction based pedagogy (Reimer, 2009).

Keeping this conflict of theory and practice in mind, I recall a particularly salient experience in my own teaching practice where I encountered tension between these two curricular approaches. At the time I was a middle-school music teacher who really wanted to "buy in" to the music-education paradigm shift. I concentrated on incorporating informal and non-traditional music learning systems (Green, 2002) in my classes and giving students opportunities to make their own meaningful experiences when they engaged with music. I watched proudly as my students collaborated to write a rock song about acceptance and inclusion. I guided them as they experimented with different instrumentation and vocals, worked with them through the tough areas where the lyrics did not quite flow, and praised them for their hard work after they performed at the school concert. I felt like I was finally engaging in the characteristics of constructivist pedagogy by working with my students as they discovered their own understandings and knowledges of music (Richardson, 2003).

At the end of the school year we were invited to perform our song in a song-writing competition. This was a first for our school. I was prepared to approach this performance as any other with my students and watch them share their passion with the audience. But at the competition, I morphed from a supportive educator who privileges positive student engagement to a teacher who was critical of mistakes and driven by the desire to win. I thought that I had overcome this way of being by embracing a student-centred way of teaching and learning, but the competition brought out the personal drive that was instilled in me through a musical tuition situated in the need to remain in control and reproduce repertoire (Allsup & Benedict, 2008).

I realized that to fully embrace a new way of thinking about music meant I needed to understand how to situate myself and my relationship with music within my teaching practice. As I explored this concept, additional questions arose, such as: How do I negotiate the pluralistic nature of my music classroom in a way that embraces who I am and where I have been? How can I understand my complex identities of teacher and musician as well as the paradox of how these roles can be in conflict but also shared at the same time? And how can these ways of knowing shape my desire to live truthfully with myself and my students in music education?

I knew I needed a method of approaching these questions that would allow for reflection on my own experiences as a musician while connecting them to my experiences as a teacher. *Currere* (Kanu & Glor, 2006) is a method of turning to the autobiographical nature of teachers' experiences through four steps, or moments, that depict both temporal and reflective movements in the study of educational experience. *Currere* returns educational experience to the person who lived it, so that the experience can be examined for latent and manifest meanings by attending to four stages: the regressive, progressive, analytical, and synthetical (Pinar, 1975/1994). In terms of my own music tuition, the regressive stage uses my lived experience as a data source in order to understand the phenomenon of transformation from music student to music teacher. I recalled my own experience as a university-level music student and the definite focus on performance ability to demonstrate an understanding of the subject matter that was determined by the classical Western musical canon. In terms of subject matter for music education, there has been a traditional hierarchical privileging of *what* is taught over *how* it is taught. There is benefit to following the classical Western musical canon. It has provided a stable basis for music and instruction by clarifying expectations and establishing standard ideals. However, being extremely rigid about these ideals can stifle imaginative action and make it difficult for musicians and educators to forge new approaches and react to societal changes (Jorgensen, 2003). In this case, the reactions to societal changes were evident in my actions when I encountered them in a competitive field with my students.

But the question still remains: why do my past understandings of music making affect my pedagogical choices in the present despite my educational training? Lori Dolloff (1999) looks at the perspectives of teacher candidates in music education and how their image of teachers affects their own educational approaches as pre-service teachers. Many teacher candidates come to formal teacher education with their own understanding of what it means to be a "good" teacher based on their many years of study in school and studio classes. They have many images of teachers competing to be role models for their own teacher image, and they all come with vastly different perspectives on the role of the teacher.

In order to assess my own perspective on the role of the teacher in the regressive stage of *currere*, I first established an element of abstraction. Abstraction describes the process of framing an issue and establishing boundaries that define a discrete phenomenon within an always interconnected reality (Sears & Cairns, 2010). I remember my personal perspective on the role of the teacher included performing at competitions or in the school community and being ranked on achievements set up by the standards of practice of musical performance. While this is not indicative of every student's experience within musical training, nor does it completely and wholly reflect my total musical experiences, abstraction allows for the placement of specific boundaries to hone in on these particular experiences in relation to the problem at hand in order to better understand the connections between past and present-day experiences. Through regression, I see that my initial expectation of music teaching was that it would reflect a state of music making with which I was comfortable and familiar. And while my current teaching practice has grown to include new multiple perspectives, I cannot deny the influence these initial music-making experiences will continue to have on my current teaching practices.

Moving through to the progressive stage of *currere* involves looking toward the possibility of the future. This is challenging, as teachers are so often concerned with the immediate present, looking for instructional strategies that can be applied to the current classroom model rather than at how this reactionary type of teaching could affect students as individual meaning makers (Kanu & Glor, 2006). Music-teacher training specifically considers the use of existing instructional tools for teaching instead of looking at whether they are applicable to the evolving nature of music practices (Bowman, 2012). As progressive as we have become in our music-teaching pedagogies, the view of the expert musician will always stand as the main frame of measurement against which most music education is conceptualized in our current curriculum (Gaztambide-Fernandez, 2010). Engaging with the progressive stage within my own practice means trying to understand how to work within a new music-education paradigm while still being situated in the current understanding of musical achievement as defined by our planned curriculum.

Turning to the analysis stage of *currere* involves a certain amount of bracketing in order to understand this phenomenon of working in between the two worlds of planned and lived curriculum. Planned curriculum involves the fundamentals of music education; the curriculum of what we are expected to teach our students. However, lived curriculum, which is enacted daily in our classrooms, needs equal attention from curriculum makers. If focus is only on the curriculum planners, then teachers become installers of the curriculum. It ignores the teacher's own skills to engage with the matters of the deeply situated world of the classroom "doings" (Aoki, 2012). In terms of my own exploration of *currere*, I have discovered the importance of being comfortable working in between these two worlds as a way to negotiate the pluralistic nature of myself as musician and teacher. Living within this *tensionality*, dwelling in the zone between curriculum-as-plan and curriculum-as-lived-experiences, allows good thoughts and action to arise out of that tension (Aoki, 2012). For me, living in this tensionality means that I do not have to value myself as a teacher based on my students' ability to perform the curriculum-as-plan, but also that I do not have to let go of the curriculum-as-lived-experiences that has and will continue to form my identity as a musician and teacher.

By synthesizing these understandings, bringing them all together in order to re-enter the lived present, I can use them as a lens for my current teaching practice. Music-education philosophy suggests there are not only varied kinds of music inside the classroom (Benedict, 2012) but also individualized approaches to understanding these different kinds of music. Small (1998) explains that the purpose of music-education performance is engagement. His theory of *musicking* is that music is not just for those who can perform at an elite standard; rather it is an important aspect of understanding ourselves and our relationships with other people. Not only is everyone's musical experience valid, but musicking creates meaning out of the relationship between the performers rather than out of the performance itself.

Meaning making, then, can be seen as collective collaboration with each other beyond the subject matter. Incorporating this into my teaching practice means that I can only focus on performance standards that are student-driven in nature and I can only work toward a musical goal if my students are invested in the same goal. If my students want to win a competition, then I can support them in that goal; however, if they are interested in pursuing other musical pathways, then I need to focus my teaching pedagogies on those particular outcomes. That essential component was missing in my previous conception of what a "student-centred" curriculum actually entails.

Teaching students with alternative musical goals is a challenge for myself as an educator because I learned under the traditional paradigm that part of the teacher's responsibility is to push their students to perform to a high standard at competitions. And contesting that very musical authority by inviting students to consider their own legitimacy as musical decision makers means, as a teacher, leaving myself open to working in a vulnerable, in-between place (Lamb, 1996). It is possible that I will be judged by others as incompetent in terms of traditional music performance rather than transformative as a music educator. Although this process of opening up ourselves and our professional practice to examination seems threatening, fear needs to be examined as a practice that stops transformation from occurring (Kanu & Glor, 2006), especially if our goal is to set up situations where students can also be transformed through their musical experiences.

The method of *currere* has given me an opportunity to actively reflect on my experiences with music education while analyzing how they have shaped my views as an educator today. While rehearsal methods are concerned with techniques that lead to an ending (Allsup & Benedict, 2008), this ending needs to be established as a common goal among all participants, teachers, and students, in order for an authentic student centred curriculum to be enacted. As I near the end of my reflective practice, I would like to also take a moment to consider my students' experiences at the songwriting competition. We did not win the competition; however, my students were happy to participate and interested in returning next year. If we do return to the competition, I hope to approach it with a different lens—one that is situated within a clearer understanding of myself and my students within the music curriculum.

REFERENCES

Allsup, R., & Benedict, C. (2008). The problems of band: An inquiry into the future of instrumental music education. *Philosophy of Music Education Review, 16*(2), 156–173.

Aoki, T. T. (2012). Teaching as in-dwelling between two curriculum worlds. In S. Gibson (Ed.), *Canadian curriculum studies* (pp. 38–44). Vancouver, BC: Pacific Educational Press.

Bartel, L. (2004). *Questioning the music education paradigm*. Waterloo, ON: Canadian Music Educators' Association.

Benedict, C. (2012). Critical and transformative literacies: Music and general education. *Theory Into Practice, 51*(3), 152–158.

Bowman, W. (2012). Manitoba's success story: What constitutes successful music education in the twenty-first century? In C. Beynon & K. Veblen (Eds.), *Critical perspectives in Canadian music education* (pp. 49–69). Waterloo, ON: Wilfred Laurier University Press.

Dolloff, L. (1999). Imagining ourselves as teachers: The development of teacher identity in music teacher education. *Music Education Research, 1*(2), 191–207.

Elliott, D., & Silverman, M. (2015). *Music matters: A philosophy of music education*. New York, NY: Oxford University Press.

Gaztambide-Fernandez, R. (2010). Wherefore the musicians? *Philosophy of Music Education Review, 18*(1), 65–84.

Gould, E., Countryman, J., Morton, C., & Stewart Rose, L. (2009). *Exploring social justice: How music education might matter*. Waterloo, ON: Canadian Music Educators Association.

Green, L. (2002). *How popular musicians learn: A way ahead for music education*. Burlington, VT: Ashgate Publishing Company.

Jorgensen, E. (2003). *Transforming music education*. Bloomington, IN: Indiana University Press.

Kanu, Y., & Glor, M. (2006). *Currere* to the rescue? Teachers as amateur intellectuals in a knowledge society. *Journal of the Canadian Association for Curriculum Studies, 4*(2), 101–121.

Lamb, R. (1996). Discords: Feminist pedagogy in music education. *Theory Into Practice, 35*(2), 124–131.

Pinar, W. F. (1975/1994). The method of "currere." *Counterpoints, 2*, 19–27.

Reimer, B. (2009). *Seeking the significance of music education: Essays and reflections*. Lanham, MD: Rowman & Littlefield Education.

Richardson, V. (2003). Constructivist pedagogy. *Teachers College Record, 105*(9), 1623–1640.

Sears, A., & Cairns, J. (2010). *A good book, in theory: Making sense through inquiry*. Peterborough, ON: Broadview Press.

Small, C. (1998). *Musicking: The meanings of performing and listening*. Middletown, CT: Wesleyan University Press.

Wasiak, E. (2013). *Teaching instrumental music in Canadian schools*. Don Mills, ON: Oxford University Press.

Wiggins, J. (2001). *Teaching for musical understanding*. New York, NY: McGraw-Hill.

Yilmaz, K. (2008). Constructivism: Its theoretical underpinnings, variations, and implications for classroom instruction. *Educational Horizons, 86*(3), 161–172.

INVOCATION

Curriculum-as-Living-Experience

Rebecca Lloyd

My contribution to curriculum studies may be summarized in one phrase: *curriculum-as-living-experience*. Curriculum within this conception is not a noun, a thing, as in fixed content that is to be delivered by a teacher-as-postal-worker. It is also not a reflective, past-tense "lived" phenomenon, a moment that can be contained, described, and then understood through visual means—reflection.

Curriculum-as-living-experience evokes a kinetic and kinesthetic consciousness directed toward the omnipresent verbs and adjectives that live within the temporal dynamics of each moment. Such a focus affords a motion sensitivity in the way we etymologically orient to curriculum, the race course, and the verb to which curriculum is premised upon, *currere*, to run. To approach curriculum with motion sensitivity is to delve deeply into the various possibilities such motile metaphors hold. A run may be construed as so much more than a means-end activity, an act that can be quantified in units of time or distance. A run can be heavy, light, quick, effortless, effervescent, agile, rhythmical, plodding, laborious ... hence, subtle changes in force, tempo, and posture have profound implications in the way one's curricular course is experienced.

In partnership with Stephen Smith, much of my curricular thinking has been directed toward the creation of a framework, the www.Function2Flow.ca model. Such an integrative approach to curriculum theorizing invites us to delve beyond the physiological aspects of human motility in terms of our baseline functions, and the shapes or forms our bodies make, and consider what it might be like to orient toward the feeling and flowing dimensions of movement potentiality. Such an offering to the Canadian landscape of curricular theorizing offers both a tangible and metaphorical structure to further explore moments that matter, moments that lift us out of the mundane and have the potential to transform our day-to-day consciousness, with motion sensitivity.

A4

Listening to the Earth

Diana B. Ihnatovych

We are immersed in music.
> (John L. Adams, 2009, p. 140)

I like to listen. I have learned a great deal from listening carefully. Most people never listen.
> (Ernest Hemingway, as cited in Grant, 2006, p. 51)

There is an expectancy to the ears, a kind of patient receptivity that they lend to other senses whenever we place ourselves in a mode of listening.
> (David Abram, as cited in Adams, 2009, p. 107)

INTRODUCTION

Three years ago, my spouse decided to advance his professional career and move to northern Alberta to work in the energy-services industry. At that time, I was working on my master's degree at the University of British Columbia in Vancouver and planned to move to Edmonton right after I completed my program requirements. Before finalizing this life-altering decision, I researched the Edmonton and northern Alberta region. I found a history of disturbing environmental issues transpiring on a massive level in Alberta. Then, after watching David Suzuki's (2011) documentary, *Tipping Point: The Age of the Oil Sands*, I refused to move to Alberta because of my concern for the health of our children.

The Age of Oil
clouds of lead-infused smoke
rise above the Earth
covered in toxic sludge
ruptured by pump jacks
screech da ka bong
screech da ka bong
disrupting the Earth's heartbeat

As a result of this experience, I became passionate about exploring the relationship between nature and humanity in our contemporary society. Currently, especially with the development of technology and social media, many people feel "a global sense of utter rootlessness—we are at the same time everywhere at home and nowhere at home" (Davis, 2009, p. 173). Humans became "homeless" and estranged in their relationships to all beings and the world (Davis, 2009). We have forgotten where we are and also who we are (Adams, 2009). It is crucial for humanity to reconnect with nature and learn to live in harmony with the earth, especially now, because our ability to dwell on this earth is at stake (Barbaza, 2009, p. 196). Humans now have the power to alter and destroy nature: "We know that we can kill all humankind with a single bomb. We can destroy the ozone. We can blow up the planet. This means the current rules of the game must change. These are not win or lose, power and control scenarios any longer. With the current circumstances, we all lose" (Adamson, 2008, p. 33).

To save ourselves, we must focus our attention, look inside ourselves, and rediscover the holistic, poetic way of dwelling on the earth. To be able to "live poetically" (Leggo, 2004), we must learn how to live mindfully. Goldstein (2003) wrote: "Mindfulness is the quality of mind that notices what is present without judgement, without interference. It is like a mirror that clearly reflects what comes before it" (p. 89). According to Greaves (2009), this reflective awareness or reflective mindfulness is the essence of the caring human's relation to its surrounding world (p. 112). But what does it mean to be in the world with care? I think we should start by listening.

Canadian composer and sound artist R. Murray Schafer (1977) suggested that to understand the earth, we could attempt to listen to the acoustic environment as a musical composition, because then we would feel more ownership for this composition. By listening, we discover our own unique, sonic way of knowing and being in the world. By listening to sounds, we open our senses and immerse ourselves in the place within our immediate environment. Listening is "the deepest mode of perception" (Adams, 2009, p. 107). Schafer (1992) developed the concept of sound education. He composed numerous listening activities for children to facilitate their learning and listening to their environment and the world around us. Schafer (1992) emphasized the seriousness of a culture of listening. He documented our tendency to focus on certain sounds and overhear others. Are the sounds discriminated against culturally so they are not heard at all? "And how does the changing acoustic environment affect the kinds of sounds we choose to listen to or ignore?" (p. 7). Even a cursory trial of his exercises reveals how our sense of hearing is overloaded with sound pollution in our contemporary urban environment. In an attempt to protect ourselves from unwelcomed intrusions of sound pollution, we have developed selective listening.

Attentive listening reintegrates us into the environment and constructs an understanding of nature as a living and breathing being, not merely an exploitable natural resource for human consumption (Riley-Taylor, 2010, p. 287). Turner and Freedman (2004) wrote:

> Consideration of the musical sounds of animate and inanimate objects can add a novel element of appreciation for, and identification with, the natural world. Acknowledging nature as a musical entity increases its standing, providing additional justification of its intrinsic value and reasons for its preservation. (p. 48)

We must tune our ears to the sounds of the earth to rediscover the connection between ourselves and our own environment, to reconnect humans to the place where they live so they can take good care of it for future generations. We have to learn how to listen and tune our minds to the musical harmony of the earth.

Music of the Forest
at the heart of the mixed forest
next to the Baltic Sea
where the wind
cues the orchestra of oak, birch and pine
I learned to recognize their voices
listening to the music of the forest

Indigenous peoples' attention to place is centred around sound and song (Diamond, 2008). The organic and holistic relationship between earth, the water, plants, wildlife, and the human spirit becomes a song. Songs of indigenous peoples from different parts of the world frequently have similar beats and rhythms because their natural environments have something in common (Diamond, 2008, p. 27). Humans are mirroring the sounds of nature. Song as a mirror of nature is present in the Inuit throat-singing tradition. In addition to imitating the natural environment, it also imitates human-made sounds, like snowmobiles (Diamond, 2008). As a result, young children from those communities develop an attentive awareness of the sounds in their environment and a deep connection to the place where they live and grow up:

> As she listened, she came to hear the breath of each place—how the snow falls here, how the ice melts—how, when everything is still—the air breathes. The drums of her ears throbbed with the heartbeat of this place, a particular rhythm that can be heard in no other place. (Adams, 1998, p. 35)

Knowledge specific to these indigenous communities about their place is frequently taught through song (Kulnieks, Longboat, & Young, 2013, p. 143). Indigenous peoples describe and preserve their culture and knowledge of their environment through music:

> We are told by our grandfathers and grandmothers that for as long as there are Indians there will be song, and as long as there is song there will be Indians. As long as we sing our songs and someone learns from them, there will be new Indian people, for song is our survival tool as people. (Sijohn, 1999, p. 48)

The lifestyle of indigenous peoples is rooted in song: "We sing songs, dawn songs, morning songs, thanksgiving-coming-up-soon songs" (Lyons, 2008, p. 25). Song is an oral tradition that is being handed down from one generation to the next. There is also another way that songs come to indigenous people: "They are delivered to us.... For us, messengers are the Owl, the Eagle, the birds, the Fish, the Ant, the Little Mouse, the Weasel, and so on.... We go outside and sing in the morning when we wake up and in the evening when we go to bed" (Sijohn, 1999, p. 47). Although there is no musical score, no written notes, there is a rhythmical communion with the sound of natural music (Vasquez, 1998, p. 176). When we listen very carefully we hear that music is around us all the time: "It is the breath of the world" (Adams, 2009, p. 4).

SOUNDSCAPE

On my walk through the forest, I inhale the crisp, autumn air. Warm rays of sun peek through the red leaves. I stop by the old nursing log. I close my eyes and listen. The bird songs surrender to the monotonous hum of the highway. Planes claim their acoustic space with relentless confidence, silencing the gentle whispering of the trees. The lawnmower interrupts the woodpecker, and drowns out the sound of the squirrel's paws climbing the tree. I sketch my soundscape. The highway hum becomes a thick black circle, without a beginning, without an end. The descending straight lines represent planes cutting across the faint swirls of the wind. The lawnmower turns into an ugly grey cloud, and the squirrel's tiny scratches against the tree bark become invisible. I compose my soundscape to learn about the place where I live.

Adams (2009) believes that paying attention to music and sound in nature can contribute to the awakening of our ecological understanding. Instead of being a vessel for self-expression, music becomes a mode of awareness. Soundscape studies directly connect to the studies of economic development, quality of life, and environmental sustainability (Allen, 2012, p. 197). Listening to human and non-human sounds introduces us to variety of different perspectives on natural and human worlds and relationships between them (Allen, 2012, p. 201). Perhaps we need to learn from indigenous people how to listen to the song of nature and learn to recognize the "interconnectedness and interdependence of all living beings" (Adamson, 2008, p. 34). Perhaps we should learn how to listen with our hearts.

It is time to slow down and listen to the world around us. It is time to quit calculating and measuring, being everywhere and nowhere, placeless, rootless, "hurrying here and there out of breath" (Leggo, 2004, p. 34). It is time to learn how to surrender and let go of our control. It is time to change "the quality of our *attention* to the world" (Adams, 2009, p. 103). It is time to rethink our human-nature relationship and become caretakers for all beings in nature. It is time to acknowledge and recognize our differences with respect, attentively listening our way to a more harmonious future on this earth.

REFERENCES

Adams, J. L. (1998). The place where you go to listen. *The North American Review, 283*(2), 35.

Adams, J. L. (2009). *The place where you go to listen: In search of an ecology of music.* Middletown, CT: Wesleyan University Press.

Adamson, R. (2008). First Nations survival and the future of the earth. In M. K. Nelson (Ed.), *Original instructions: Indigenous teachings for a sustainable future* (pp. 27–35). Rochester, VT: Bear & Company.

Allen, A. S. (2012). Ecomusicology: Music, culture, nature ... and change in environmental studies? *Journal of Environmental Studies and Sciences, 2*(2), 192–201.

Barbaza, R. (2009). There where nothing happens: The poetry of space in Heidegger and Arellano. In L. McWhorter & G. Stenstad (Eds.), *Heidegger and the earth: Essays in environmental philosophy* (2nd ed.) (pp. 186–200). Toronto, ON: University of Toronto Press.

Davis, S. (2009). The path of a thinking, poeticizing building: The strange uncanniness of human being on earth. In L. McWhorter & G. Stenstad (Eds.), *Heidegger and the earth: Essays in environmental philosophy* (2nd ed.) (pp. 169–185). Toronto, ON: University of Toronto Press.

Diamond, B. (2008). *Native American music in Eastern North America: Experiencing music, expressing culture.* New York, NY: Oxford University Press.

Goldstein, J. (2003). *One Dharma.* New York, NY: HarperOne.

Grant, I. (2006). Creative approaches to new media research. *Young Consumers, 7*(3), 51–56.

Greaves, T. (2009). The world's silent spring: Heidegger and Herder on animality and the origin of language. In L. McWhorter & G. Stenstad (Eds.), *Heidegger and the earth: Essays in environmental philosophy* (2nd ed.) (pp. 103–122). Toronto, ON: University of Toronto Press.

Kulnieko, A., Longhoat, D., & Young, K. (2013). Engaging literacies through ecologically minded curriculum: Educating teachers about Indigenous knowledges through an ecojustice education framework. *in education, 19*(2), 138–152.

Leggo, C. (2004). The curriculum of joy: Six poetic ruminations. *Journal of the Canadian Association for Curriculum Studies, 2*(2), 27–42.

Lyons, O. (2008). Listening to natural law. In M. K. Nelson (Ed.), *Original instructions: Indigenous teachings for a sustainable future* (pp. 22–26). Rochester, VT: Bear & Company.

Riley-Taylor, E. (2010). Reconceiving ecology: Diversity, language and horizons of the possible. In E. Malewski (Ed.), *Curriculum studies handbook: The next moment* (pp. 286–298). New York, NY: Routledge.

Schafer, R. M. (1977). *The tuning of the world.* New York, NY: Knopf.

Schafer, R. M. (1992). *A sound education: 100 exercises in listening and sound-making.* Indian River, ON: Arcana.

Sijohn, C. (1999). The circle of songs. In W. Smyth, E. Ryan, & V. Hilbert (Eds.), *Spirit of the first people: Native American music traditions of Washington state* (pp. 45–49). Seattle, WA: University of Washington Press.

Turner, D. (1999). Humanity as shepherd of being: Heidegger's philosophy and the animal other. In L. McWhorter & G. Stenstad (Eds.), *Heidegger and the earth: Essays in environmental philosophy* (2nd ed.) (pp. 144–166). Toronto, ON: University of Toronto Press.

Turner, K., & Freedman, B. (2004). Music and environmental studies. *The Journal of Environmental Education, 36*(1), 45–52.

Vasquez, G. R. (1998). Education in the modern west and in the Andean culture. In F. Apffel-Marglin (Ed.), *The spirit of regeneration: Andean culture confronting western notions of development* (pp. 172–192). New York, NY: Zed Books.

INVOCATION

Rumination on Pedagogical Rhythm

Claudia Eppert

Perhaps deeper relationships with rhythm, rhythm of breath, heart, seasons, shall become reclaimed as a pedagogical imperative. Rhythm etymologically derives from the Sanskrit *sru*, meaning to stream, current, or flowing waters. The root field *sru* becomes *rhéō* in Greek, with aspiration following *r*, and *r* replacing *s* (Rendich, 2015). From here emerges Greek *rhythmós*, indicating flow, motion, or time, and Latin's measured *rhythmus*, connoting harmony in post-classical renderings. Ancients held that, in rhythm, joy/sorrow, sound/silence, light/dark, work/rest interminably interplay, while also embedding themselves within the wholistic nondual, where distinctions dissolve without being lost. I venture the present-day human spirit longs for kinship with nature's interplay, and with the non-linear, immeasurably empty-abundant Whole, understood not as totality, system, thing, or object of thought, but rather as that ineffability that "allows us to relate everything with everything without doing violence to the related things" (Panikkar, 2010, p. 29). For Panikkar, rhythm engages all qualities of life, encompassing *intraconnection*, "the dwelling of all in all" (p. 34). Rhythm, thus, is not a static, repetitive, eternal return, but rather a generative dance between the concrete, manifest *Umwelt*, and the ineffable, within which the concrete assumes ever new expressions of the whole (p. 33). Panikkar notes Plato's near inclination to equate education, *paideia*, with bringing forth rhythmic consciousness (p. 40). Yet, in the modern age, senses of rhythm, not progressing anywhere, and eschewing any narrow objectifying episteme, have largely been restricted to music (p. 38). And so, I wonder, in our diverse curricula, might we re-attune to rhythm, within, on the earth, and in the immensity of space? In life, learn skillfully to play, to "dance with the rhythms of situations," ever aware of the transformational nature of the dance itself (Trungpa, 2004, p. 116)? In wisdom, finally, come to abide in full embrace, and in moving communion with the entirety?

REFERENCES

Panikkar, R. (2010). *The rhythm of being: The Gifford lectures*. Maryknoll, NY: Orbis.

Rendich, F. (2015). *Comparative etymological dictionary of classical Indo-European languages*. (G. Davis, Trans.). Charleston, SC: CreateSpace Independent Publishing.

Trungpa, C. (2004). The six states of Bardo: Allenspark, 1971. In C. R. Gimian (Ed.), *The collected works of Chögyam Trungpa* (Vol. 6) (pp. 11–153). Boston, MA: Shambhala.

A5

Artful Portable Library Spaces: Increasing Community Agency and Shared Knowledge

Amélie Lemieux and Mitchell McLarnon

INTRODUCTION

This community project explores the impact, documented research, and processes of building and introducing a Little Free Library (LFL) to a physical location of the Faculty of Education at McGill University. We undertook this sustainable literacy initiative for two main purposes: (1) to create an eco-friendly space for books that are recycled or often left alone on benches of university hallways; and (2) to contribute to art, literacy, and place-based studies (Graham, 2007; Howard, 2007) that address the collective sharing of knowledge through a medium—in our case, printed books. Our goal was to develop a space for university students, faculty, and staff, a space designed to revitalize printed books through viewed, displayed, and embodied experiences. Our idea originated from our observations during numerous strolls in our respective neighbourhoods of Villeray (northern Montreal) and Place Saint-Henri (southwest Montreal), where there were several established examples of LFLs, or *croque-livres*, as they are called in French. Contributing to recent studies urging academics to pursue research on the impacts of implementing LFLs in communities (Snow, 2015), our study presents a collaborative inquiry into the reflections around crafting and implementing a LFL for positive change, agency, and knowledge sharing within an academic space. In this chapter, and in the context of Canadian curriculum studies, we invite you to consider how our processes are based on parity with the product and outcomes, as well as how a sustainable project can be replicated in order to impact literacy practices in a learning community.

BACKGROUND AND FRAMEWORK

In Montreal, the first LFL was set up in Rosemont in April 2014. Its debut spread enthusiasm across communities and, soon after, little crafted birdhouses filled with books appeared in other parts of the city. Primarily catering to children and youth, LFLs entice communities to (re)discover books, with the aim of encouraging literacy practices. The LFL concept is based on sharing, that is, all books are donated or exchanged, as opposed to loaned, as is the case in a regular library.

LFL efforts are directed toward pushing communal engagement, accessing different forms of knowledge by occupying physical and tangible spaces for public good (Mattern, 2012; Springer & Turpin, 2015), fostering community agency (Naidoo & Sweeney, 2015), and developing democratic engagement (Cantor, 2012). In undertaking this project, we suspected that it would provoke the conventional understanding of a traditional library space. However, with our arts-based and literacy backgrounds, we felt that our academic community would engage with our newly installed LFL, at least to a certain extent. We trusted that the LFL movement within the walls of our faculty would rouse a level of emotion, in the same way that Mattern (2012) has observed:

> Given the rise of proprietary platforms and ephemeral content, the LFL believes that the tactility, the originality, the *aura* of these structures—plus the fact that they're communal property—generates an *affective* response. Ideally, that affect would translate into politics; it would inspire citizens to question why the presence of freely accessible books in public space elicits such emotion. (para. 26)

As our observations suggest, people tend to leave books on benches or tables in the hallways of our faculty building (photos 1 and 2), it makes sense that LFLs have generated a powerful impact in our university community. That is, our LFL offers a space where these books could be left. Our hope is that our initiative promoted positive feelings about the revitalization and sharing of printed books in the Faculty of Education.

ARTFUL CREATIVE PROCESS

Our discussions about the building of the library box took place over 10 weeks, starting in August 2015. After spending the summer discussing potential artful-, literacy-, and curriculum-related research initiatives, we introduced the LFL to McGill's campus. In our discussions, and in reviewing community approaches

Photo 1. Amélie Lemieux (2015). *Books left in the hallway.* Digital photograph

Photo 2. Amélie Lemieux (2015). *A dozen books left in a box in the hallway.* Digital photograph

to the history and ethos of LFLs, we considered two options: (1) purchasing the model from the LFL collective; or (2) building it ourselves from new and recycled materials. We inquired about prices of pre-designed LFL models, which cost around $260, both in the United States and in the province of Quebec. We chose the second option.

Although it seemed straightforward at first, we encountered difficulties when we attempted to purchase new materials such as wood, hinges, glue, nails, and other items. The list of necessities kept expanding, and it seemed counter-productive and illogical to buy new pieces, as we wanted this to be a project based on reusing materials. For cost and environmental purposes, we decided to use only recycled or second-hand resources (cf. photo 3) for our project. With this chapter, we felt it was important to document our process through picture-taking. This way, we share our process visually so that other campuses and schools can replicate the project at a low cost, with sustainable ethics. That is, we opted for a wooden six-pack wine box, a white stool with a removable top purchased at a thrift shop, two hinges, screws and nails from our personal supplies, and a doorknob kept in one of our toolboxes. The coloured tints came from previous purchases. The total cost of our artfully crafted LFL was less than 10% of the original suggested retail price advertised by both the American and Canadian LFL organizations.

Photo 3. Amélie Lemieux (2015). *White stool and wooden box*. Digital photograph

During December 2015, we constructed our LFL as documented in the following steps. In the building and research process, we included field notes addressing each step of the construction so we could share the process with other educational researchers. Specifically, we first removed the textile cover from the stool's removable top (cf. photo 4), and turned it upside down as a base for the box. Then, Mitchell drilled through the box, into the bench, so that the removable top would be fixed, connecting the two parts together as an ensemble (cf. photo 5). We removed the sliding door of the wooden box, installed the metal hinges (cf. photo 6), and created a door with the knob. The next day, Amélie applied a preliminary coat of gold paint on the box, covering the bottom white legs and doorknob with recycled newspaper (cf. photo 7). After a second coat, we wrote "Books," "*Livres,*" and "*Prends ou donne un livre*" on the sides of the box, and "Little Free Library" on the top (photo 8). Important to our LFL and our research project was to: (1) have a sustainable and artful process; (2) advance literacy and multiliteracy throughout this initiative; and (3) be inclusive of McGill's and Montreal's two main linguistic communities: French and English. As such, we created the first bilingual LFL.

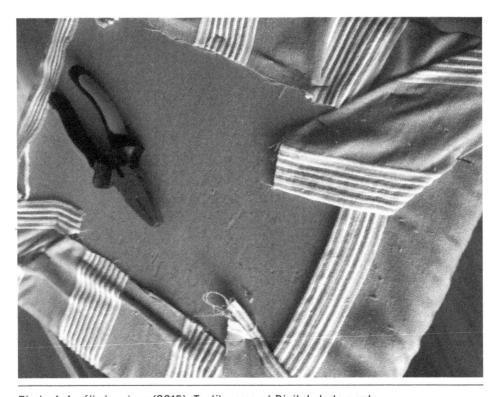

Photo 4. Amélie Lemieux (2015). *Textile removal.* Digital photograph

Photo 5. Amélie Lemieux (2015). *Juxtaposition*. Digital photograph

Photo 6. Amélie Lemieux (2015). *Assemblage*. Digital photograph

Photo 7. Amélie Lemieux (2015). *Golden library*. Digital photograph

INAUGURATION

We inaugurated our LFL at noon on Tuesday, January 5, 2016, near the elevators on the first floor of the Faculty of Education at McGill University. We selected this location because it is one of the most frequented by students, staff, and faculty. There was sufficient space to place the LFL. The surrounding billboards and university research advertisements also created a convenient space where the LFL did not feel out of place. We donated 16 books in a range of languages, including English, French, German, and Czech. The selection ranged from grammar notebooks, literary theory handbooks, translation studies research, French literature, and books on the history of reading, to accounting notebooks and culinary anthologies. After putting our donated books into our artful exhibit, we walked the hallways and found six books left on random benches and in strange locations of the building. We added each found book to the library box. Of the books found in McGill's Faculty of Education building, there were course packs for McGill's Bachelor of Education courses, along with recent *Educational Researcher* journals. In total, we filled our box with 22 books for the purpose of sharing, reusing, and re-homing.

Photo 8. Amélie Lemieux (2015). *Bilingual LFL*. Digital photograph

When we returned to McGill later that week (Thursday, January 7, 2016), there were only seven books left. Therefore, in less than 48 hours, a total of 15 books had found new homes. While we were inspired by this outcome, we took a critical stance on what took place in the first few days as we realized that community members were quick to *take* the free books, and slow to *leave* unused books. However, we received a couple of email messages from community members willing to offer books to the LFL. These members donated the books for our project, and gave them to us so that we would fill the box ourselves.

DISCUSSION AND OUTCOMES

As we reflected on and exchanged ideas about our progress in building and establishing the LFL, we realized that our processes were synonymous with creative analytical practices (Richardson & St. Pierre, 2008). When one engages in creative and artistic methods of inquiry, one is also in an analytical mode of thought. This resonates with the multiple approaches and hybrid research methods used in arts-based educational research and literacy studies because creative and pedagogical inquiries often overlap multiple disciplines while concurrently focusing on specific aspects of inquiry (Springgay, Irwin, Leggo, & Gouzouasis, 2008). What might this mean in and for contemporary curriculum studies? We see the LFL initiative as an opportunity for cross-curricular learning. Through the budgeting and building processes, we attempted to draw links to multiliteracies while avoiding the trope of scholarly competition and the inherent comparison of performance. Through collaboration, we prioritize learning through inquiry.

We are currently living in a high-speed, ever-changing world. As provincial curriculum and educational policies shift across Canada toward competency-based learning, these renewals aim to address these everyday complexities that learners experience. Future generations will need people who have been educated to address socio-cultural and political issues that involve engaging with complex interpersonal relationships within diverse groups of people. One way we can offer this opportunity is through literacy, and a sustainable way of doing so is through offering an open access to books that people want to discard. Others may well find a good use for them. Our sustainable premise builds on Kate Pahl's (2014) idea that "repurposing and remaking can become an active process of meaning making" (p. 60). With this philosophy, we offer ways for our community to pursue literacy practices in the university. Objects such as the LFL can have that "power" to convey meaning and foster literacy practices (Pahl & Rowsell, 2010).

Engaging in curricular projects like the LFL can provide learners of all ages with an escape from memorizing content while allowing for authentic critical engagement. In other words, it is not productive to memorize the rules to the game when the game keeps changing. Our transitional society will require autonomous and creative thinkers, not *test-takers*. With the aims of provoking curriculum, the

LFL adopts a philosophy that is based on sustainability, that is, working on what we already have, and learning from it for durable futures. As the number of books and community reaction changed each time we walked by the LFL, we had to find different ways of keeping pace with our internal and external demands.

Situating our work in Canadian curriculum studies, our collective topos has brought us to where we live, work, and play (Chambers, 1999). Our attempts to develop community within our faculty are in line with Putnam's (2000) idea of social capital. Specific to Putnam's (2000) understanding of social capital is that only communities can possess and wield its use. The agency of communities is exemplified by concepts like bonding, bridging, and reciprocity. Putnam argues that only through social relations can we obtain personal benefits. His notion of bonding is internally generated within a specific group of individuals. In our case, we bonded through our own discourse and analysis while building the LFL but also bonded with several members of McGill's community who showed interest in our initiative. On the other hand, bridging has extrinsic principles. The premise of bridging is hallmarked by interactions between diverse people from different social groups (Beames, Higgins, & Nicol, 2012). Therefore, by extending communication and establishing invisible networks—at McGill, with students, staff, and faculty—bridging describes how potential social divisions can be negotiated by demonstrating that through community-oriented initiatives, individuals can advance their interests in many areas of their lives, in our case through free, unused, or recycled books. The idea of reciprocity is more straightforward, although worthy of analysis. According to Putnam (2000), reciprocity involves social trust whereby past interactions inform future collaborations. As we started from nothing to establish our LFL, we hope that our efforts serve as a benchmark for future initiatives. We trusted and envisioned that members of McGill's community would share their own books and want to contribute to ongoing collective action in the context of our university.

From a reciprocity perspective, at first, we remarked that McGill's community was better at taking books than leaving them. In the early stages, we made efforts to keep the LFL full and kept track of the coming and going of books. During the first two weeks, over 50 books were taken and used by community members but hardly any were dropped off. As the guardians of this initiative, we happily found books from a variety of outlets, including groups of friends and local businesses. After our first unsolicited book drop came from an anonymous donor who left 38 books on January 21, 2016, we sent an email to all addresses on McGill's Faculty of Education email list thanking the anonymous donor, while outlining how our LFL is there for everyone, requiring no registration, and encouraging all those interested in participating to get involved.

CONCLUSION

In our project, we wanted to: (1) use recycled materials to build the box; (2) create an eco-friendly space for books that are recycled or often left on benches, outside of offices, and in random locations of university hallways; and (3) contribute to art, literacy, and learning for sustainable development by addressing the collective sharing of knowledge. By using art in this sustainable-development literacies project, we have noticed that the box has had an influence on the space. For example, the artfulness of the LFL attracts more attention than a random pile of books, or books piled in a brown archive box. We contend that the brown archive box would not attract the same attention, and might not evoke the same receptiveness or response from community members.

This LFL initiative is ongoing and evergreen. We plan to continue to document our process and experience and have expanded the initiative across schools and faculties in and around our university. It is our hope that through our work, others will join in recycling books, and in reusing material to build their own LFLs, instead of seeking a ready-made LFL, as this process allows for potential connections across the curriculum. Furthermore, by considering creative and artful approaches to project-based learning and curriculum studies, we also transcend traditionally understood literacies.

REFERENCES

Beames, S., Higgins, P., & Nicol, R. (2012). *Learning outside the classroom: Theory and guidelines for practice*. London, England: Routledge.

Cantor, N. (2012). Intensifying impact: Engagement matters (paper 50). Office of the Chancellor, Syracuse University. Available at: surface.syr.edu/chancellor/50

Chambers, C. (1999). A topography for Canadian curriculum theory. *Canadian Journal of Education, 24*(2), 137–150.

Graham, M. A. (2007). Art, ecology and art education: Locating art education in a critical place-based pedagogy. *Studies in Art Education, 48*(4), 375–391.

Howard, P. (2007). The pedagogy of place: Reinterpreting ecological education through the language arts. *Diaspora, Indigenous, and Minority Education, 1*(2), 109–126.

Mattern, S. (2012, May). Marginalia: Little libraries in the urban margins. *Places Journal*. Available at: placesjournal.org/article/marginalia-little-libraries-in-the-urban-margins/

Naidoo, J. C., & Sweeney, M. E. (2015). Educating for social justice: Perspectives from library and information science and collaboration with K–12 social studies educators. *Journal of International Social Studies, 5*(1), 196–207.

Pahl, K. (2014). *Materializing literacies in communities: The uses of literacy revisited*. London, England: Bloomsbury.

Pahl, K., & Rowsell, J. (2010). *Artifactual literacies: Every object tells a story*. New York, NY: Teachers College Press.

Putnam, R. D. (2000). *Bowling alone: The collapse and revival of American community*. New York, NY: Simon and Schuster.

Richardson, L., & St. Pierre, E. A. (2008). Writing: A method of inquiry. In N. K. Denzin & Y. S. Lincoln (Eds.), *Collecting and interpreting qualitative materials* (3rd ed.) (pp. 473–500). Thousand Oaks, CA: Sage.

Snow, M. (2015). Little free libraries: A call for research into the tiny book depositories. *Children and Libraries: The Journal of the Association for Library Service to Children, 13*(4), 30–32.

Springer, A.-S., & Turpin, E. (2015). *Intercalations 1: Fantasies of the library*. Berlin, Germany: K. Verlag & Haus der Kulturen der Welt.

Springgay, S., Irwin, R. L., Leggo, C., & Gouzouasis, P. (Eds.). (2008). *Being with a/r/tography*. Rotterdam, The Netherlands: Sense Publishers.

A6

The Spacing of the Hegemonic *Chora* in the Curriculum of First-Language Attrition

Wisam Kh. Abdul-Jabbar

> *The foreigner's mother tongue is that language of the past that withers without ever leaving you.*
>   (Julia Kristeva, 1991, p. 15)

INTRODUCTION

Many studies have focused on the process of language acquisition for newcomers' children and the ways in which linguistic acculturation can be achieved. Fewer studies, however, have looked at the insidious effects of learning a new language upon one's mother tongue and ethnic identity within the context of immigration. This study draws on Julia Kristeva's conceptualization of "the chora" in *Revolution in Poetic Language* (1984) to illustrate how acquiring a new language can trigger a process of ethnic erosion in terms of one's first language and identity. This study argues that schools enunciate a new *chora*, a maternal surrogate that generates a process of "spacing," which can cause ethnic values to erode. Over time, this duplicate *chora* dominates the learner's world through language. The ethnic *chora* dissipates, giving room to the new one, as the first language becomes a relic that everybody appreciates but no one understands.

Many scholars have explored the correlation between the loss of ethnic language and cultural ties: "In general, as immigrants become progressively more like the native born (especially in terms of language), there may be a gradual loosening of their ethnic social and cultural ties, and a change in ethnic identity (Pigott & Kalbach, 2005, p. 5). According to Lily Wong Fillmore (1991), "Few American-born children of immigrant parents are fully proficient in the ethnic language, even if it was the only language they spoke when they entered school ... even if it is the only one their parents know" (p. 324). Moreover, Sandra Kouritzin (1999) points out that "language loss now occurs suddenly between two generations rather than more slowly across several generations. As a result, some individuals are losing the means with which to maintain relationships with their parents, their families, and their cultures" (p. 11). Schools focus mainly on developing mainstream languages in newly arrived school-age children, with an eye toward efficiency and performance. However, in what ways does the loss of one's ethnic language help or hinder the condition of living congenially between two cultures? What role does the school play to accelerate the lamentable loss of one's first language? Young immigrant children's first language degenerates into an accepted form of collateral damage as a result of the desired process of learning mainstream language. The loss of first language isolates children from their ethnic roots and marginalizes their ethnic communities. Over time, with Kristeva's *Strangers to Ourselves* (1991) in mind, do young immigrant children grow up to become strangers to their own parents and culture?

KRISTEVA'S *CHORA*: STRANGERS TO OUR LANGUAGE AND CULTURE

In *Strangers to Ourselves*, Julia Kristeva (1991) speaks of the dissipation of one's mother language as a "memory" that "has been cut off from the body ... from the bittersweet slumber of childhood" (p. 15). For the newcomer, this language becomes both "cherished and useless," a language that "withers without ever leaving you" (p. 15). The new language, on the other hand, does not necessarily, or successfully, fill the vacuum. Rather, it can be very deceptive and provokingly frustrating: "You have a feeling that the new language is a resurrection, new skin, new sex" (p. 15). Kristeva asserts that "the illusion bursts" when the speaker realizes that this new feeling is "artificial and sublimated" (p. 15). Thus, the intrusion of a new language functions as a constant reminder of what has been lost.

In *Revolution in Poetic Language* (1984), Kristeva argues that the infant develops a relationship with its mother prior to birth, and establishes a connection defined by pre-birth language. For Kristeva, the subject and language are products of a maternal process that continues to inform the life of the subject, who develops a dialogical relationship, which she calls "the semiotic 'chora'" and which informs his or her capacity as a speaking subject:

> The semiotic "chora" ... registers the first imprints of experience and is a rudimentary signal of language that is to follow. The chora is an articulation of bodily drives, energy charges and psychical marks which constitute a non-expressive totality, one that does not give way to form, but is known through its *effects*. (Barrett, 2011, p. 9)

The *chora*, therefore, chronicles and animates language, and informs the psyche and identity formation through "effects" that it observes and absorbs from its nurturing surroundings. I argue that Kristeva's reconceptualization of the *chora*, a notion initially introduced by Plato in *Timaeus*, provides a way to explore the loss of the first language among young immigrant students, due to the rise of a new, reborn *chora* generated by the hegemonic curriculum of the receiving country.

Drawing on Lacan's distinction between the imaginary and the symbolic order, Kristeva introduces a distinction between the semiotic and the symbolic. "The interaction between these two terms (which, it must be stressed, are processes, not static entities) then constitutes the signifying process" (Moi, 1986, p. 12). Kristeva argues that the semiotic is basically primordial with an "endless flow of pulsions ... [that are] gathered up in the *chora* (from the Greek word for enclosed space, womb)" (Moi, 1986, p. 12). Kristeva attempts to extract the *chora* from "the ontological apparatus of the Platonic system" (Huffer, 1998, p. 88) in order to move from metaphysical assumptions into the psychoanalytical realm, where she sets the distinction between the semiotic and the symbolic:

> It is, however, generated in order to attain this signifying position. Neither model nor copy, the *chora* precedes and underlies figuration and thus specularization, and is analogous only to vocal or kinetic rhythm. We must restore this motility's gestural and vocal play (to mention only the aspect relevant to language) on the level of the socialized body in order to remove motility from ontology and amorphousness where Plato confines it. (Kristeva, 1984, p. 26)

During a dialogue on cosmological notions, Plato's (1977) Timaeus introduces the concept of the *chora*, which neither represents "the unchanging model" nor "the changing copy of it" (p. 48). It is a third substratum that is "difficult and obscure," which constitutes the "receptacle and ... nurse of all becoming" providing "a position for everything that comes to be" (p. 49). Timaeus compares the *chora* to "a kind of neutral plastic material" and "the receptacle to the mother" (p. 50). Kristeva argues that Plato calls "this receptacle or *chora* nourishing and maternal, not yet unified in an ordered whole because deity is absent from it. Though deprived of unity, identity, or deity, the *chora* is nevertheless subject to a regulating process [*réglementation*]" (Kristeva, 1984, p. 26). Whereas, for Plato (1977), reality exists in the world of models and forms, and the world as we know it copies that essential reality, the *chora* is not intelligible as a space and its copy is equally inaccessible to the senses: it is "puzzling" and "very hard to grasp" (p. 50) as it baffles reasoning; and yet, for Plato, it can be nurturing as a repository. Kristeva repositions Plato's notion of the *chora* from its cosmological aspect "onto the unconscious signifying processes mediated by the intensely ambivalent pre-Oedipal relation to the mother" (Goulimari, 2015, p. 23). For Kristeva, these signifying processes both generate and animate what she calls the semiotic properties of language, such as rhyme, rhythm, and sound.

In Plato's account, the *chora* is "not matter but space," whereas Kristeva reconceptualizes it "not as space but as spacing" (Kintz, 1994, p. 145). Kristeva's definition of the *chora* as "spacing" is her point of innovative departure from the Platonic notion. For Kristeva, the *chora* "is the site of an aesthetic wobble that shows up in English in the postmodern grammatical form of choice, the gerund with its *–ing* to suggest that textuality or interpretation never stops but is always in process" (Kintz, 1994, p. 146). Kristeva (1984) borrows the term *chora* in order to suggest mobility. It is, rather, a departure from the Platonic locus of uncertainty and elusiveness into a confirmation of a "phenomenological, spatial intuition" that "gives rise to [the] geometry" of the semiotic language (p. 25). For Kristeva, it is a "signifying position" that needs to be attained. Kristeva extracts the *chora* from the Platonic system in order to explain the dynamics and semiotics of the initial stages of language processes within the Lacanian imaginary order in which the mother serves as the dominant figure. In a similar way, I attempt to extend the notion of the *chora* from Kristeva's psychoanalytic apparatus into the realm of hegemonic curriculum perpetuated by the cultural and linguistic normalization exercised by schools.

DECOLONIZING THE SPACING OF THE SCHOOL-GENERATED *CHORA*

The *chora* is a hypothetical space of convergence between language and subjectivity. It defines self-relation and informs connections with external and social objects in the world. The role of the mother signified by the *chora* is implicated in our encounters with language, culture, and identity formation. The *chora* generates a semiotic aspect of language that works within and outside the symbolic order; the latter encroaches, dominates, determines signification, and represents law and order. For

Kristeva, the semiotic works against the symbolic to "produce the dialectical tension that keeps society going" (Oliver, 1993, p. 10). The semiotic, therefore, resists social norms as it seeks to diversify and challenge uniformity and cohesion, as superimposed upon the individual by the symbolic order. Overtaking the role of the *chora* that generates the semiotic order means the end of the type of resistance that paints the social fabric with different colours.

I hypothesize that schools, in operating as hegemonic sites, become new mother figures, imposing themselves on young minds whose views about their new culture are similar to the views of infants experiencing the world through their mothers' perceptions. That act of linguistic and ethnic separation initiates a material process that begins prior to the total acquisition of the new language. Accordingly, schools enunciate a new *chora*, whose main role is to unconsciously replace the first one, which is no longer relevant as it is extraneous and alien to the new socio-cultural landscape. In effect, the enunciation of the new *chora* entails an act of severance with ethnic and linguistic ties, as it replaces the initial *chora* that appeared at birth.

Second-generation or immigrant youth are constantly challenged by institutional and other discourses to facilitate assimilation to the extent that, over time, they become divorced from their vital feelings, ultimately undermining their capacities for reconciliation with the ethnic self. This further produces the general perception "that living between two cultures is psychologically undesirable because managing the complexity of dual reference points generates ambiguity, identity confusion, and normlessness" (Lafromboise, Coleman, & Gerton, 1995, p. 489). Likewise, a "dual pattern of identification and a divided loyalty ... [may lead to] an ambivalent attitude" (Stonequist, 1935, p. 96), which is often perceived as an unfavourable departure from an assumed set of values or an expected transition into something "like us" (Abdul-Jabbar, 2015, p. 2). That sense of ambiguity is often feared, either for its capacity to destabilize the socio-political and hegemonic agenda of developing an elusive mainstream cohesive identity, or because of the alleged long-term threat of this growing sense of uncertainty that may undermine the imaginary of nationalistic allegiance.

In this capacity, Kristeva's semiotic *chora* has the potential to resist, even threaten, hegemonic orders and subvert established rules or popular trends. The semiotic *chora* is a crucible of the first language, which, if lost, results in the loss of a substantial part of the ethnic identity of both the individual and the community:

> A person who speaks an ethnic language is thought to be more ethnically
> connected than one who is more assimilated, in that h/she speaks mainly
> English or French. Thus, as the use of their ethnic language declines,

individuals may tend to be less ethnically connected. (Kalbach & Kalbach, 1995, p. 31)

By teaching only the mainstream language and not encouraging or providing opportunities for students to learn minor languages, schools generate a spacing *chora* that is ostensibly but efficiently accommodating as "it destroys the threatening other in its midst by literally incorporating him into itself. This is the extreme gesture of xenophilia: the devouring embrace that takes the other in until there is nothing left of 'them' but us" (Bammer, 1995, p. 47). Schools have therefore shifted from the oppressive and xenophobic residential/boarding model into a more contemporary bent. Yatta Kanu (2006) notes that

> the purpose of school is to create a form of consciousness that enables the inculcation of the knowledge and culture of dominant groups as official knowledge for all students, thereby allowing dominant groups to maintain social control without resorting to overt mechanisms of domination. (p. 5)

Ultimately, for young immigrants, the language learned at school, even if acquired at a very early age, is not motherly but instructive; not maternal but acquired; not genuine but devoid of emotional ties. The school presents itself as a surrogate mother, a *chora* that speaks its own appealing language, which in due course swallows or appropriates the students' family values. It declares itself the nurturing mother. Thus the sometimes ironic nickname "alma mater" (literally, "nurturing mother") for one's school. This surrogate mother should be appreciated and followed, as opposed to the biological parents, who are now seen as distant and foreign, even incompatible with the encroaching symbolic order.

CONCLUSION

Few studies have explored key components in how second-generation participants identify with elements of their ethnic culture, such as language, ethnic community involvement, visiting country of origin, and continued family ties. Brooke S. Pigott and Madeline A. Kalbach (2005) argue that speaking an ethnic language underpins ethnic identity (p. 3). They point out that "research reveals that ethnic connectedness declines as the use of the ethnic language decreases" (p. 5). Maintaining ethnic language positively reinforces ethnic identity, as individuals are thought to be less culturally connected if they do not know how to speak their first language.

There is a tendency toward a departure from one's cultural ties if modern institutions and academic life do not provide social and linguistic sites to facilitate connections with one's ethnic community. Due to an increasing sense of uselessness and irrelevance to school life, the ethnic self and its fading language, as implicated in Kristeva's conceptualization of the *chora*, become abstracted from the particularities of daily life. The language of new schools and institutions, on the other hand, strives to generate a new *chora* that is drained of emotional and memory traits.

A complex set of tensions and interactions generate the operations of the *chora*, whose actuality and "spacing" contextualizes and supplements the acquisition of the new language. This process starts with a non-verbal site that gravitates toward the mother's body. Schools regenerate a *chora* whose position eliminates the role of the ethnic self and eventually forms a symbolic alliance of signification between language acquisition and the life of the subject. Since "the operation of the semiotic within signification continually proliferates cultural possibilities" (Oliver, 1993, p. 10), the hypothetical severance of the semiotic *chora* is necessary in order to prepare for the intrusive encroachment of the second language as the only means of signification. Significantly, since the creation of a new *chora* that functions against the authentic one seems inevitable, curriculum writers need to think of more ways to salvage the ethnic *chora* so it does not dissipate into a symbolic order that essentially aspires toward multiculturalism. In a complex multicultural educational system marked by tensions and interactions, future directions in Canadian curriculum should hopefully strive to generate a "spacing" that negates and resists first-language attrition.

REFERENCES

Abdul-Jabbar, W. Kh. (2015). Pedagogical reflections on internalizing geopolitical representations in print media. *The Canadian Journal for the Scholarship of Teaching and Learning, 6*(2), Article 4.

Bammer, A. (1995). Xenophobia, xenophilia, and no place to rest. In G. Brinker-Gabler (Ed.), *Encountering the other(s): Studies in literature, history, and culture* (pp. 45–64). New York: State University of New York Press.

Barrett, E. (2011). *Kristeva reframed: Interpreting key thinkers for the arts.* New York, NY: I. B. Tauris.

Goulimari, P. (2015). *Literary criticism and theory: From Plato to postmodernism.* London, England: Routledge.

Huffer, L. (1998). *Maternal pasts, feminist futures: Nostalgia, ethics, and the question of difference.* Palo Alto, CA: Stanford University Press.

Kalbach, M. A., & Kalbach, W. E. (1995). The importance of ethnic-connectedness for Canada's post-war immigrants. *Canadian Ethnic Studies/Études ethniques au Canada, 27*(2), 16–33.

Kanu, Y. (Ed.) (2006). *Curriculum as cultural practice: Postcolonial imaginations.* Toronto, ON: University of Toronto Press.

Kintz, L. (1994). Plato, Kristeva and the chora: Figuring the unfigurable. In S. Shankman (Ed.), *Plato and postmodernism* (pp. 145–161). Eugene, OR: Wipf and Stock Publishers.

Kouritzin, S. G. (1999). *Face[t]s of first language loss.* Mahwah, NJ: Erlbaum.

Kristeva, J. (1984). *Revolution in poetic language.* New York, NY: Columbia University Press.

Kristeva, J. (1991). *Strangers to ourselves.* (L. S. Roudiez, Trans.). New York, NY: Columbia University Press.

Lafromboise, T., Coleman, H., & Gerton, J. (1995). Psychological impact of biculturalism: Evidence and theory. In N. R. Goldberger (Ed.), *The culture and psychology reader* (pp. 489–536). New York: New York University Press.

Moi, T. (Ed.). (1986). *The Kristeva reader.* New York, NY: Columbia University Press.

Oliver, K. (1993). *Reading Kristeva: Unraveling the double-bind.* Bloomington, IN: Indiana University Press.

Pigott, B. S., & Kalbach, M. A. (2005). Language effects on ethnic identity in Canada. *Canadian Ethnic Studies, 37*(2), 3–18.

Plato. (1977). *Timaeus and Critias.* (D. Lee, Trans.) Harmondsworth, England: Penguin.

Stonequist, E. V. (1935). The problem of marginal man. *American Journal of Sociology, 7,* 1–12.

Wong Fillmore, L. (1991) When learning a second language means losing the first. *Early Childhood Research Quarterly, 6,* 323–346.

INVOCATION

Old Mournings, New Days

Robert C. Nellis

I teach a Family Studies course in our Teacher Education program. I remember looking at the topic of love and showing clips from Baz Luhrmann's 1996 film *Romeo + Juliet*. I turn the lights back on to moist, secreted eyes, amplified by the silence of the room's sterile lights and hum. How curious, I pose, that this play, as per the movie's trailer, "The greatest love story the world has ever known," is, of course, not a romance but a tragedy. What's with that? Some pause from the class. I'll ever remember once, one of my student-colleagues offering, heartfully, gingerly, that it's because love is structured from the beginning as a looming, impending tragedy! Whether between lovers, spouses, parents and children, humans and animals, every love—sooner or later—somehow, will end. Some pause again—only now, from me! I hear Jacques Derrida's *The Gift of Death*, *The Work of Mourning*. I remember John Caputo's imagining that perhaps this is why lovers cling so tightly to each other in the night.

I read into Jean Piaget's notion of *accommodation*, of how one brings new information into existing schemas or understandings of the world. When a novel idea, possibility, suggestion, or even prayer does not match my received narratives, if I am to bring the new within, I'll need new stories to accommodate it. This is inherently transformational. If I am to open my mind, heart, and arms to new possibilities, I am called upon to change, to say hello to new selves and goodbye to old. This is a loss, and loss calls for mourning. *Morning?* New days, turning to new pages upon which to write new tales of kindness, inclusiveness, democracy, justice, responsibility, possibility, hope. After loss, it's the love we remember ...

A7

Navigating a Curriculum of Travel through Geneva: Museums, Gardens, and Governance

Rita Forte

INTRODUCTION

Guten Tag, bonjour, bongiorno, allegra, and hello. I sat in the viewing gallery of the Federal Palace in Bern. It was the opening day of the national government, also known as the Federal Assembly. The speaker opened the session with a greeting in five different languages. Bern is approximately a two-hour train ride from Geneva, the city also known as "the peace capital." In an attempt to interpret my travel to Geneva, I discuss the use of travel writing as a way to support and challenge Canadian curriculum studies.

THE CURRICULUM OF TRAVEL WRITING

Travel writing is described as a "non-fictional rather than fictional form" (Thompson, 2011, p. 15). An interaction between the "human subject and the world" (Korte, 2000, p. 5), this genre of writing allows an opportunity to reflect on a journey while moving between space and time. Drawing on the disciplines of "history, geography, anthropology and social science" (Thompson, 2011, p. 12), one is allowed to travel across borders and enter new places and spaces. Both Chambers (2006) and Talburt (2009) discuss "the border" as a metaphor among countries, peoples, nation-states, and cultures. More importantly, the implication is that the formation of borders can create "physical, emotional and spiritual places" (Chambers, 2006, p. 8). Talburt (2009) poses the question, "In what ways does it open selves to new perspectives on difference, reinforce received opinions, or encourage a return to self?" (p. 109). Thinking through the travel, and combining description and exposition (Korte, 2000), a curriculum of travel emerges, especially about a multitude of locations.

For Chambers (2006), the concept of the border suggests connections to citizenship, nationhood, and identity. She suggests:

> The border has been a high-end metaphor in the reconceptualization of curriculum around politics, identity, and difference. Curriculum theorists have used the metaphor as currency as they moved the politics of difference from its origins in class and the material conditions of our lives across the border to a place where difference embraces the libidinal, the racial/cultural, and the individual, sometimes almost eclipsing the historical and the economic. (p. 7)

For Talburt (2009), the border coincides with boundaries that are created and undone, "however real or imagined" (p. 116). According to Talburt,

> The curricular question becomes how subjects are invited to imagine self and other in relation to boundaries. Positionality and location can at once appear as real and as always dynamic, and travel can appear not as the meeting of two distinct identities or cultures but as productive of emergent social formations. (p. 116)

These two interpretations of the border tend to focus on place, the local and the national, "as mutually implicated events" (p. 116). As a researcher, I believe that travel writing provides more than a narrative because it embeds the journaling notes and images within the theoretical context. In turn, this body of literature enables me to engage my chosen curriculum artifact, travel to the museums, gardens, and the spaces of governance that inhabit Geneva, in a fluid, unsolidified way.

MULTICULTURAL, COSMOPOLITICAL, AND GLOBAL

In Geneva, a multicultural citizenship within a strong Swiss citizenship has developed rather than an assimilationist ideology. Although Banks (2009) refers to Kymlicka's interpretation of multiculturalism, he states that "[n]ations throughout the world are trying to determine whether they will perceive themselves as multicultural" (p. 3). Interestingly, the preservation of the French canton of Geneva within a multilingual nation-state of French, German, Italian, and Romansh languages seems to clearly lend itself to a cosmopolitan view. What exists in this city-state is a focus on being a citizen of Geneva. Each of the street signs whose names are derived from notable Genevan public figures include the name and the reason for reverence. For example, Boulevard Carl-Vogt and Rue François-Dussaud. Carl Vogt believed in polygenist evolution where each race evolved differently. François Dussaud was one of the first researchers to synchronize sound and cinema. On Rousseau Island, the tribute on a sculpture states "Jean Jacques Rousseau, Citoyen de Genève." Rousseau (1750) argues that "even from our infancy an absurd system of education serves to adorn our wit and corrupt our judgment" (p. 147) and then maintains that "our minds have been corrupted in proportion as the arts and sciences have improved" (p. 133). Despite their esteem and repute, their provocative views challenge traditional Western theories such as Darwinian evolution, the potency of the arts, and the sciences.

Two tenets related to cosmopolitanism are offered by Sobe (2009). One refers to identity and self-definition beyond the local. The other aspect relates to political action for locating the self and the community at both the local and global levels. These two tenets are different because the first tenet talks about identity and the second tenet dialogues about a mechanism that moves. Cosmopolitanism encourages multiple perspectives and depicts a sage way of life where all human beings have equal worth and coexist. Hansen (2010) refers to the "the capacity to fuse reflective openness to the new with reflective loyalty to the known" (p. 151). As Held (2010) makes clear:

> Cosmopolitanism elaborates a concern with the equal moral status of each and every human being and creates a bedrock of interest in what it is that human beings have in common, independently of their particular familial, ethical, national and religious affiliations. (p. x)

Cosmopolitanism is not an idolization of one culture in comparison to another. Rather it is an overall appreciation for difference and how variation can contribute to one's understanding of the self, others, and the world. This ties into making a new space within curriculum that invites the recognition and embracing of diversity. Hansen, Burdick-Shepherd, Cammarano, and Obelleiro (2009) state that

> cosmopolitanism is a name for an orientation toward self, others, and world. In this orientation, a person or community juxtaposes reflective openness to new influences with reflective loyalty toward the tried and the known. Put another way, cosmopolitanism is a name for an outlook toward the

challenges and opportunities of being a person or community dwelling in a world of ongoing social transformation. (p. 587)

Generally, there are three underlying aspects of globalization: economy, polity, and culture (Waters, 1995). Cosmopolitanism connects to globalization because of the spillovers of culture. Globalization can also be related to connectivity and deterritorialization (Tomlinson, 1999) as a network of interconnections and interdependencies that involve wholeness, multidimensionality, capital markets, and a dialectic of opposed principles and tendencies. Wang (2006) offers a definition of globalization related to space that consists of the local, the global, and the autobiographical:

> Both the challenges and possibilities for teaching in an era of globalization lie in a space in which cultures and identities mutually—if not equally—impact one another. Such a space is not free from conflicts but is filled with ambiguity, paradoxes, and complexity, and as it shifts, a network of hybrid movements brings new shapes to both the local and the global. (p. 13)

In terms of connecting globalization to the environment, Jickling and Wals (2008) recognize the neoliberal energies, ways of favouring free-market capitalism, that can impact education and at the same time benefit global changes in education that can be implemented quickly through international non-governmental organizations.

Cross-culturalism, denoting different cultures, and/or multiculturalism, expressing several cultural groups within a society, in Canada offers newcomers the opportunity to carry on their own traditions and values; however, multiculturalism, within the Canadian context, precludes actions toward changing our system of government as a constitutional monarchy. Inevitably, people who choose to live in Canada bring their own values and add to Canadian identity. With reference to multiculturalism, Pinar (2010) notes four elements of multiculturalism: identity, recognition, rights, and redistribution (p. 26). There are many ways to define the discourse of cross-cultural research, which relates to universalism and particularism, diversity, and the embracing of varying cultures' coexistence.

SWITZERLAND AS A COSMOPOLITICAL STATE

"Switzerland is a patchwork of four linguistic regions: German, French, Italian and Romansh-speaking. This blend is an important element of our country's cultural diversity," articulates the website of the Swiss Confederation (2007). The city of

Geneva is divided by Lake Geneva (Lac Léman), resulting in the Rive Droite and Rive Gauche sections. Among the many cantons in Switzerland, Geneva is both a city and a canton, resulting in both a regional-type government and a municipal-type government.

Travelling to Geneva thematically based on museums, gardens, and governance, I visited museums that demonstrated a cosmopolitan effect. Located on Avenue de la Paix, the International Red Cross and Red Crescent Museum (ICRC) sits atop a hill. At the entrance I encountered the statues referred to, collectively, as "The Petrified."

Ten individual sculptures wearing whitish-grey cloaks covering their bodies and faces stood upright in a pod. Did they represent prisoners of war? Did they represent the frightened from the atrocities of war who are unable to move? I learned that the shrouded figures denounce the violation of human rights that occur during war. Already, one is prompted to start contemplating the purposes of the Committee of the Red Cross before entering a museum characterized by artifacts and exhibits depicting its founder, Henry Dunant, using glass display cases, guidebooks, digital film, and interactive technology to present the work of the ICRC. On the day I went, an exhibit called *Sang, Sang, Sang* was part of the collection. In English, the translation was *All About Blood*.

Other museums I visited included the Natural History Museum of Geneva and the Art and History Museum. In the rotunda of the Natural History Museum, the skeleton of a prehistoric creature was constructed. I recalled a visit to the Canadian Museum of Nature in Ottawa. This type of museum usually exists in a nation's capital, but Geneva, a city-state, possesses one also. At the Art and History Museum, paintings depicted the main figures of the Reformation. Consistent with the myriad of exhibits, "'multiculturalism' becomes a 'museum'" (Pinar, 2010, p. 35) and observing difference, at times, prompts a search for likeness.

At Parc La Grange, green spaces covered the grounds with a prominent rose garden consisting of a wooden structure that had stairs leading up to it. Rose bushes surrounded the structure, with narrow pathways to walk through the rose garden. In the background, the Swiss Alps could faintly be seen. Next to the park was the Parc des Eaux Vives. I tried to follow the running water around the trees and beneath the rocks, but it seemed cavernous, especially with the growing plants surfacing from the water. It was so green, so clean, so large, so picturesque, and so calm, especially with its international array of plants and flowers. When Wang (2009) references "cultural difference as the difference between types of society" (p. 42), the inclusion of multinational references in the park through the art and/ or practice of garden cultivation addresses multicultural representations. I could

Rita Forte (July 25, 2005). *The petrified*. Digital photograph. Artist: Carl Bucher (1979)

see the small signs randomly emerging from the soil depicting the names of the originating countries. One read *Tibet*.

In the Conservatoire et Jardin Botaniques, green spaces covered the grounds with an encased greenhouse exhibiting exotic plants. The park included a library, a herbarium, and plants/trees from various continents. In one part of the park was a flower wall. Flowers and greenery flourished from a wall that seemed to block an industrial area. Adjacent to the flower wall were rectangular ponds surrounded by flowers. From the centre of the ponds emerged green plants and metal sculptures of two swans on a platform. At times the exoticism of the plants made them look like an island. Palm trees, many varieties of orchids, cacti, and pineapple, along with water lilies and huge plants with thick fleshy stems, were surrounded by direct sunlight, and the heat of the sun felt tropical. Travel writing has often been characterized by "the contrasts, the distance and shares with the reader astonishment, surprise and amazement" (Cintrat, Massau, Barreiro, & Soares, 1996, p. 48). By articulating this experience, I realize that the inclusion of several different continents in the gardens lent itself to cosmopolitanism, globalization, and multiculturalism.

As I was walking, crossing Lake Geneva from the right bank to the left bank, I found *l'horloge fleurie*, the flower clock.

Rita Forte (July 23, 2003). *The flower clock*. Digital photograph

Situated on a hill, the functioning clock's numbers consisted of flowers. The clock consisted of a hybrid of a Venn diagram and concentric circles. Some numbers of the clock were situated within the main circle, while other numbers looked randomly dispersed outside the main circle, inside smaller, random circles. The entire exhibit pristinely existed in a relatively high-traffic walking area surrounded by green trees and shrubs. It combined art, flowers, a garden, and technology to epitomize the "imaginary and physical landscape" (Chambers, 1999, p. 147).

The United Nations headquarters for social issues and human rights issues is in Geneva. While Geneva is known for its strong banking presence, anything relating to the financial organs of the United Nations is housed in New York. When I visited this building, before entering, I had to hand over my passport to the security guard. We were shown several rooms. One was where the General Assembly sits. The symbol of the United Nations, with its olive branches and modified globe to provide equal space for each continent on the two-dimensional surface, was posted prominently on the front wall. According to the United Nations' (2012) official description, the emblem "consists of a map of the world on a polar azimuthally equidistant projection surrounded by two olive branches. These two symbols speak for themselves: the olive branch is a symbol of peace, while the world map represents the Organization in its quest to attain world peace."

Since the Conference on Disarmament was not sitting, we entered the room where disarmament treaties are negotiated. The countries' name plates were positioned at the desk-like tables in the square room: Myanmar, Mongolia, Mexico, Malaysia.... We entered from the door above and had an aerial view of the room. The tour guide explained that the negotiations for the removal of anti-personnel land mines started in this room before Canada initiated the Ottawa Process, which expedited the formation of the anti-personnel land mine treaty. After spending time in the United Nations building without any belongings and/or identity, I returned to the security area and obtained my passport.

As the security guard carefully looked at my bilingual driver's licence before I entered the viewing gallery of the Federal Palace, I realized that Canada's legislated bilingualism, which is a source of debate at times in Canada, may not be readily known to citizens of other nation-states. Canada has two official languages, but Switzerland has at least four. Given that Geneva is a French canton, elementary-school children learn to speak German, French, and English as additional languages. While Canada is bilingual, where ideally we switch interchangeably between English and French, Geneva could be characterized as French, while other cantons are characterized based on another language, exclusively. These two ways of approaching multilingualism characterize the culture and the conflict with multiple perspectives. As I see the connections between this curriculum of travel and the orders of questions posed by Dillon (2009), such as "What is it?" "What is it like?" and "How is it defined?" (p. 344), some answers begin to emerge relating to content, time, space, location, and actions. A curriculum of travel allows me to make connections and, hopefully, take the reader on the journey.

REFERENCES

Banks, J. (2009). Diversity and citizenship education in multicultural nations. *Multicultural Education Review, 1*(1), 1–28.

Chambers, C. (1999). A topography for Canadian curriculum theory. *Canadian Journal of Education, 24*(2), 137–150.

Chambers, C. (2006). "Where do I belong?" Canadian curriculum as passport home. *Journal of the American Association for the Advancement of Curriculum Studies, 2,* 1–18.

Cintrat, I., Massau, M., Barreiro, C. M., & Soares, L. (1996). Travel writing. *Language, Culture and Curriculum, 9*(1), 35–50.

Dillon, J. T. (2009). The questions of curriculum. *Journal of Curriculum Studies, 41*(3), 343–359.

Hansen, D. (2010). Chasing butterflies without a net: Interpreting cosmopolitanism. *Studies in Philosophy of Education, 29,* 151–166.

Hansen, D., Burdick-Shepherd, S., Cammarano, C., & Obelleiro, G. (2009). Education, values, and valuing in cosmopolitan perspective. *Curriculum Inquiry, 39*(5), 587–612.

Held, D. (2010). *Cosmopolitanism: Ideals and realities.* Malden, MA: Wiley.

Jickling, B., & Wals, A. (2008). Globalization and environmental education: Looking beyond sustainable development. *Journal of Curriculum Studies, 40*(1), 1–21.

Korte, B. (2000). *English travel writing from pilgrimages to postcolonial explorations.* New York, NY: St. Martin's Press.

Pinar, W. F. (2010). Hand in hand: Multiculturalism, nationality, cosmopolitanism. *Multicultural Education Review, 2*(1), 25–53.

Rousseau, J.-J. (1750). *Discourse on the arts and sciences.* London, England: J. M. Dent & Sons.

Sobe, N. (2009). Rethinking "Cosmopolitanism" as an analytic for the comparative study of globalization and education. *Current Issues in Comparative Education, 12*(1), 6–13.

Swiss Confederation. (2007). The Federal Authorities of the Swiss Confederation. Available at: www.infoclio.ch/en/node/132446

Talburt, S. (2009). International travel and implication. *Journal of Curriculum Theorizing, 25*(3), 104–118.

Thompson, C. (2011). *Travel writing.* New York, NY: Routledge.

Tomlinson, J. (1999). *Globalization and culture.* Chicago, IL: University of Chicago Press.

United Nations. (2012). Fact sheet: United Nations emblem and flag. Available at: ask.un.org/loader.php?fid=2800&type=1&key=4e33d55b2d943764e5085a395d74ccd6

Wang, H. (2006). Globalization and curriculum studies: Tensions, challenges, and possibilities. *Journal of the American Association for the Advancement of Curriculum Studies,* *2*(February), 1–17.

Wang, H. (2009). Life history and cross-cultural thought: Engaging an intercultural curriculum. *Transnational Curriculum Inquiry, 6*(2), 37–50.

Waters, M. (1995). *Globalization.* London, England: Routledge.

A8

A Quantumeracy Reading List

Kyle Stooshnov

Since presenting *Quantumeracy: Teaching Fiction as Virtual Reality* at the 2015 Provoking Curriculum Studies Conference, each novel I read seemed to further my argument that current fictional literature has an intrinsic connection to quantum physics. Emily St. John Mandel's (2014) *Station Eleven*, recommended by another Provoking Curriculum Studies participant, has two characters discussing alternate realities connected to Everett's "Many Worlds Interpretation" (Gribbin, 2014). William Gibson's (2014) novel *The Peripheral* has a plot that hinges upon what protagonist Wilf Netherton mentions as "something to do with quantum tunnelling" (p. 39). Karim Alrawi's (2015) *Book of Sands* also has characters casually mentioning quantum physics without making an explicit connection to events in the narrative. In a book club gathering with the author, I offered up my opinion that quantum theory was at the heart of his narrative structure and Alrawi very eagerly replied that it was. Like Netherton's dialogue, however, it is difficult to explain specifically how fiction blends with quantum theory. My notion of quantumeracy examines this blending of theoretical science with artful literacy: readers imagine worlds that are the basis of everyday reality, yet the closer they examine quantum events or fictional stories, the greater the uncertainty becomes and the more the readers must rely on interpretation rather than objective reality. The intrinsic connections between science and humanities are entangled in the portmanteau *quantumeracy*, where the uncertain quantum reality informs the emergent literacy taught in schools. This chapter looks back on a number of texts I presented as a reading list of examples of this concept, and

Kyle Stooshnov (2015). *Provoking Curriculum Studies conference presentation.* Digital slide

expands upon each author's connection to quantum theory with reflections upon Louise Rosenblatt's (1978, 2005) transaction theory and how such a reading list can provoke 21st-century K–12 curriculum.

A reading list is typically a collection of texts grouped together in an effective if not simple way of demonstrating various ideas based upon the availability of the texts. The German philologist Erich Auerbach (2013) toured through libraries in order to create a list of classical books and included them in *Mimesis: The Representation of Reality in Western Literature.* Likewise, the Swiss narratologist Marie-Laure Ryan immersed herself in computer science in order to explore hypertext, which she discusses in her books *Possible Worlds, Artificial Intelligence, and Narrative Theory* (1991) and, more recently, *Narrative as Virtual Reality 2* (2015). Every list gives details of how each text relates to the overarching idea explored. For the purposes of this chapter, I will continue the trajectory of literary studies that starts with ink on the page and shifts over to pixels on a screen by going deeper inside the computer, into the semiconducting transistors and quantum mechanics of an electron that comprise all media, including the paper-bound books[1] I mention on my reading list. Valentine, one of the characters in Tom Stoppard's (1993) play *Arcadia*, sums up the transition between print and electronic media when he comments on the electronic calculator near the end of Act One, Scene Four. He alludes to the mere months needed to compute complex algorithms that would have taken "the rest of my life—thousands of of pages—tens of thousands!" (p. 74) to solve with paper and pencil. It is possible to think of the influence of "the Quantum Moment" described by Robert Crease and Alfred Goldhaber (2015, p. 24) reflected in fictional literature when probability and uncertainty change the meaning of texts that I define as quantumeracy, and Louise Rosenblatt discusses as the poem.

As a researcher and educator who explored literature, Rosenblatt (1978, 2005) developed the theory of transaction between the reader and the text to create the poem. Much of her theory derives from pragmatist scholar John Dewey and reflects the new paradigm at the start of the 20th century sparked by "Einstein's theory and the developments in subatomic physics" (2005, p. 2), otherwise known as quantum mechanics, where the observer is just as much a part of the process as the phenomenon observed; so the reader transacts with a text. These texts can be any mode of storytelling, in some cases switching from one to the other, as Douglas Adams' (1978–2005) *Hitchhiker's Guide to the Galaxy* began as a radio drama, then became a novel, television series, video game, and eventually a feature film.[2] Other texts are so well suited to one medium, like the stage of Stoppard's *Arcadia*, that it would be difficult to transpose or adapt them to another mode. Both examples are notable for being popular and critically praised texts that blend the aesthetic artistry of their respective media while also including efferent details about mathematics and science related to their plots. Rosenblatt (2005) distinguishes between two types of reading:

> Efferent reading will select out the desired reference and ignore or subordinate affect. Aesthetic reading, in contrast, will fuse the cognitive and affective elements of consciousness—sensations, images, feelings, ideas— into a personally lived-through poem or story.... In the transactional model, efferent and aesthetic are parallel or coordinate modes. (p. 98)

The 21st century's pragmatism[3] in current K–12 education has a sharp divide between the hard sciences and the fine arts, with educational policy-makers pushing an agenda in favour of the STEM subjects (science, technology, engineering, and mathematics) as the more marketable skills for their students (Michaels, 2011). While ministries of education and school districts work toward foundational skills and a more efferent stance toward understanding texts, each Rosenblattian poem on the following list transacts between the outer limits of scientific theory and the aesthetic yet uncertain elements found in novels suitable to provoke quantumeracy in the K–12 curriculum.

The reading list of novel-sized poems to begin building a sense of quantumeracy includes Jasper Fforde's books, in particular the *Last Dragonslayer* (2010–2014) series. The Welsh author Fforde writes prolifically in a number of genres, often crossing over from a fantasy-based detective series *Thursday Next* (2001–2012) and gritty potboiler parody *Nursery Crimes* (2005–2006) to dystopian romances *Shade of Grey* (2009) and *Early Riser* (forthcoming). The *Last Dragonslayer* series is one of the first specifically aimed at the young adult audience and, much like his other series, where the settings are familiar locations within Great Britain, every novel presents an alternate-history version of the nation, perhaps most tellingly the "Ununited Kingdoms" for the *Last Dragonslayer* series. It would satisfy enough curiosity within the readers already familiar with the many-worlds interpretation of quantum theory to determine the points of departure in Fforde's fiction from standard British history. Jennifer Strange, the series's Dragonslayer, lives in a fractured country comprising "kingdoms, duchies, socialist collectives, public limited companies and ramshackle potentiates" (Fforde, 2011, p. 28) that are the result of numerous wars and injustices.[4] Once-powerful wizards, greedy industrial conglomerates, and ineffectual political leaders are all part of the parody Fforde creates, and an efferent reading of each "relative state" leads back to the quantum many-world interpretation developed by Hugh Everett in his 1957 doctoral dissertation (Osnaghi, Freitas, & Freire, 2008).

There is a playful sense of quantumeracy in the many worlds of Jasper Fforde's novels, especially for the *Thursday Next* series, most particularly in *First Among Sequels* (2007) and the often-delayed follow-up *Dark Reading Matter* (forthcoming),[5] but perhaps the most direct quantum theory applied to Fforde's novels comes with the Quarkbeast itself. A loyal pet belonging to Jennifer Strange, this fearsome yet friendly creature is one of several created by wizards, in this case to win a wager for most eccentric non-evolutionary animal. There are six types of Quarkbeast; although each one is identical to all the others, they closely match the six "flavors" of the subatomic particles called quarks detailed by Hawking (1996) as "up, down, strange, charmed, bottom, and top ... modern physicists seem to have more imaginative ways of naming new particles and phenomena" (p. 85). There is much efferent information to be pulled from descriptions of the Quarkbeast, yet an aesthetic account of its song would be difficult to recreate in another medium:[6]

It was a lonely song. One of lament, of unknown knowledge, a song of resignation, and of love and poetry given and received. The small movements the Quarkbeasts made as they padded around one another altered the hum so subtly that it sounded like an alto bassoon, but with one single note, infinitely variable. (Fforde, 2011, p. 257)

One final comment about the Quarkbeast, before getting to the next book on the quantumeracy reading list, is its passing reference in Fforde's first novel, *The Eyre Affair* (2001, p. 32), demonstrating yet another of the many worlds Fforde's characters and creations can occupy.

Ruth Ozeki's (2013) novel *A Tale for the Time Being* also has a few of its main characters crossing over from one world to another, transcending time and space through the written word and Zen Buddhism: Japanese American teenager Nao writes about her experiences moving back to Japan with her family due to her father's career change; former Silicon Valley programmer Haruki #2 (Nao's father) is so named after his uncle who was a kamikaze pilot, and whom the family refers to as Haruki #1; Jiko is a Zen Buddhist nun and great-grandmother to Nao, whose diary crosses the Pacific Ocean along with a Jungle Crow who may be Jiko's animal-spirit; and Ruth is a Japanese American author living on the west coast of British Columbia who discovers Nao's diary and the quantumerate issues it presents. Firstly, there is the superpositioned states of both authors, Nao and Ruth, the former being a suicidal teenager who may have died in the 2011 tsunami that devastated the Pacific Tōhoku region of Japan, the latter being a fictional version of the novel's author, who discovers the diary and begins transcribing it. Ruth's double role as novel-author and diary-reader is further complicated by her ability to enter into Haruki #2's and Jiko's lives,[7] and like the observer in the Heisenberg uncertainty principle (Polkinghorne, 2002, pp. 32–34), she affects the outcome of a story that for Ruth should already be written.

The themes of extreme bullying and wartime atrocities presented in Ozeki's novel may be too graphic for younger readers, even with the teenage protagonist Nao narrating most of the story. Similar topics are explored in other quantumerate novels, such as Margaret Atwood's (1989) *Cat's Eye* or Kurt Vonnegut Jr.'s (1969) *Slaughterhouse Five, or the Children's Crusade*, with unreliable narrators and protagonists becoming unstuck from a conventional timeline, adopting instead four-dimensional space-time first put forth by Hermann Minkowski and mentioned in Albert Einstein's (2015) "The Special Theory of Relativity." More age-appropriate series for younger students to explore similar themes are the *Time Quintet*, Madeleine L'Engle's (1963–1989) science fantasy novels that begin with *A Wrinkle in Time*, and the three-volume epic adventure *The Lord of the Rings* by J. R. R. Tolkien (1954–1955). Both series are otherworldly, with the children in the

Time Quintet being transported through the fifth dimension to visit other planets and distant ages: one instance has teenage protagonist Charles Wallace visiting an American Civil War author, Matthew Maddox, who reflects on how "myth and matter merge. What happens in one time can make a difference in what happens in another time, far more than we realize" (L'Engle, 1981, p. 256). A similar sentiment permeates *The Lord of the Rings*, a narrated account of Frodo Baggins' attempt to rid Middle-earth of the evil of Sauron's ring. A former ally in Frodo's quest becomes corrupted by Sauron's influence when Saruman the White reveals to Gandalf the Grey that he is now "Saruman of Many Colours!" Gandalf confronts his peer, telling him that broken white light "is no longer white.... And he that breaks a thing to find out what it is has left the path of wisdom" (Tolkien, 1999, p. 339). Chad Orzel (2012) argues that Gandalf is in the wrong by mentioning many of the innovations in the field of quantum mechanics by early atomists like Niels Bohr and Louis de Broglie. In a quantumerate sense, soon after the discovery of Saruman's treachery in *The Fellowship of the Ring*, the fellowship itself begins to break apart, and the narrative fractures into separate storylines throughout the following two volumes.

The last two books on my list trace back to the same early days of quantum mechanics in the 20th century (Crease & Goldhaber, 2015), and these modernist novels count as prototypes of quantumeracy. Virginia Woolf's (1992) novel *To the Lighthouse* attracted the critical attention of Auerbach (2013), who notes her stylistic disruption of the narrative "verges upon a realm beyond reality" (p. 532). While the literary scholar mentions the radical changes happening in the field of science and technology at the start of the 20th century, he does not go into specific detail about the connection between the author and other modernists like her, including Marcel Proust[8] and James Joyce, nor the new quantum realities being discovered about time, space, and subjective consciousness. Woolf describes her process, known currently as stream-of-consciousness, initially as her "tunneling process," which would later be echoed in the study of radioactive decay with the concept of quantum tunnelling emerging in 1927 (Nimtz & Haibel, 2008), the same year as Heisenberg's uncertainty principle was formulated (Polkinghorne, 2002) and *To the Lighthouse* was originally published.

Shortly before these groundbreaking scientific discoveries, however, installments of James Joyce's *Work in Progress* (Van Hulle, 2016) began to appear in Europe that would eventually, in 1939, become *Finnegans Wake*, the first example of quantumeracy and the last novel I presented on my reading list. Like the subatomic processes physicists can only theorize over, Joyce's dense text and tightly woven allusions seem to defy interpretation. Ryan (2015) mentions that some "people ... find the language of *Finnegans Wake* highly dysfunctional, while others admire it as a synthesis of different languages" (p. 140), including quantum theorists themselves. In parentheses, Joyce writes about "working out a quantum theory" for the often-abused word *talis*, "for it is really a most tantumising state of affairs" (Joyce, 1992, p. 149). Several other allusions to the work of Einstein and other physicists are lurking in the story, but the strongest case came a few decades after the novel was published. Part of the "imaginative ways" for naming subatomic particles Hawking (1996) mentions is how physicist Murray Gell-Mann got the name for quarks as an "enigmatic quotation from James Joyce" (p. 85), which starts as:

> Three Quarks for Muster Mark!
> Sure he hasn't got much of a bark
> And sure any he has it's all beside the mark. (Joyce, 1992, p. 383)

The reiterative nature of quantumeracy returns to the top of my reading list and layers another interpretation for Jasper Fforde's Quarkbeast.

How far back into literature do readers need to go? *Finnegans Wake* may be a prime example of quantumeracy, yet even Joyce (1992) reaches further back to rewrite familiar stories from earlier ages: his Burrus and Caseous episode retells the story of Shakespeare's *Julius Caesar* "to equate the *qualis* equivalent ... irrumi-nate the quantum urge" (p. 167). Many of the events in Shakespeare's play are a fictional (and anachronistic) recreation of historical reality, and Rosenblatt (1978) distinguishes how "the 'real world' becomes irrelevant or secondary" (p. 31) to the aesthetic parallel for an different textbook history of Caesar, Brutus, and Cassius. A similar retelling of historical events happens in Robert Harris' (2015) novel *Dictator*, which fictionalizes the life of Roman senator and philosopher Marcus Cicero, as recorded by his secretary, Tiro.[9] The assassination of Caesar is condensed into a couple of paragraphs, with Harris (2015) going against the long-held tradition of Caesar's dying words, changing "Et tu, Brute?" to "Even you?" and making them not directed at Marcus Brutus but "a bitter reproach to Decimus [Brutus], who had tricked him" (p. 297). This example of uncertainty fits into my evolving sense of quantumeracy, and *Dictator* became another late addition to the reading list as it was presented in my *Virtual Narrative Inquiry into New Narrative* presenta-tion at the 2016 Canadian Society for the Study of Education Conference.

The purpose of this quantumeracy reading list is to urge transactional readers of all texts to move beyond STEM-based curriculum toward a fusion of foun-dationless quantum-literate elements. From the development of the quantum computers occurring at Burnaby's D-Wave Systems, to Prime Minister Trudeau's "impromptu lecture on quantum mechanics" (Koprowski, 2016) at Waterloo's Perimeter Institute for Theoretical Physics, Canada is poised to become an international centre advancing into the uncertain realm of science. There are a number of Canadian-authored novels on my quantumeracy reading list, and the hope is that including more of these thought-provoking texts into K–12 curriculum will assist in preparing students for the Quantum Moment. Neil Turok (2012), the director of the Perimeter Institute, considers how human "bodies and our senses work in smooth, continuous ways, and we most appreciate music or art or natural experiences that incorporate rich, continuous textures" that he likens to an analog human nature: "We are analog beings living in a digital world, facing a quantum future" (p. 230). Crease and Goldhaber (2015) explore the educational implications calling for a new framework for 21st century learners, one that "requires crossing many traditional disciplinary boundaries, but such is the entangled state of literacy in the modern world" (p. 278). As educators face the uncertain future with their students, my intention with this chapter is to provide a set of reading materials, mostly in the familiar print-based books mentioned on my reading list, that are both fact-based efferent depictions of reality and aesthetic responses to the virtual nature of the written word.

NOTES

1. Unless examining hand-printed texts in a rare-collection library or auction house, every book available in shops today would have had a computer's word processor as part of its creation, from the author's hard drive to the bookseller's inventory. Bruce Rosenblum and Fred Kuttner (2011) discuss in Chapter 9 (pp. 115–123) how one-third of America's economy is based upon products created through applied quantum mechanics: the transistor powering the author's laptop, the laser printer that produces the book's pages, and even the barcode-scanning laser at bookstores and libraries are just a few quantum imprints on the traditional paper-bound book.

2. Given the original radio series closely follows the release of the film *Star Wars* (1977), a parody screenplay may have been the author's initial attempt. Adams humorously writes in his wry "Guide to the Guide" (1992, pp. 7–12) the process of producing the radio show and how the BBC's attitude toward it became "very similar to that which Macbeth had towards murdering people" (p. 9).

3. A more economic-driven form today compared to the idealistic philosophy of John Dewey, who sought the value of intellectual inquiry in itself. Flora Michaels (2011) describes the shift toward the accountability focus in the current "economic story" that she calls *monoculture*.

4. A brief description of each nation can be found on the author's website, under *The Last Dragonslayer* heading "Where's Where": www.jasperfforde.com/dragon/where.html.

5. The title of this novel is one of several that appear under the heading "Thursday Next will return in:" to follow *First Among Sequels* (2007, p. 399). The title of the next in the series was *One of Our Thursdays Is Missing* (2011), with no mention of a follow-up title. *Dark Reading Matter* was also the working title for another part of the series, *The Woman Who Died a Lot* (2012), which at least contains dialogue that describes "an unknown region of story that we call Dark Reading Matter" (p. 81).

6. Many of Fforde's novels are challenging to adapt into more visual media, having many literary puns and imaginary spaces, such as *Thursday Next*'s BookWorld. In December 2016, however, *The Last Dragonslayer* became the first book to be adapted for television as a Sky1 miniseries.

7. Much uncertainty occurs around the lives or deaths of the Yasutani family in Japan: Nao may already be dead when Ruth finds her diary; Haruki #2's unemployment in Japan leads him to suicide; Jiko's reincarnation as a Jungle Crow indicates that she also may be in the afterlife; and even Haruki #1's account of his final days during the Battle of Okinawa survive in letters to his mother, Jiko, despite his not being able to send them. The name given to Ruth's cat, Schrödinger, foreshadows how the death of a character is not certain until it is observed, collapsing the quantum-narrative wavefunction.

8. Proust's seven-volume poem, *À la recherche du temps perdu* (1913–1927), is featured prominently in Ozeki (2013) as the palimpsestic book into which Nao writes her diary as a Time Being.

9. Harris (2015) mentions that there was once such a multi-volume history written by the historical Tiro, referred to by later historians Pedianus and Plutarch, that "disappeared amid the collapse of the Roman Empire" (Author's Note, p. xi).

REFERENCES

Adams, D. (1992). *The hitchhiker's guide to the galaxy: A trilogy in four parts*. London, England: Pan Macmillan.

Alrawi, K. (2015). *Book of sands*. Toronto, ON: Harper Avenue.

Atwood, M. (1989). *Cat's eye*. New York, NY: Doubleday.

Auerbach, E. (2013). *Mimesis: The representation of reality in Western literature*. Princeton, NJ: Princeton University Press.

Crease, R. P., & Goldhaber, A. S. (2015). *The quantum moment: How Planck, Bohr, Einstein, and Heisenberg taught us to love uncertainty*. New York, NY: W. W. Norton & Co.

Einstein, A. (2015). *Relativity: The special & general theory*. Princeton, NJ: Princeton University Press.

Fforde, J. (2001). *The Eyre affair*. London, England: Hodder & Stoughton.

Fforde, J. (2007). *First among sequels*. London, England: Hodder & Stoughton.

Fforde, J. (2011). *The song of the Quarkbeast*. London, England: Hodder & Stoughton.

Fforde, J. (2012). *The woman who died a lot*. London, England: Hodder & Stoughton.

Gibson, W. (2014). *The peripheral.* New York, NY: Berkley Books.

Gribbin, J. (2014). *Computing with quantum cats: From Alan Turing to teleportation.* London, England: Black Swan.

Harris, R. (2015). *Dictator.* London, England: Hutchinson.

Hawking, S. (1996). *The illustrated* A Brief History of Time*: Updated and expanded version.* New York, NY: Bantam Book.

Joyce, J. (1992). *Finnegans wake.* London, England: Penguin.

Koprowski, E. (2016, May 13). The quantum mechanics of Canadian politics. *Masterstudies.ca.* Available at: www.masterstudies.ca/news/The-Quantum-Mechanics-of-Canadian-Politics-877/

L'Engle, M. (1981). *A swiftly tilting planet.* New York, NY: Bantam Doubleday Dell.

Mandel, E. S. (2014). *Station eleven.* Toronto, ON: Harper Avenue.

Michaels, F. S. (2011). *Monoculture: How one story is changing everything.* Canada: Red Clover Press.

Nimtz, G., & Haibel, A. (2008). *Zero time space: How quantum tunneling broke the light speed barrier.* Weinheim, Germany: Wiley-VCH.

Orzel, C. (2012). Gandalf was wrong: Middle-earth needs science. *Tor.com.* Available at: www.tor.com/2012/10/11/why-gandalf-is-wrong

Osnaghi, S., Freitas, F., & Freire, O. Jr. (2008). The origin of the Everettian heresy. *Studies in History and Philosophy of Science, 40*(2), 97–123.

Ozeki, R. (2013). *A tale for the time being.* Toronto, ON: Viking.

Polkinghorne, J. (2002). *Quantum theory: A very short introduction.* Oxford, England: Oxford University Press.

Rosenblatt, L. M. (1978). *The reader, the text, the poem: The transactional theory of the literary work.* Carbondale, IL: South Illinois University Press.

Rosenblatt, L. M. (2005). *Making meaning with text: Selected essays.* L. Luedeke (Ed.). Portsmouth, NH: Heinemann.

Rosenblum, B., & Kuttner, F. (2011). *Quantum enigma: Physics encounters consciousness.* New York, NY: Oxford University Press.

Ryan, M.-L. (1991). *Possible worlds, artificial intelligence, and narrative theory.* Bloomington, IN: Indiana University Press.

Ryan, M.-L. (2015). *Narrative as virtual reality 2: Revisiting immersion and interactivity in literature and electronic media.* Baltimore, MD: Johns Hopkins University Press.

Stoppard, T. (1993). *Arcadia.* London, England: Faber and Faber.

Tolkien, J. R. R. (1999). *The fellowship of the ring: The lord of the rings, part 1.* London, England: Harper Collins.

Turok, N. (2012). *The universe within: From quantum to cosmos.* Toronto, ON: House of Anansi Press.

Van Hulle, D. (2016). *James Joyce's "Work in Progress": Pre-book publications of* Finnegans Wake *fragments*. Abingdon, England: Routledge.

Vonnegut, K. Jr. (1969). *Slaughterhouse five, or the children's crusade*. New York, NY: Delacorte Press.

Woolf, V. (1992). *To the lighthouse*. London, England: Penguin.

INVOCATION

Reading the Water for the Wind:
On the Remnants of Curriculum

Lisa Farley and RM Kennedy

" I love the wind, Mother, but does the wind love me?" (Obed & Steffler, 1990). We take this question from a children's collection of environmental poems set on the Newfoundland coast as a metaphor for encountering that which is always slightly beyond our grasp. Its expression of the uncertainty of love translates, for us, into the fine risk of learning that involves staking a relationship with knowledge that sweeps away staid meanings and promises no certainty in return. Its gusty referent, too, reminds us of Socrates' observation of the invisible element of the wind that appears only in the impressions it leaves behind. "The winds themselves are invisible," he writes, "yet what they do is manifest to us and we somehow feel their approach" (cited in Arendt, 1971, p. 174). Wind is slippery stuff, catchable only in traces: worn cheeks, windmills, jet trails, swollen waves, and flotsam washing against the shore.

The same may be true of curriculum, such that ideas, words, thoughts, and meanings are after-effects of a blustery encounter. From the perspective of the wind, teaching and learning can be neither predicted nor measured, but rather glimpsed as ripples in the water of signification. Windswept curriculum tousles set pathways, exposing the elusive and unconscious elements of meaning brought to the surface from the deep. The metaphor of wind invites curriculum scholars to lean into the gale and be carried into the stark conditions of teaching, learning, and thinking itself. There, we may find unspoken meanings held in the traces left in its wake. From the perspective of the wind, curriculum is an invisible labour of thought, and words are its remnants that invite the work of reading and renewing our shared world.

REFERENCES

Arendt, H. (1971). *The life of the mind*. New York, NY: Harcourt.

Obed, E. B., & Steffler, S. (1990). *Wind in my pocket*. St. John's, NL: Breakwater Books.

A9

The Character of Contemporary Curriculum Studies in Canada: A Rumination on the Ecological and Metaphorical Nature of Language

Kelly Young

> *All education is environmental education.*
> (David Orr, 1992, p. 81)

At the end of the 20th century, Cynthia Chambers (1999) revisited challenges facing Canadian curriculum theorists in her groundbreaking article, "A Topography for Canadian Curriculum Theory." She proposed that Canadian curriculum theorists must continue to question the *topos*, "the particular places and regions where we live and work" (p. 147). When I reflect on Chambers' question about the *topos* in relation to the character of a contemporary understanding of curriculum studies in Canada, I am reminded of the complex conditions of the development of ecological habits of mind and the importance of the literary imagination in pedagogical practices (Pinar, 2011). By ecological habits of mind, I mean our perceptions of our relationship with place that are formed through metaphorical language and lived experiences in natural settings (Young, 2008).

I have ruminated on this subject, both theoretically and pedagogically, in an exploration of what it means to provoke curriculum in this *place*. Trent University resides on a beautiful natural landscape on the Otonabee River in Peterborough, Ontario. The School of Education at Trent is my pedagogical setting. It is in the university classrooms, as well as outside in this particular place surrounded by wild woodland, that I imagine how particular spaces of pedagogy expose our complex relations to place as we explore particular forms of knowledge and lived experience.

The development of ecological habits of mind involves the enhancement of an ecological consciousness that brings notions of interdependence, co-implicated relationships and the natural world into focus in daily educational practices that involve, among other things, literary explorations of root metaphors (Bowers, 2002, 2004, 2011). It is through the literary imagination that ecological habits of mind can be fostered in teacher education. (Young, 2008, p. 1)

Gary Nabhan and Stephen Trimble's (1994) insightful understanding of *The Geography of Childhood* helps to outline the importance of the natural world in human development:

> For ourselves, and for our planet, we must be both strong and strongly connected—with each other, with the earth. As children, we need time to wander, to be outside, to nibble on icicles and watch ants, to build with dirt and sticks in a hollow of the earth, to lie back and contemplate clouds and chickadees. These simple acts forge the connections that define a land of one's own—home and refuge for both girls and boys. (p. 75)

By examining our relations with the natural world we are also considering the discourses that create both sustainable and unsustainable practices that profoundly influence child development in terms of children's perceptions of their relationships to their environment (Cobb, 1959; Coles, 1990; Nabhan, 1997; Nabhan & Rosenberg, 1997). In order to help students become ecologically literate (Orr, 1992) and develop ecological habits of mind (Young, 2008), I consider root metaphors embedded in eco-mythical narratives in order to reveal the ways that language carries forward anti-ecological ways of knowing and being (both culturally and naturally) in the world (Bowers, 2002).

> There are no windows in our cold basement classroom. We cannot see the wind moving through the tree branches or hear the birds sing. It is here that we play with language. Nouns. Verbs. Metaphors. We move between two words on the board: drain and stream. What do they mean? What are the associations we make when we read them? We reveal the ways in which one of these words has a mechanistic analog = drain, and one has an ecological analog = stream. Both lead to the same place, yet they are not conceptualized in the same way. In this classroom we start to look at ecologies of communication that are based upon a human-centred world where enlightenment metaphors continue to be pervasive. (Writing Excerpt, September 21, 2015)

Within these stark concrete walls we peel back the layers of language to see that words have a history and particular associations as they encode earlier thought processes and are carried forward through taken-for-granted ways of thinking (Bowers, 2002, 2006, 2011; Martusewicz, Edmundson, & Lupinacci, 2011; Young, 2009). There is an urgent challenge for educators to engage a contemporary curriculum that teaches about the cultural and linguistic roots of ecological and social crises. How do we ask difficult questions about social misconceptions and cultural biases in Western language that encode earlier patterns of taken-for-granted thinking? How do we engage a curriculum that challenges enlightenment principles where metaphoric language describes a world that is fixed, abstract, and rational? How do we engage a curriculum that challenges misconceptions of a paradigm of "endless progress"? What is lost when we cannot name these analogs as interpretive frameworks that prevent us from seeing how words have a history? Understood from an ecological perspective, human relations with the natural world are conceived by others and by our own internalized histories through mechanistic metaphors that have a particular history.

There can be no "outside" without "inside" and vice versa. One cannot comprehend one's complex identity without understanding how it is interdependent upon the natural world. All humans are embedded in an ecosystem, and our relationship to the earth involves a story we inherit and reinterpret. In this sense, curriculum—our construction and reinterpretation of this ecological knowledge for conversation with youth—becomes a form of ecological analysis. Understanding curriculum as ecological analysis implies that knowledge enables us to see the *topos* and our complex relationship to it. Children are being denied access to their *topos* or what we might call their ecological curricular rights. William F. Pinar and Madeleine Grumet (1976) understand curriculum as autobiographical text, and they trace the meaning of *curriculum* to its Latin infinite *currere*, as a course to be run or

> to run the course: Thus *currere* refers to an existential experience of institutional structures. The method of *currere* is a strategy devised to expose experience, so that we may see more of it and see more clearly. With such seeing can come deepened understanding of the running, and with this, can come deepened agency. (p. vii)

With a reconceptualization of contemporary curriculum understood as environmental autobiographical text (Doerr, 2004), we can begin to question our curricular relationship to the *topos*. Gary Nabhan and Stephen Trimble (1994) write:

Our world today is one in which we are losing ways of speaking about plants and animals as rapidly as we are losing endangered species themselves. Oral traditions about plants, animals, treacherous waters, and complex topography depend upon specific vocabularies that encode particularities which may not be recognized in the lexicons of commonly spoken, widespread languages. (p. 94)

I engage creative non-fiction as a form of rumination to help me answer questions about our relationship with the *topos*.

AN ECOLOGICAL CURRICULAR INQUIRY: CULTURAL MYTHOLOGIES AND EVENTS OF IDENTIFICATION

From a bird's-eye view, we sit in a circle surrounded by pine trees as we consider the complexity of curriculum studies. In response to Chambers' (1999) call for a rumination about our relationship to place, we spend time outside the classroom walls and contemplate questions about landscape and identity. We delve into (a) exploring a reconceptualist framing of ecological curriculum where we inquire into the ways in which curriculum participates in the making of identity; (b) exploring a reconceptualist approach to the complexity, ecology, culture, and character of curriculum studies; and (c) questioning identification experiences concerned with complex relations among past, present, and imagined experiences in natural settings. We engage in our inquiries through writing pedagogies framed within a liberating-constraint method (Davis, Sumara, & Luce-Kapler, 2000, p. 87). That is, we engage in writing practices that are at once creative and restrictive to explore questions about the development of our ecological habits of mind (Young, 2009). A liberating-constraint method enables participants to follow a prescriptive writing exercise while at the same time inserting free writing as a form of narrative stream of consciousness. The exercise becomes an important site to explore and interpret complex relations among landscape, identity, and curriculum.

In our circle, underneath the vivid blue sky, surrounded by the smell of cedar trees, and the sounds of rushing water from the Otonabee River, we ruminate on our own relationship with place. What are our oldest memories of being in the natural world? Where is our favourite place? We write about our encounters in prose through timed-writing activities as we engage in a stream-of-consciousness that brings together memory, history, and language, and exposes the complex relations of place and knowledge. As

a site of pedagogical interpretation, we explore identity-formation—being
in place—through aesthetic practices. (Writing Excerpt, October 4, 2015)

After our writing session, we engage in a further discussion about the stories that
frame our understanding of the development of our ecological habits of mind.
Students are invited to share their narratives and make connections between particular forms of knowledge represented in their prose. We then play with the form
through Brent Davis, Dennis Sumara, and Rebecca Luce-Kapler's (2000) conceptualization of a liberating-constraint method and moderate our lengthy texts
by eliminating excess adverbs, adjectives, and expressions through poetic inquiry
that distills prose into poetic form. Poetic inquiry serves as a way to draw out
and provoke experience (Prendergast, Leggo, & Sameshima, 2009). Poetic inquiry
brings to the forefront a discourse of imagination and possibility involving an exploration of pedagogy with/in place. We envision tracing pathways our ancestors
have walked and remember stories retold where history and memory help in the
meaning-making process. Ancestral pathways are places where Elders dwelled in
our natural world, leaving imaginable footprints for us to follow. The stories conjure
up images as poetic inquiry allows for an expression of our perceptions of history
and memory. It is where stories and interpretations of these stories are revisited
from a time long ago. In this vein, what follows is a poem that emerged from my/
our class writing activities.

Seeds of Memory
In the clamour of the backwoods
lives a story
of bearers of light
who came before us

we know our way to the circle
across logs, past hollow trees
to a mythical place
where we gaze into history
absorb tales that bind us
flowing across tongues

song-poems at twilight
wash over us
as we dream of sandpipers

who gather shiny stones
cradle found treasures
offerings from the earth

where seagulls swoop
slicing through air
plunging into waves
forming ripples
that dissolve into silence

Engaging in writing activities allows for a creative outlet as we engage in discussions about our shared understandings of our human place in the natural world. We share our writing, continue our dialogue about the interrelatedness of all things, and recant cultural myths about our understanding of the ways in which schooling is mainly an indoor activity separate from the natural world. We delve into our insights about our own identifications with place.

By examining the complex conditions of contemporary Canadian curriculum studies through ecology, it is possible to consider how anti-ecological habits of mind may be interrupted during a writing event. In this chapter, I have explored the ways in which my students and I engage in questions of the character of contemporary curriculum studies in relation to the *topos*—that is, questioning what it means to provoke curriculum in this place through an analysis of our own development of ecological habits of mind through aesthetic writing activities. We considered how a cultural and linguistic analysis of our knowledge and understanding of our relations with natural places is embedded in stories that we inherit and reinterpret over a lifetime. It is in a special place that we are able to inquire into the ways in which language plays a role in the making of ecological habits of mind and consider how cultural mythologies play into the making of identity. By spending time considering the complex conditions of contemporary Canadian curriculum through ecology, we can begin to understand the interrelatedness of all life in deeper ways through our individual and collective stories.

REFERENCES

Bowers, C. A. (2002). Toward an eco-justice pedagogy. *Environmental Education Research*, *8*(1), 21–34.

Bowers, C. A. (2004). *Eco-justice dictionary*. Available at: www.cabowers.net

Bowers, C. A. (2006). *Revitalizing the commons: Cultural and educational sites of resistance and affirmation*. Langham, MA: Lexington Books.

Bowers, C. A. (2011). *Perspectives on the ideas of Gregory Bateson: Ecological intelligence and educational reforms.* Eugene, OR: Eco-Justice Press.

Chambers, C. (1999). A topography for Canadian curriculum theory. *Canadian Journal of Education, 24*(2), 137–150.

Cobb, E. (1959). The ecology of imagination in childhood. *Daedalus: Journal of the American Academy of Arts and Sciences, 88*(Summer), 537–548.

Coles, R. (1990). *The spiritual life of children.* San Diego, CA: Houghton Mifflin Harcourt.

Davis, B., Sumara, D., & Luce-Kapler, R. (2000). *Engaging minds: Learning and teaching in a complex world.* Mahwah, NJ: Erlbaum.

Doerr, M. (2004). *Currere and the environmental autobiography: A phenomenological approach to the teaching of ecology.* New York, NY: Peter Lang.

Martusewicz, R., Edmundson, J., & Lupinacci, J. (2011). *Ecojustice education: Toward diverse, democratic, and sustainable communities.* New York, NY: Routledge.

Nabhan, G. (1997). *Cultures of habit: On nature, culture, and stories.* Washington, DC: Counterpoint Press.

Nabhan, G., & Rosenberg, J. (1997). Where ancient stories guide children home. *Natural History, 106*(9), 54–61.

Nabhan, G., & Trimble, S. (1994). *The geography of childhood: Why children need wild places.* Boston, MA: Beacon Press.

Orr, D. (1992). *Ecological literacy: Education and the transition to a postmodern world.* Albany, NY: State University of New York Press.

Pinar, W. F. (2011). *The character of curriculum studies: Bildung, currere, and the recurring question of the subject.* New York, NY: Palgrave Macmillan.

Pinar, W. F., & Grumet, M. (1976). *Toward a poor curriculum.* Dubuque, IA: Kendall Hunt Publishing.

Prendergast, M., Leggo, C., & Sameshima, P. (Eds.). (2009). *Poetic inquiry: Vibrant voices in the social sciences.* Rotterdam, The Netherlands: Sense Publishers.

Young, K. (2005). Developing ecological literacy as a habit of mind in teacher education. *The EcoJustice Review: Educating for the Commons, 1*(1), 1–7.

Young, K. (2008). Ecological habits of mind and the literary imagination. *Educational Insights, 12*(1), 1–9.

Young, K. (2009). Reconceptualizing elementary language arts curriculum: An ecojustice approach. In L. Iannacci & P. Whitty (Eds.), *Early childhood curricula: Reconceptualist perspectives* (pp. 299–325). Calgary, AB: Detselig.

INVOCATION

Siren's Ghost Net

Pauline Sameshima and Sean Wiebe

The marine glow catches her cheek
a fleeting snapshot as she moves abandoned
in and out of my frame pushed, propelled
by the currents, she dances
comforted in darkness.

I watch her exhaling, absolved,
she drifts while I am bounded here,
her spine is strong ribbed and striated,
unhindered by her billowing dress
miles of nylon flowing, orchestrated

in careful moon choreography,
her elegance so far from me
arising in glory, prismic liquid light,
a glistening silhouette
that blinds my downward gaze.

And then her Prussian wedding dress trails
into view, a tangled carrion of
lifeless weights. Her face
surprised as if she's unprepared
for the burden of Dorian Gray.

Against thrashings of the new catches
she knows fate, arms soft
waning against the slipstream
willing the dead to drag her down
to the scavengers and bottom feeders.

There, translucent, she waits
to be cleansed of her waste, her curse,
urges her glass floats to raise her again

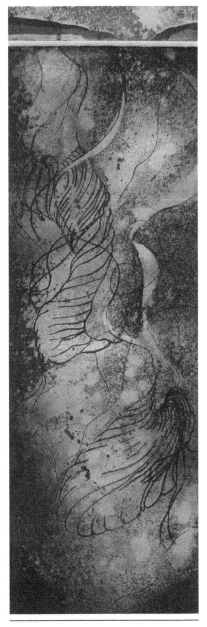

Jenn Whitford Robins. *Driftnet abstraction.* Intaglio print

where I might hear her shimmering song
come to me, oh lover, come.

Mortality and immortality are both unknown
she would pull me up and down
to rise and fall eternally
ensnared, her slow dance of dross
with no refrain

I am white-knuckled in this fog
its anesthetic shutting down my will
I wear my hat pulled down,
afraid of the dark, afraid to be alone,
my feet mostly stumbling
to a music that leads me home.

With sustained engagement in the artwork and research into the vast implications of lost and abandoned drift nets, our response to "Driftnet Abstraction" by Canadian printmaker Jenn Whitford Robins illustrates how the collaborative model Parallaxic Praxis (Sameshima & Vandermause, 2008) can generate repair through multi-perspective views.

REFERENCE

Sameshima, P., & Vandermause, R. (2008). Parallaxic praxis: An artful interdisciplinary collaborative research methodology. In B. Kožuh, R. Kahn, & A. Kozlowska (Eds.), *The practical science of society* (pp. 141–152). Grand Forks, England: The College of Education and Human Development & Slovenian Research Agency.

MÉTISSAGE B

B1

Provoking the Intimate Dialogue: A Path of Love

Samira Thomas

I recognized her by her hands. There was something unseeable in my mother's face when she passed away, but her hands, those I recognized. I sat with her a while, crying over her body, whispering, "I love you," again and again.

I recognized her by her hands.

There is an intimacy of knowledge when you can know somebody in this way—by their feet, their gait, their shrug. It is a knowledge of the way a person moves through the world, experiences the world, bound by their skin, the inflexibility of their muscles, the delicate nature of their wave. It is the way I knew my mother, a knowledge that was born out of love for her and a decades-long intimate dialogue that remains ongoing. It wasn't just a physical knowledge, but also one of the imagination.

Some in education may recoil at the idea of drawing intimacy into the class-room. Indeed, a quick search of the existing work on intimacy and education demonstrates the use of the words *intimate* and *intimacy* to indicate a sexual nature (Miller & Larrabee, 1995). A select few relate to the idea of small class sizes (Wynne & Walberg, 1995), but fewer still consider the need for intimacy in the knowing of things. Perhaps the suggestion of intimacy is dangerous. And yet, there is a vibrant world of intimate engagement in curriculum studies, from *currere* (Pinar, 2011) to a/r/tography (Irwin, 2013), from poetic inquiry (Prendergast, Leggo, & Sameshima, 2009) to life writing (Chambers, Hasebe-Ludt, Leggo, & Sinner, 2012). Intimacy is not only a sexual act, it is an act of depth, closeness, and love. It is the knowing of another by their hands.

The Intimate Dialogue is a "prayerful act" (Macdonald, 1995), born out of the notion of prayer theorized by the 12th-century Sufi scholar Ibn 'Arabi. He developed the contours of his Sufism—a particular path of love that calls for considering the Beloved only through love. Love is a central part of the Islamic doctrine broadly (Chittick, 2014), with almost 30 different kinds of love exhibiting themselves in the Qu'ran (Muhammad, 2013). We may think of love in Islam through three broad strokes. The first is the path of *Shariah*, the path of jurisprudence. This comes as a means of mandated behaviours, but "there is no possible way to enforce the edicts, 'Love God' and 'Love your neighbor'" (Chittick, 2014, p. 230). We may find ways to understand these edicts as being realized, for example, through kindness to neighbours or good deeds done in the name of God, but in reality, we have no way to measure a mandate to love. The second path is that of *Kalam*, which can be roughly understood as theology. In essence, the word *kalam* means "the word" and in this case, the word of God, making this path a series of commandments, and our demonstration of our "love for God is that we obey" (Chittick, 2014, p. 3). The third path is that of *Sufism*, the goal of which is "to achieve a profound transformation in the very substance of the human soul, changing the way we see ourselves and the world" (Chittick, 2014, p. 231), a transformation that Ibn 'Arabi believed was found through prayer, the Intimate Dialogue between the lover and the Beloved.

Love in Islam and its paths illuminate our understanding of curriculum. Too often we seek the *shariah* of education, that which is mandated and measured through proxies like acts of kindness, never fully grasping the spirit of those we seek to educate. What if, instead, we approached learning through the *Sufi* path, enabling educators and learners to take on the roles of lover and Beloved, enabling an Intimate Dialogue?

Where do you go when you sit in prayer? When you read a poem? When you are confronted by a ballerina of Degas or the lilies of Monet? Where do you go when you write and paint and dance and sing these worlds of your own? And when you feel mathematics stir your soul as al-Khwarizmi did? When you are confronted by the earth-as-a-pale-blue-dot in the cosmic sea that Carl Sagan enlivened for us? Where do you go when you have reached the limit of your intellectual and sensual journey? Just imagine.

It is the Realm of the Imagination, that world that Maxine Greene (1995) saw allowed us to see that "things can be actually 'otherwise'" (pp. 78–79). It is not the world of the intellect, nor the world of the senses, but an intermediary world; "it is the world through which spirits are embodied, and bodies spiritualized" (Bloom, 1998, p. xiii). It is the place where we find ourselves and the Beloved able to meet, enter into communion, engage in an intimate dialogue. It is the place we visit when we meet art, the wonder of the cosmos, the incredible magnificence of our world, and all that live around it. It is where teacher and student meet in a gasp of wonder, together. The world of the imagination is not a world in which things are created out of nothingness, but rather, a world that allows us to witness a process of increasing illumination (Bloom, 1998, p. xiv). It is in this place that intimacy is found.

Spirit(ual). Spirit, "the nonphysical part of a person regarded as a person's true self, the seat of emotions and character; the soul" (Spirit, n.d.). Spirit once simply meant *breath*. To learn someone intimately is to learn her breath, to reach her spirit.

What if we thought of our truest selves dwelling in our inhalation and exhalation?

Inhale. This is your spirit, your truest self. We are *that* fragile, each one of us.

It is here we can consider our first breath and our last. Upon our first breath, we take in the world. We are offered it all:

> The aggregate of our joy and suffering, thousands of confident religions, ideologies, and economic doctrines, every hunter and forager, every hero and coward, every creator and destroyer of civilization, every king and peasant, every young couple in love, every mother and father, hopeful child, inventor and explorer, every teacher of morals, every corrupt politician, every "superstar," every "supreme leader," every saint and sinner in the history of our species. (Sagan & Druyan, 2011, p. 6)

Our first breath takes it all in.

"To speak of the 'spirit' and the 'spiritual' is not to speak of something 'other' than humankind, merely 'more' than humankind as it is lived and known" (Huebner, 1985/1999, p. 342). When we speak of the spirit and the spiritual, we allow ourselves to live for a moment and witness "more than the material, the sensory, and the quantitative" (Huebner, 1985/1999, p. 342). It is here that we perhaps live in the Imaginal Realm, where we take in one another in each breath, where we let go of our truest selves with every breath. And in our inhaling and exhaling together, we begin the Intimate Dialogue. Henry Ford believed so strongly that our spirit, what he called our souls, exists in our breath that he tried to preserve the last breath of his best friend, Thomas Edison. This testament to a friendship and the life of one spirit lives now at the Henry Ford Museum (Alexander, 2015). Though invisible, the relic of Edison's breath is the world of friendship and love, treasured by Ford always. In our last breath, perhaps we exhale every story we ever told, every inch of wisdom we gained in our lifetime, every foible and folly, our every laugh, tear, and eye-roll. That last breath holds our truest self with our hopes and fears, heartbreaks, memories, things we have forgotten along the way, every sigh of sadness and every hiccup; it is all there. There to be taken in by others, there for the newborns about to take their first breath.

Exhale.

My mother's name meant "light" and when I was born, she called me "companion." This was the first story I ever held, the first story that ever held me: Light's Companion. Companion of the Light. When she was killed in the evening light in Kabul, the sun was shining brilliantly in Vancouver. I stepped outside after hearing the news and was blinded. The light was illuminating every blade of grass, every speckle in the pavement, every leaf in every tree. Light was kissing the whole world. Light was kissing me, perhaps, goodbye.

Samira. *Companion.* Together, with bread. Vanier (2008) describes what it means to be a companion. It is an aspirational definition:

> It implies sharing together, eating together, nourishing each other, walking together. The one who accompanies is like a midwife, helping us to come to life, to live more fully. But the accompanier receives life also, and as people open up to each other, a communion of hearts develops between them. They do not clutch on to each other but give life to one another and call each other to greater freedom. (Vanier, 2008, p. 129)

Ultimately, a companion is one who "loves us and understands our life" (Vanier, 2008, p. 128). An Intimate Dialogue embraces the subjective histories and landscapes of the participants, the unknown entities of their lives. It exists between companions, under the shade of love, in the midst of understanding. Understanding is different from knowing. In understanding another we find compassion, patience, empathy, and space to grow and explore. In knowing another, we find answers, expectations, and rules that are more often than not misplaced. In knowing, there is the assumption that the boundaries of a being are known, defined, unchanging, and perhaps most laughably, knowable.

As a path, the Intimate Dialogue seeks to internalize Pinar's (2011) *currere* as it "occurs through conversation, not only classroom discourse but also dialogue among specific students and teachers and within oneself in solitude" (p. 1). It holds the spirit of *currere* as its consequence is certainly an "intensified subjective engagement with the world" (Pinar, 2010, p. 178). The Intimate Dialogue emphasizes the relational in achieving a deeper subjective engagement with the world, and, indeed, understanding the world to be both beyond and within oneself.

As a/r/tography "became an unanticipated integrative strategy for student and teacher learning" (Irwin, 2013, p. 201), the Intimate Dialogue is not about the growth of the student or the teacher, the researcher or the subject, but of both, concurrently. It is a way of reaching together for the quiet places within that take searching to find.

The Intimate Dialogue liberates dreams from the realm of dismissed unreality they dwell in today. It frees the imagination to become an avenue from which we can learn. It enables us to share our realities without needing to be known, but yearning to be understood. It allows us to become companions for a moment or a lifetime, and beyond, on the path we walk each day.

There is a reason I refer to the Beloved in this way. It opens up a space to recognize many as Beloved, to adopt, in a sense, the Hindu concept of *Namaste*. This term is one that has been translated as: *I bow to the divine in you*. We begin, therefore, by treating the others in our dialogue as our Beloved.

It must first and foremost be welcomed. Invited.

It begins in love, within the two beings. The participants must take on the role of lover and Beloved, honouring the subjective beings that they each are, embracing the complexity of the lives that are entering the dialogue. They must become conspirators, knowing that they will never know all of the stories that each holds or the names the other answers to, but will seek to understand one another, to love one another, to liberate one another.

Like other prayerful acts, the Intimate Dialogue is enacted in places that offer themselves to meditative work; it is your sacred place, that place "where you can find yourself/ again and again" (Campbell, 2011, p. 89). Is it your studio? The dark room? The woods? Beneath the night sky? Your CathedralMosqueSynagogue? For me and my mother, it was our kitchen. I was the sous-chef to her chef, meticulously chopping things as I shared my innermost thoughts, and she hers. Between conversations, I admired her precision in measuring ingredients by their feel in her palm, a palm that I came to know through the taste of my food, its grasp crossing the street, its wiping away of my tears. She would dance with a spoon in her hand as she concocted our favourite meals. Our hands were busy, our conversations varied from lighthearted to deeply felt. This was our place where we found ourselves again and again. In the wisdom of a/r/tography, it is often a conversation over an activity of co-creation or exploration. Find your place where you find yourself, again and again. Use your hands, write your stories, go fishing. Leave the office spaces, flee the florescent hum of the old research rooms.

The Intimate Dialogue blooms like a flower. Have you ever watched a flower bloom in the spring? Some take longer than expected, while others bloom before anticipated; some last for days, growing steadily stronger until they are gone, while others last months. Spend a year or two watching the flowers bloom and wilt, and you will begin to understand the timelessness of the Intimate Dialogue. It cannot be rushed, but happens in its own time. Perhaps after a decade of watching, we will both have more wisdom on the matter.

In intimacy, there is compassion and mercy. Compassion, to suffer with. Mercy, a reward. Because the Intimate Dialogue does not simply touch the joys and sorrows of our lives but meets them where they reside, we become more-than-witness to these joys and sorrows. We hold them alongside our own stories, integrate them into our biographies, tell and retell their narrative arcs, and find ourselves transformed in the process.

The Intimate Dialogue asks us to share the same air. To be conscious of this. To recognize that our breath is a shared breath, that our joys can offer scaffolding in moments when the other's joy has collapsed. It asks us to be cognizant of the other's mortal and divine sigh. To inhale the breath of the other. To exhale yourself into the other.

Go together to the Imaginal Realm. Here let your face, body, memories, stories, blood, images, ancestors, ghosts, inhabitants, habits, habitats, relations, spirits, monsters, familiars come to life (Jardine, 2012, p. 161). Take the awe-filled and the awful moments and enact them in ways that feel physically impossible. Give life to the fairies, the ballerinas, the lilies, and sit with them in the afternoon sun. The Intimate Dialogue asks for the participants to share, to articulate this to another. It asks for us to meet in the ecotone of the imagination,

> the space where diverse ecological habitats, such as a meadow and a forest, intersect, a space of tension, or fecundity, a space of complex and intense liveliness, only possible with the overlapping and intersecting of distinct differences. The ecotone is tangled and messy, defying simple formulae for order and organization. (Leggo, 2002, n.p.)

It is not a space that offers ease initially. We will find challenges and swerves (Retallack, 2003, p. 1) along the way. We arrive in this space without a numbered list of questions to be checked off. We arrive with openness, ready to share our breath, and to learn together.

In this place, we may come to recognize our curriculum by its hands, its gait, its way of moving through us, and through this world.

REFERENCES

Alexander, E. (2015). *The light of the world: A memoir.* New York, NY: Grand Central Publishing.

Bloom, H. (1998). Preface. In H. Corbin, *Alone with the alone: Creative imagination in the Sūfism of Ibn 'Arabī* (pp. ix–xx). Princeton, NJ: Princeton University Press.

Campbell, J. (2011). Living in the world. In R. Walter (Ed.), *A Joseph Campbell companion: Reflections on the art of living* (pp. 27–106). [Kindle version]. Available at: Amazon.com.

Chambers, C. M., Hasebe-Ludt, E., Leggo, C., & Sinner, A. (Eds.). (2012). *A heart of wisdom: Life writing as empathetic inquiry.* New York, NY: Peter Lang.

Chittick, W. C. (2014). Love in Islamic thought. *Religion Compass, 8*(7), 229–238. doi: 10.1111/rec3.12112

Greene, M. (1995). *Releasing the imagination: Essays on education, the arts, and social change.* San Francisco, CA: Jossey-Bass.

Huebner, D. E. (1985/1999). Spirituality and knowing. In V. Hillis (Ed.), *The lure of the transcendent: Collected essays by Dwayne E. Huebner* (pp. 340–352). Mahwah, NJ: Erlbaum.

Irwin, R. L. (2013). Becoming a/r/tography. *Studies in Art Education, 54*(3), 198–215.

Jardine, D. W. (2012). *Pedagogy left in peace: Cultivating free spaces in teaching and learning.* New York, NY: Continuum.

Leggo, C. (2002). Living with hope in schools. *Alberta Teachers' Association Magazine, 83*(2). Available at: www.teachers.ab.ca/Publications/ATA%20Magazine/Volume%2083/ Number%202/Articles/Pages/Living%20with%20Hope%20in%20Schools.aspx

Macdonald, B. J. (Ed.). (1995). *Theory as a prayerful act: The collected essays of James B. Macdonald.* New York, NY: Peter Lang.

Miller, G. M., & Larrabee, M. J. (1995). Sexual intimacy in counselor education and supervision: A national survey. *Counselor Education and Supervision, 34*(4), 332–343.

Muhammad, G. B. (2013). *Love in the holy Quran.* Cambridge, England: The Islamic Texts Society.

Pinar, W. F. (2010). Currere. In C. Kreidel (Ed.), *Encyclopedia of curriculum studies* (pp. 177–178). Thousand Oaks, CA: Sage.

Pinar, W. F. (2011). *The character of curriculum studies: Bildung, currere, and the recurring question of the subject.* New York, NY: Palgrave Macmillan.

Prendergast, M., Leggo, C., & Sameshima, P. (Eds.). (2009). *Poetic inquiry: Vibrant voices in the social sciences.* Rotterdam, The Netherlands: Sense Publishers.

Retallack, J. (2003). *The poethical wager.* Berkeley, CA: University of California Press.

Sagan, C., & Druyan, A. (2011). *Pale blue dot: A vision of the human future in space.* New York, NY: Ballantine Books.

Spirit. (n.d.). In *Oxford English dictionary online*. Available at: en.oxforddictionaries.com/ definition/us/spirit

Vanier, J. (2008). *Becoming human*. New York, NY: Paulist Press.

Wynne, E. A., & Walberg, H. J. (1995). The virtues of intimacy in education. *Educational Leadership, 53*(3), 53–54.

INVOCATION

Three Invocations That Provoke:
Strangler Figs, Madness, and Earthquakes

Peter P. Grimmett

Three things have struck me during my leave here in Australia and New Zealand. First, in the Daintree Rainforest, on the tropical northeast coast of Queensland (after boating in crocodile-infested waters and quickly realizing that lifejackets were but a symbolic reference to lifesaving), my wife and I came across the strangler fig phenomenon within the dense rainforest trails.

The strangler fig has an aggressive growth habit that ensures its survival in the rainforest. Beginning life as a sticky seed left on a high tree branch by an animal such as a bird, bat, or monkey, the young strangler lives on the tree's surface. The seedlings grow slowly at first, getting their nutrients from the sun, rain, and leaf litter that has collected on the host. The stranglers send out many thin roots that snake down the trunk of the host tree or dangle as aerial roots from its branches. When the roots reach the ground, they dig in and put on a growth spurt, competing with the host tree for water and nutrients. They also send out a network of roots that encircle the host tree and fuse together. As the roots grow thicker they squeeze the trunk of their host and cut off its flow of nutrients. In the canopy the strangler fig puts out lots of leaves that soon grow thicker than the host tree's and rob it of sunlight. Eventually the host dies from strangulation, insufficient sunlight, and root competition, and the strangler fig stands on its own. A hollow centre is all that remains of the host.

Second, while in Adelaide, Australia, my wife and I saw the 15th world performance of John Numeier's controversial ballet *Nijinsky*. It was actually my wife's gift for my 70th birthday! The ballet choreographs Nijinsky's descent into madness. Cavorting between vivid reminiscences of his homosexual affair with his famed teacher, Serge Diaghilev, and his subsequent heterosexual marriage to Romola de Pulszky, the woman who had pursued him, Nijinsky's creative urges are danced out in this gripping human exposition. In Nijinsky's eyes, it is the world around him that has gone mad, not Nijinsky himself. It is as if Nijinsky's own creative forces have strangled his life-world.

Third, while in Blenheim, New Zealand, we found ourselves far too close to the epicentre of the 7.8 earthquake two minutes after midnight on November 13, 2016. Three minutes of violent seismic activity left us feeling hopelessly out of control and terrified.

What could this mean for curriculum? Sometimes we may become so caught up with all sorts of legitimate pursuits that we do not realize that the roots of such preoccupations are diverting the focus away from the academic curriculum. Without a firm grounding in the academic curriculum, we are prone to losing sight of the important focus on the subject and our subjectivity that enables both "the making present of content to persons" (Huebner, as cited in Grumet, 1978, p. 278) and the making of "persons who are made present through the contact with curriculum" (Grumet, 1978, p. 278). When that happens, our creative forces have possibly begun to strangle our life-world, inviting a descent into madness, leaving us feeling hopelessly out of control.

REFERENCE

Grumet, M. (1978). Songs and situations. In G. Willis (Ed.), *Qualitative evaluation* (pp. 274–315). Berkeley, CA: McCutchan.

B2

Eros, Aesthetics, and Education: Intersections of Life and Learning

Boyd White

INTRODUCTION

This chapter examines links between eros and aesthetics and their place in education. I am arguing for an aesthetic foundation to all levels of education—for attention to the sensuous qualities of daily existence and the combined affective/reflective/corporeal resonance that results from such attention.

I teach in a faculty of education. One of my goals is to encourage my students to define who they are as individuals and as teachers—to know themselves. As Parker Palmer (1998) has insisted, "We teach who we are.... When I do not know myself, I cannot know my subject—not at the deepest levels of embodied, personal meaning" (p. 2). My challenge, then, is to develop pathways that guide students toward self-definition. In this chapter I argue that aesthetic encounters can provide one such pathway. Further, I argue that eros is the driving force underlying those encounters. Thomas Alexander (2013) notes, "We are erotic beings. Our Eros ... is distinctively human" (p. 135). Alexander argues further that our individual meaning making derives from interactions with our communities. Thus I try in my teaching to draw attention to the influences that our private lives have on our outwardly focused perspectives. If Palmer is right about the need to know ourselves, then our students need to become aware of the inevitable mix of the public and private (Bullough, 1998; see also Griffin, 1995).

Above, I have introduced two concepts, aesthetic experience and eros. Both terms deserve further clarification.

AESTHETIC EXPERIENCE

Kathleen Abowitz (2007) has asserted, "Perception and imagination, self-knowledge, and creative expression are qualities enlivened and deepened through aesthetic experiences" (p. 289). Surely the qualities Abowitz mentions are ones to which those of us in teacher-education faculties hope teachers aspire. But what are aesthetic experiences? As Richard Shusterman (2006) has pointed out, both words in the phrase *aesthetic experience* have multiple meanings and perspectives. The word *aesthetic*, for example, "ambiguously refers not only to distinctive but also diverse objects of perception ... or even distinctive qualities such as beauty, grace ... that can be found in these objects" (p. 217). *Aesthetic*, Shusterman continues, "also applies to the distinctive discourse used to discuss those objects and modes of perception" (p. 217). What unites all of these variables, however, is the emphasis on perception—more specifically, perception by the senses, a concept that originated in the ancient Greek word *aisthetikos*.

Shusterman noted that the concept of experience is "even more elusively vague, problematic, and confusingly controversial than the aesthetic" (p. 217). That is, *experience*, like *aesthetic*, has objective and subjective possibilities; in addition, *experience* can be used as "both a noun and a verb" (p. 217). Shusterman concluded his overview of aesthetic experience by insisting that, though both words have a multiplicity of meanings, "vague terms still signify, and their rich and varied uses can compensate for their lack of precise, univocal meanings" (p. 218). Thus, he argued for acceptance of a pluralistic concept of aesthetic experience.

I argue that it is the pluralism that makes aesthetic experience beneficial in the classroom. There is no singular route that must be followed, no absolutes. Indeed, as Marcia Muelder Eaton and Ronald Moore (2002) have suggested, it is the variables, as they accumulate, that make aesthetic experience the special experience that it is. Aesthetic experience typically involves the whole self in empathic interaction with objects and events. That is, the interaction is not just intellectual, or corporeal, or even temperament-oriented. It is a dynamic force of communication between the individual and some specific feature of the world in which one finds oneself. I suggest, too, that Martin Buber's (1937/2004) *I-Thou* concept, although more spiritually oriented than corporeal, has certain affinities with aesthetic experience insofar as both emphasize reciprocal interaction, a dialogue. I will return to this possibility in a later section of this chapter.

EROS

The word *eros* derives from the ancient Greek *erasthai*, to love or desire. The Greeks distinguished four different kinds of love, only one of which, *erao*, had to do with sexual pleasure. The others are *phileo*—to have affection for; *agapao*—to have regard for or be contented with; and *stergo*—love between children and parents, or a ruler and his subjects (Eros, n.d.).

Some educational philosophers have equated eros with a passion for wisdom and goodness (Abowitz, 2007; Burch, 1999; Garrison, 1994, 1995, 1997; hooks, 1994; Hull, 2002; Rose, 2009; Russon, 2000; Schwab, 1954; Thøgersen, 2011; Tsabar, 2013; Tushnet, 1999). Kathleen Hull (2002) captured the general sentiment: "Passions are real and they can be important to a person's learning experience" (p. 20).

But, just as aesthetic experience is variable, so too is eros. Kerry Burch (1999, 2000) presented one variation that corresponds with Hull's position. He (2000) observed that eros is "a connecting agent between people ... compelling one to the aesthetic and the ethical" (p. 1). That impulse to connect is essentially a response to a sense that something is not yet achieved. It is in that sense of addressing the incomplete that Burch (1999, 2000) argued for the recognition of eros as an organizing principle of John Dewey's notion of democratic education. Thus, for Burch, eros is unequivocably a positive force.

In contrast, Ulla Thøgersen (2011) noted that while Plato, in the *Symposium*, "marks the dynamic force of eros as the starting point for our learning about the world" (p. 402), that learning is not necessarily always positive. There is another side as well. Thøgersen stated, "Our desires—like a musical chord—carry the fundamental notes on which our life is built" (p. 401). And those notes are variable. Thøgersen then offered two differing views of eros, one introduced in the ninth book of Plato's *Republic* and the other in *Phaedrus*. In the former, Eros is a tyrant "who rules according to his own pleasures and hence ignores any form of reason" (p. 405). Thøgersen noted that Socrates' first speech in *Phaedrus* appears to support that initial view. But then Socrates makes a second speech, apparently "intended to correct the 'false stories' in his first speech" (p. 406). Here Socrates speaks of the "divine character which can direct us to the highest form of happiness and wisdom" (p. 406). So, yes, eros can lead us to the good. It can also lead us astray. Eros needs careful management. Thøgersen noted Socrates' metaphor for eros: "The human soul can be compared to a union of two horses and a charioteer. One horse is good and the other bad; (sic) making the job of the charioteer necessary, but difficult" (p. 406). I suggest that our task as educators is to acknowledge and manage the two divergent forces. In a similar vein, Alexander (2013), quoting Paul Tillich (1956), cautioned:

No love is real without a unity of *eros* and *agape* [self-sacrifice]. *Agape* without *eros* is obedience to a moral law, without warmth, without longing, without reunion. *Eros* without *agape* is chaotic desire, denying the validity of the claim of the other one as an independent self, able to love and be loved. (p. 398)

EXEMPLIFICATION: PREAMBLE

To prompt students in their efforts at self-definition and awareness of their connections with the world around them, I like to provide examples, ones that I feel exemplify connections to eros and aesthetics. Here, I offer one such example. The occasion was an invitation from the Baltimore Museum of Art to local writers to choose any piece in the museum's collection and respond to it. Dan Fesperman is a professional writer, but not a professional art critic. He chose Rodin's *The Thinker*.

> As a boy, I could never get past the cliché of this big brooding fellow. He was a sitcom prop, an ad logo, a stand-in for dime store philosophy or for any cheap problem solvable within the half-hour span of *The Dobie Gillis Show*.
>
> I took it on faith without a single, well, *thought* that here resided such lofty intellect that none of us could ever warm up to him. With age and experience, I've come to empathize with the old boy. Look at those toes, curled like fish hooks into the rock, or the elbow crossed awkwardly to the opposite knee. The bewildered stare, the hair in disarray.
>
> Is he a sculpture or a mirror? He is the blocked writer, the baffled lover, the befuddled father, the misunderstood employee and spouse. And his failure to reach a conclusion, much less a solution, has turned him into a human pretzel.
>
> When he finally stands, every muscle will ache. Pass him in the street and you'll be appalled by his hunch and his hobble. The red imprint of his knuckles will still be inflamed upon his chin, a scarlet letter of indecision. Yet still he sits, buckled by the weight of his troubles, which are our troubles, not as a vast brain working inevitably toward an answer but as an eternal question mark.
>
> (Transcribed from the audio presentation, written and narrated by Dan Fesperman, which accompanied the work at the Baltimore Museum of Art)

To me, the author of this critique provides us with an opportunity to meet anew this well-known work. While the critique is obviously well reflected, it is also corporeal. Then, too, in his recognition of himself (and by extension, us) in the Other, I think he approached Buber's *I-Thou* moment to which I alluded earlier.

Auguste Rodin (1904–1917). *The thinker*. Bronze cast, Baltimore Museum of Art

I turn now to a poem by a graduate student, Cristina, whose self-identity is, perhaps for her, too, an eternal question mark. Born to Taiwanese parents and brought up in a South American country and then Canada, she has always felt like an outsider. In what follows, she visits Taiwan, the country of her parents' births.

I gasp   for   air
grey air   in a   grey city   with no
maple trees.
Alone   in
*   a sea of faces*
I walk,   in shock.
This is
my mother's land
my father's country
*   not mine.*
When will I cross
over
Until then,   pretend
to be   like them
same eyes, same skin
but   they know
I'm the   outsider
always on the threshold
ever in-between.

Unlike the previous example, in this case the young woman is having difficulty in making the connections she so clearly desires. But the attempt is valiant and offers us a moment of gut-felt reflection on our own moments of otherness.

In an undergraduate class, I asked students to look at a photographic portrait and describe what they felt was the general mood of the sitter. They made astute observations, which led them to wanting more information about the image. The photograph shows Lewis Powell (a.k.a. Payne), shackled in a ship's holding cell (essentially a metal tank), awaiting execution, by hanging, for his role in the Lincoln assassination conspiracy. Having provided the context of the photograph, I then asked the students to adopt the mindset of Powell and write a brief monologue. Here is Paul's effort. He was approximately the same age Powell was when he sat in the cell:

Alexander Gardner (1865). *Lewis Powell (a.k.a. Payne) in holding cell.* Albumen silver print photograph

I did it ... Yes I did it.
The only thing worse than my looming death is the waiting.
The rocking, the rolling, day-in, day-out, is driving me to insanity.
I have but one regret in life—that I was not successful.

If I'd succeeded and gotten caught, I would have been a hero.

Instead, that bastard walks free while I wait to die.

Here, the student did enter into the spirit of the exercise—to enter into a Martin Buber–type meeting with a misguided young man. Paul enjoyed the drama of the exercise and was able to enter into an empathic relationship with the protagonist while, at the same time, grappling with the historical context and the nation's continuing struggles toward justice. The monologue demonstrates a life lived vicariously—emotionally, intellectually, and even physically.

CONCLUSION

Teachers, by and large, endorse the concept of empathy and its desirability in the classroom. So it is perhaps not surprising that when I introduce an artwork into a discussion, or suggest an art-related activity, students tend to be receptive. Artworks require empathy as a condition of engagement. And as David Swanger (1990) insists, "The epistemology of art is empathy" (p. 76). The examples above are meant to demonstrate people's capacities in that direction, and the challenges therein. The extent to which those examples demonstrate eros is variable. That is, Alexander (2013) elaborates on just how demanding Buber's *I* and *Thou* interaction is. The point he makes requires quoting at length:

> Insofar as *one* person only is taking the standpoint of the other, we may have simply a situation which aims at manipulative control. Even if we both take the role of the other, if an "I-It" relationship holds there is only mutual manipulation, not genuine communication. But when the other *also* takes the "standpoint of the other," a mutual, shared, participatory dialogic space is established.... Not only may the Other become a "Thou" to my "I" (and my "I" changes in being genuinely related to a "Thou"), but both become a "We." (p. 411)

The challenge, as I now see it, is to strive toward articulation of the "We." I think Dan Fesperman's critique of *The Thinker* does indeed attain the *We* state, however momentarily. The two student examples demonstrate the challenges inherent in Buber's *meeting*. Cristina's poem vividly demonstrates her aching desire to arrive at the *We* and just how difficult that is. The final example could be considered as step one in the *I-Thou* meeting, a reaching out. While a photograph cannot literally reciprocate, to the extent that one can say, "The image (or the situation) speaks to me," there is an effort toward communication taking place. But to arrive at the *We* state, Paul's narrative would have to acknowledge his original self as well as that of the Other. A quest for the *We* in educational interactions remains an ongoing challenge.

What attention to eros and aesthetics has to offer to education is a reassertion of the importance of attention to well-directed passion for life and learning, for self-awareness and awareness of one's connections to others and the world at large, to what it means to be a human being with all our weaknesses, fears, and aspirations, as well as our strengths.

ACKNOWLEDGEMENTS

I owe a debt of gratitude to my students Cristina Hsyu and Paul Stewart and to Dan Fesperman for their gracious permission to include their work in this chapter. It is my delight as a teacher to have learned from each of you.

REFERENCES

Abowitz, K. K. (2007). Moral perception through aesthetics: Engaging imaginations in educational ethics. *Journal of Teacher Education, 58*(4), 287–298.

Alexander, T. M. (2013). *The human eros: Eco-ontology and the aesthetics of existence.* New York, NY: Fordham University Press.

Buber, M. (1937/2004). *I and thou.* New York, NY: Charles Scribner's Sons.

Bullough, R. (1998). Musings on life writing: Biography and case studies in teacher education. In C. Kridel (Ed.), *Writing educational biography* (pp. 19–32). New York, NY: Garland.

Burch, K. (1999). Eros as the educational principle of democracy. *Studies in Philosophy and Education, 18*(3), 123–142.

Burch, K. (2000). *Eros as the educational principle of democracy.* New York, NY: Peter Lang.

Eaton, M. M., & Moore, R. (2002). Aesthetic experience: Its revival and its relevance to aesthetic education. *Journal of Aesthetic Education, 36*(2), 9–23.

Eros. (n.d.). In *Online etymology dictionary.* Available at: www.etymonline.com/index.php?term=Eros

Fesperman, D. (2012). Narration on Auguste Rodin's *The Thinker.* In *60 objects: Countless stories—Antioch Court.* By the Baltimore Museum of Art. Retrieved December 17, 2017, from: itunes.apple.com/pa/itunes-u/60-objects-countless-stories-antioch-court/id535496429?l=en&mt=10

Garrison, J. (1994). Dewey, eros and education. *Education and Culture, XI*(2), 1–5.

Garrison, J. (1995). Deweyan prophetic pragmatism: Poetry and the education of eros. *American Journal of Education, 103*(4), 406–431.

Garrison, J. (1997). *Dewey and eros: Wisdom and desire in the art of teaching.* New York, NY: Teachers College Press.

Griffin, S. (1995). *The eros of everyday life.* Toronto, ON: Anchor Books/Doubleday.

hooks, b. (1994). Eros, eroticism, and the pedagogical process. In H. Giroux & P. McLaren (Eds.), *Between borders: Pedagogy and the politics of cultural studies* (pp. 113–118). New York, NY: Routledge.

Hull, K. (2002). Eros and education: The role of desire in teaching and learning. *The NEA Higher Education Journal, 18*(Fall), 19–31.

Palmer, P. (1998). *The courage to teach.* San Francisco, CA: Harper & Row.

Rose, R. (2009, April 27). Education, wonder and eros. *Huffington Post.* Available at: www.huffingtonpost.com/robert-rose/education-wonder-and-eros_b_191396.html

Russon, J. E. (2000). Eros and education: Plato's transformative epistemology. *Laval théologique et philosophique, 56*(1), 113–125. Available at: id.erudit.org/iderudit/401227ar

Schwab, J. (1954). Eros and education: A discussion of one aspect of discussion. *The Journal of General Education, 8*(1) 51–71.

Shusterman, R. (2006). Aesthetic experience: From analysis to eros. *Journal of Aesthetic Education, 64*(2), 217–229.

Swanger, D. (1990). *Essays in aesthetic education.* San Francisco, CA: ETM Text.

Thøgersen, U. (2011). Desire, democracy and education. *Educational Philosophy and Theory, 43*(4), 400–410.

Tillich, P. (1956). *The dynamics of faith.* New York, NY: Harper.

Tsabar, B. (2013). "Poverty and resourcefulness": On the formative significance of eros in educational practice. *Studies in Philosophy of Education, 33*(1), 75–87. Available at: link.springer.com/article/10.1007%2Fs11217-013-9364-5#page-1

Tushnet, E. (1999, September 1). Eros and education: Escaping the tyranny of the present. *The Yale Free Press.* Available at: yalefreepress.sites.yale.edu/news/eros-and-education

B3

The Question Holds the Lantern

Margaret Louise Dobson

*Only where things can be seen in a variety of aspects without changing their iden-
tity, so that those who gather around them know that they see sameness in utter
diversity, can worldly reality truly and reliably appear.*
   (Hannah Arendt, 1974, p. 57)

*The curtain rises slowly to reveal a dimly lit, sparsely furnished living room. Seated com-
fortably on a wooden chair at centre stage is the main character, a young woman
wearing Lululemon. Her glowing countenance and self-assured demeanour beam
in stark contrast to the otherwise shadowy stage setting. In fact, the radiant face of
the young woman is the scene's principal source of light. From the cavernous wing
at stage left, a voice, barely audible at first, but louder and more persistent with each
succeeding articulation, breaks through the silence and poses the central question.*
The Voice: Who are you?
*Main Character, nonchalantly fiddling with the yellow rubber bracelet on her right
wrist, at first appearing distracted and disinterested, then reluctantly, but with a
growing sense of self-assuredness, begins to answer the question. She becomes increasingly mesmerized by her own words, as if caught in a trance of a well-rehearsed
credo:* I am Jane Catherine Marsden. I am 39 years old. I was born and raised
in Everton, Ontario. I graduated from North View High School with honours. I attended Southwestern University, where I graduated with an MBA.
Today I am CEO of Deerfield Canada, Inc., a green enterprise that invents

and produces alternative energy solutions. I practice yoga daily and I exercise at a nearby fitness club twice weekly. As you can see, I am in excellent shape. I live a well-balanced, eco-friendly lifestyle. All in all, I am a well-educated, health-conscious, socially well-adjusted, environmentally aware, highly qualified, gainfully employed Canadian. In fact, by today's standards, I would say that I am a very successful individual.

The Voice, sounding surprised: Are you sure a "successful individual" is who you are? Who would you be if an unfortunate accident, or some dire circumstance, were to befall you? What if you were to lose your job, and along with losing your job, you were to lose your healthy lifestyle and your enviable social status? Would you be the "successful individual" you claim to be? Or, would you then consider yourself to be a failure by today's standards?

Main Character, holding her ground: In that hypothetical and improbable scenario, I suppose, yes, I would become a victim of my circumstances. I would lose everything I have worked hard to achieve. Certainly, in that case, yes, I would be devastated.

The Voice, gaining momentum: Is it really *you* who would be devastated? Or, is it the person you think you are—the one you have made yourself out to be—that would be victimized? I'll ask the question again. Who are you, *really*?

Main Character, nonplussed, starts to recite a summary of the mantra: I am Jane Catherine Marsden. I am a Canadian citizen. I am CEO ...

The Voice, cutting her off mid-sentence, sounding impatient: "Jane Catherine Marsden" is the name given to you by your parents. "Canadian" is the citizenship you were born into. "CEO" is your occupation. Your name, your citizenship, and your occupation describe what you have acquired and what you do for a living, but such monikers do not tell me who you are. I am not asking *what* you are; I am asking *who* you are. So, you see? You have not yet addressed the question. You are still beating around the bush.

Main Character, becoming defensive: All right, then. I suppose I haven't told you the whole story. As I said, I am a successful career woman, but I am also a wife and mother. I am married to Bob Marsden, who is a software developer, and we have three children, ages nine, seven, and five. I am a member of the governing board at my children's school, and I am a soccer mom who attends most of her son's games. Considering the time constraints imposed upon me by my career, I do my best to be a good wife and mother.

The Voice, calmly, this time more patiently: Hmmm.... Have you finished? Is that it? Is that who you think you are: a "good wife and mother" with a time-consuming career?

Main Character, beginning to show signs of exasperation due to the annoying persistence of the provocation; now sitting on the edge of her chair: Okay. Okay. I see what you're getting at. I *do* have a life of my own, you know. I *can* think for myself despite appearances to the contrary. You are implying by your questions that I am mindlessly going along with the latest societal trends. You are insinuating that I don't know who I am because of the busy life I lead. But you are wrong. I may look like a typical modern woman on the outside, but on the inside I have my own private thoughts, which I keep to myself. I have always been an avid reader, although I do confess there isn't much time for books these days. As for any core religious beliefs or any fundamental political or philosophical theories I may adhere to—*if* that is what you are driving at by suggesting I am "beating around the bush"—I was raised as a Protestant Christian in the United Church of Canada, but I don't follow any particular religion today. I enjoy the privileges of living in a democratic country, but I don't belong to a right-wing or left-wing political party, nor am I enamoured with any particular school of thought. This is not to say that I don't experience a deep sense of meaning and purpose to my life. I do! *After a long pause, takes a deep breath; is visibly shaken, yet remains resolute:* To be honest, your relentless questioning is starting to get on my nerves. You are going too far with your probing. In fact, I think you are being downright nosy. This is really none of your business! Besides, I don't have time for all this nonsense. I am much too busy to think.

The Voice, seizing the moment: I understand your frustration. You are peeved because you are being put on the spot. You feel yourself being squeezed into a corner and you are running out of answers. Let me assure you that the question I am posing is not nonsense. There is no question more urgent than the question of identity. You will soon discover that your business *is* my business, and *vice versa*! We are intimately connected in our dialogic identity. You will come to realize that "much too busy" is a temporary state of distraction that has nothing to do with the reality of time. You are about to see that everything you tell me *about* yourself cannot possibly be who you are. And so, I ask you one more time, *who* is telling me the story about you?

Main Character, automatically, in a reflexive response: *I* am!

The Voice, gleefully jumping in: At last we are getting somewhere!

Main Character: Yes, but ... *I* am ... *what* I have become.... Can't you see that?

The Voice: By persisting in the belief that you are *what* you have become, are you not losing sight of *who* you really are? Has not a tragic cover-up occurred?

Main Character, after a lengthy pause, stubbornly refusing to acknowledge even the slightest possibility of a new and different perspective: Not really.... I know myself by reason of *what* I have become, by measure of *what* I have achieved. That's what I know.

The Voice, vulnerable to the blow, feels the chill of rejection personally, yet persists in mounting the tension; quietly reiterates: There is a critical difference between knowing and thinking (Arendt, 1971, p. 418). I am not asking *what* you know; I am asking *who* you are.

Main Character, for the first time openly listening to the undeniable validity of the question, begrudgingly yields, and finally allows The Voice a voice: Then *you* tell me: *who* am I?

The Voice, having now gained the full attention of the main character, proceeds with carefully chosen, deliberate words: No one other than you can reveal the answer to that question for you. Who you are is some*one* felt inwardly and expressed outwardly through your words and actions, not some*thing* you can define or evaluate, not even by today's standards! *Who* is your unique and distinct identity (Arendt, 1974, p. 180). As the source of creativity, you remain outside of the actual work process as well as independent of what you may achieve (p. 211).

Main Character, beginning to show signs of interest: What you are saying, then, is that I may *possess* certain qualities, and I may *hold* various positions and viewpoints based on my inherent talents and acquired skills. Of course! To live well and wisely in this world, I must have a character and a role of one kind or another to play. I can see that. But, *what* I know and *what* I do is not my identity, is not *who* I am. Aha! I think I get it! Like an actress performing a role on the stage, for the sake of authenticity, I may momentarily identify with the interchangeable characters of the various parts I play (Arendt, 2003, pp. 11–14). But, when the curtain comes down at the end of the play, and I remove my makeup and step out of my role, who am I then? That is the question! *Reflectively pausing between words and phrases*: When all is said and done, and when it comes right down to it ... I am ... living, breathing, feeling, and thinking. I am *being* human.

The Voice, excitedly: At last you understand the question! Calling *who* you are *what* you will does not change the reality. *Who* is your unchangeable identity (Arendt, 1974, p. 193). Wondrously, though, you may distinguish yourself in public by reason of what you say and do (p. 179).

Main Character, after a long pause, now listening very intently: Go on. Tell me more.

The Voice, continuing: As you begin to assume self-awareness as existent apart from the performance of your public *persona*, your life's energy will slowly be withdrawn from its industrious investment in a self-made identity. As your constructed identity starts to shift and change and your separate self-image begins to fade into the background, you will take a look around you and see for yourself *who* remains in-between (Arendt, 1974, p. 183). With no further inclination to project the "successful individual" or the "good wife and mother" as your identity, you are now free to disclose and experience the fullness of your reality. The end of your make-believe performance heralds a new beginning for your living story, a story with no ending (Arendt, 1977/2006, p. xiii). In sheer human togetherness you will come to see yourself reflected in a variety of aspects. You will come to know yourself in the "sameness of utter diversity" (Arendt, 1974, p. 57).

Main Character, smiling, slowly rises from her chair and walks to the edge of the stage. As her newly softened gaze moves out into the audience, the light, once emanating from a well-rehearsed confidence in the veracity of her own performance, slowly begins to expand to incorporate the audience in an increasingly generative, and eventually all-encompassing, radiance. The illusion of a separate, self-made identity is thus dispelled in the dawning light of conscious awareness. She pauses to reflect, and then quietly exits stage right. The curtain falls.

REFERENCES

Arendt, H. (1971). Thinking and moral considerations: A lecture. *Social Research, 38*(3), 417–446.

Arendt, H. (1974). *The human condition*. Chicago, IL: University of Chicago Press.

Arendt, H. (1977/2006). *Between past and future: Eight exercises in political thought*. New York, NY: Penguin Books.

Arendt, H. (2003). *Responsibility and judgment*. New York, NY: Random House.

INVOCATION

Curriculum Grammar for the Anthropocene

Jackie Seidel

As in the beginning, then also at the end, a new word bursts forth. *Anthropocene!* Singularly signalling an existential question as much as an existential threat: both yes and no, the betweentime.

Our subtle animal feet, animal hearts, soft animal bodies sense the rumble-ground. The word remembers us, what we are. A bit frightened or maybe wholly terrified. In the warm places and the cold places, many forever disappearances. Glimpsed out of the eyeblink's corner, barely. There and gone at once, extincted along with so many words and so many animalpeople. Their names are forgotten. Everything that was cracks open under power worth killing for. Its name is progress and it is hungry, amen. What is ancient and tarslick spills forth filth and we eat it, some of us eat it, yes we eat ourselves sick. We teach the children to do it too. This is the lesson: We tell them it's good for them even if they cry. Especially if they cry, then we feed them more so they'll get used to it. Even when it gets too warm, even then. Even though the taste is revolting it's so. hard. to. stop. Even I do wantneed to lick it one last time.

Or maybe this new word opens to a timeplace of rupture and responsibility. Grieflove arrives, broken-hearted. Vows are spoken. To the stars, the ground, the air, the ocean waters, the forests, one another, all the others whose names are forgottenremembered, to all the animalchildren's children with their soft bodies that fly and run and swim and breathe and sing in the futurenow as then. Vows to be gentlefierce and peacequiet so that ears can hear spiritwind and wisdomspeak. Where the offerings come from. How else, how else, would we know what to do now?

B4

Learning about Curriculum through My Self

Shauna Rak

My motivation to examine the role of the Holocaust in art education is based on my own experiences, which have shaped my understanding of my identity formation. To begin, I locate myself in my family story and my experiences in the Jewish Parochial school system. Then, I disconnect from my heritage and begin to explore Jewish culture through literature, my Bubby's stories of survival during the Holocaust, and lastly a visit to Poland. Through this process I have been able to enter into a historical lens of living inquiry and explore new perspectives in which my family story implicates my own.

MY STORY

I was raised in a predominantly Jewish community, Dollard-des-Ormeaux, a suburb of Montreal. My parents sent me to a private Jewish elementary school. In this Orthodox school I was immersed in Jewish culture and tradition, and studied the laws, the Bible, and Hebrew. The use of the creative arts within my elementary education was very limited. At this time, I was not aware of my artist identity and did not notice any creative restraint. I can only remember creating art one time throughout my entire elementary school experience. My mother remembers the same art project, as it coincided with the holiday of Passover. On Passover, at the dinner table, we place a hard-boiled egg in the centre of the Seder plate to symbolize life. The project's objective was to incorporate this hard-boiled egg into an art project. There was no theme, or guidelines; we were to have fun. From what I recall, this ended up being a competition for the mothers instead of an assignment for the children, a common occurrence in the school.

Reflecting back, I worked collaboratively with my mother on most of the projects I did in class. When I prepared for oral presentations, it was always my mother who taught me innovative ways to present them on bristol board. She helped me create three-dimensional props so that my presentations were less traditional than the rest of my classmates'. She always taught me how to be original and creative in my work.

Outside of school I remember cooking, telling stories, and creating in the kitchen as significant parts of my upbringing. It was my job to remember the recipes and stories that linked us to our past. Only now do I realize that this was the unfolding of my creative process, as well as the foundation upon which I now engage in the storytelling tradition as a form of research. The symbolism of food and story is a critical part of my memories. Today, when I hear an onion hitting a pan, smell the scent of garlic, touch the malleable texture of dough before it is turned into pastry, or taste recipes that have been passed down through generations, I am reminded of cooking in my family kitchen. These memories are crucial to my connection with my past and part of a continuously developing symbolism, as the stories contribute to my experience each time I cook my mother's recipes.

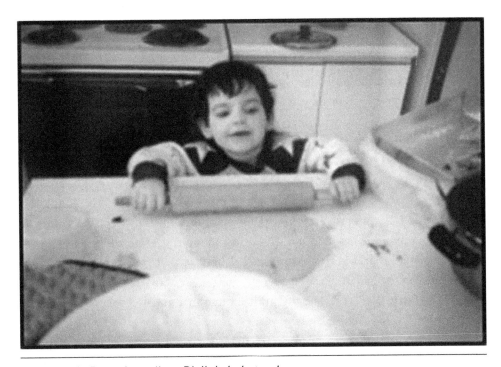

Shauna Rak. *Becoming culture.* Digital photograph

Once I reached high school I was confused about my identity and strived to develop my own story, apart from, but related to, my family. I felt detached from my internal values, achievements, and personal goals, and I started to lose interest in the curriculum. It seemed to have no direction, and my priorities changed. At the core of my story were parties, friends, popularity, boys, body weight, and good hair days—values I now see as superficial. In my high school, the Jewish program consisted of Hebrew, Yiddish, and a class in Jewish history and traditions. The funding and special events within the school were mostly geared toward the Jewish curriculum. We learned history from textbooks where the Holocaust was presented through facts and figures. The school did not encourage creative arts, nor were stories part of the history curriculum, and for me, this meant that the emotion and empathy evoked by storytelling, as I knew it in my family, was notably absent. I felt increasingly disengaged from the Jewish studies curriculum, and as a result began to withdraw from my cultural heritage. I remember describing the Jewish community as a superficial cult, disparaging toward others. We lived in such a tight-knit universe, sheltered from the rest of the world. But I kept asking myself: What value does Hebrew, Yiddish, and Jewish culture hold for my future, outside of the bubble?

During this time period, I decided that I wanted to remove myself from my family and from my Jewish identity: I stopped going to synagogue during the high holidays; lost belief in my religious values, amongst many other personal values; and I got my first tattoo. In the Jewish religion the human body is not to be manually manipulated because it is God's creation. Tattoos are further identified as a traumatic symbol since the Holocaust, when hundreds of thousands of Jews were branded with numbers. I am a granddaughter of Holocaust survivors, and my getting a tattoo was heartbreaking for my parents. My parents, being second-generation, are more profoundly affected by the Holocaust in a historical and emotional context than I felt myself to be at the time. Tattoos are still a symbol of oppression in their eyes, whereas my generation is far enough removed from the horrors of Auschwitz to consider tattoos as symbols of freedom and self-expression. For me, this tattoo was a symbol that I was my own person, with my own identity, independent of my culture and family. As an adult, I have since redone that tattoo and gotten two others. I believe that they represent expression, revealing my artistic nature; they are no longer about rebelling against my cultural identity. Nevertheless, the guilt haunts me, and I cover up my tattoos each time I visit my Bubby.

I realize today that my adolescent rebellion and struggle to change was apparent to everyone, as noted in the awards page of my high-school yearbook, where

I won for "Most Changed Since Grade 7." There is a picture of me as a young child, smiling, a space between my teeth, short messy hair, sporting an old frumpy T-shirt, followed by a picture of me as a young adult with perfect teeth, perfect hair, and the same radiant smile. I wonder if either "me" was happy or fulfilled.

During this period, my connection to my cultural identity was sustained by family time and traditions we shared in the home. Visits from my Bubby were always meaningful to me. Her infectious laughter is woven into my DNA. We are alike in many ways. She is large in her mannerisms, blunt, harshly honest, yet, at the same time, oddly chic. She repeats her stories, always conveying the same strength, language, and tone. I remember my mother would cry at the table as she listened, embodying my Bubby's revisitings of the past, while I would sit in silence, eyes wide open, enamoured with my Bubby's courage and ability to be so striking and clever. Our mutual admiration, love, and remarkable fashion sense is evident in expression, colour, and vibrancy in the picture on page 118, taken at my "Sweet 16."

Her stories about the time during and after the war connect me to my heritage. These stories were not forced upon me, and I learned about my history in a context with which I could connect. As an avid reader, I easily envisioned Bubby's story as a book. In my vivid imagination—which I probably inherited from her—scenes sprang to life. I read a number of Holocaust stories in my youth, such as *The Diary of Anne Frank* (1947/1993), *Daniel's Story* (Matas, 1993), and *Number the*

Artificial changes. Digital photograph

My "sweet 16" birthday: Two generations (2002). Digital photograph

Stars (Lowry, 1989). I still cannot define what attracted me to these novels; maybe it was a connection that I had once lost and yearned to recover.

Overall I believe, based on my experience, that the Quebec education system fails to make fundamental connections to the Holocaust that are relevant to the lives of students. A study by researchers at the Université de Montréal stated that Quebec's treatment of the Holocaust in today's high-school history curriculum is "superficial and incomplete, with no real reflection on the event's complexity" (Seidman, 2014, n.p.). This supports my lived and learned experiences in secondary school. A related study by Sivane Hirsch and Marie McAndrew (2013) discussed the treatment of the Jewish religion as a whole in the Quebec education system, and focused on the lukewarm reaction students have toward textbook representations of Jewish culture:

> Le traitement du judaïsme dans les manuels scolaires d'éthique et culture religieuse au Québec contribue-t-il à un meilleur vivre-ensemble? Les explications des pratiques juives dans les manuels restent le plus souvent

théoriques et n'établissent que rarement des liens avec la réalité de la communauté juive québécoise. Les photos sont plutôt "anonymes" elles ne permettent généralement pas de rattacher la photo à un lieu ou à un contexte particulier et montrent des pratiques provenant d'ailleurs. Les manuels manquent ainsi souvent l'occasion de situer le judaïsme dans le paysage Québécois contemporain et de rapprocher sa réalité à celle des autres élèves Québécois. (p. 107)

This is further explored in a recent article by Janice Arnold (2014), who states that "Quebec youngsters today simply cannot grasp that something so horrific could take place, and anyway it was so long ago" (p. 12). Arnold's article on the scarcity of available resources on Holocaust studies in Quebec is another account of the need to develop an engaging Holocaust curriculum here.

When I began the master's program in Art Education, I remember trying to situate myself within the field. Many of the students had a strong connection to working within the school system and others in the community. At this point in time I situated myself as a community art educator but with no clearly defined purpose. I had not yet questioned curriculum, pedagogic purpose, or intent within my own educational trajectory. I began to write my story during the first semester of the Art Education graduate program, and finally confronted my pedagogic questions and concerns about my experiences in the Jewish school system. Where were the connections between my cultural identity and my artist-researcher-teacher self? Also, what made me feel engaged as a learner? Examining my passion for storytelling, I wondered how I could incorporate storytelling and my family history into a purposeful and provoking curriculum. This is when I decided I would interview my grandmother for my research project. Through her stories I felt I would certainly develop new understandings about myself and my approach to art education.

Current pedagogical approaches that foster disassociation from the history of the Holocaust are inhibiting students' abilities to learn about its perils from first-person perspectives, and ultimately, to make a deep, personal connection to its history. This gap between the past and the present is of grave concern to me. The number of living survivors of the Holocaust is growing smaller, and we need to find innovative ways for living histories to continue. I believe this is possible by providing an entry point into innovative and critical methods for Holocaust education that use creative methods for storytelling as learning experiences.

The lack of emotion and depth within Holocaust education as it is taught in Quebec has a direct correlation to my own story. As a third-generation survivor, I believe that I am obliged to teach future generations about the Holocaust. The truth is I am part of the last generation who will hear oral stories from living survivors. It is my responsibility, therefore, to help resolve the prevalent issues within Holocaust education and ensure that future generations continue to be educated about, make connections with, and actively remember this horrific event.

As part of my research journey into my Bubby's life history, I felt obliged to see the cities, towns, and villages that she spoke of, as well as places I had learned about through film and literature. I needed to give greater context to the nuances of her stories.

MY JOURNEY: MARCH OF THE LIVING

I travelled to Poland and Israel in the spring of 2014 with the March of the Living: a two-week group trip to learn about the Jewish community that once flourished in Europe, the tragedy of the Holocaust, and the survival of the State of Israel (marchoftheliving.org). I applied to this particular program because I wanted to further the phenomenological impact of visiting the sites through the company of other multi-generation survivors. Being in the company of survivors and descendants of survivors enhanced my experience and narrative, providing a rich and foundational perspective. I travelled to these sites because I wanted first-hand experience, to connect to my past, to cultivate my own identity, and to develop a pedagogical philosophy that addressed how to educate future genera-tions about this human tragedy. During the trip, I recognized that travelling to these sites added a new dimension to my understanding of my Bubby's story. I also recognized substantial connections between the experience of being in the same geographic locations as my Bubby had been during the Holocaust, and my current efforts to embody historical contexts through storytelling. This experi-ence underscored the relationship between my Bubby's stories and my research journey. From the moment I stepped off the plane in Warsaw I was faced with an obvious contradiction: the hustle and bustle of modern life was haunted by the dead. I was unsettled by the ease with which citizens went about their business in light of their country's history. Ultimately, my unease nurtured a process of growth, the seed of which was sown on this trip.

This journey had a profound effect on my identity and I take pride in the courage, dedication, and growth that I practiced during and after this trip. I there-fore devote my journey, growth, and dedication to augmenting future Holocaust studies, and to honouring the Mezinska, Rosenfeld, Gluck, Kogut, and Lebovits families that I marched for in silence on *Yom Hashoah* in the spring of 2014.

Marching to remember (2015). Digital photograph

RE-IMAGINING MY POSITION IN TEACHING AND CREATING

The sense of shared understanding is significant within my study as I continue to engage with more and more Holocaust literary examples and survivor testimonies. Maxine Greene (1995) states the necessity for engaging with Holocaust literature: "the *Diary of Anne Frank*, the novels of Elie Wiesel, and the stories and essays of Primo Levi ... the experiences they open to informed awareness cannot be self-enclosed and cannot miseducate" (p. 101). I received this same invaluable experience as I learned about the history of the Holocaust through my Bubby's perceptions, relating to her personality, her strength, and empathizing with her heartaches, fears, love, and choices. Such insight cannot be conveyed in facts, dates, and descriptions of events alone. I believe that the practice of storytelling facilitates "opportunity to remake the story, to play with its meaning for us at that point in our life, to reinvest it with new meaning and so be touched and changed by it on so many levels" (Nash, 2014, p. 167). As my personal experience transformed me throughout this journey, so did my interpretation of it and its effect on my artist-researcher-teaching practice. Storytelling has allowed me to rethink and re-imagine my position in teaching and creating, and how I relate to others with a more inclusive pedagogical discipline.

REFERENCES

Arnold, J. (2014, November 27). Demand for Holocaust education growing in schools. *The Canadian Jewish News*.

Frank, A. (1947/1993). *Anne Frank: The diary of a young girl*. New York, NY: Bantam

Greene, M. (1995). *Releasing the imagination: Essays on education, the arts, and social change*. San Francisco, CA: Jossey-Bass.

Hirsch, S., & McAndrew, M. (2013). Le traitement du judaïsme dans les manuels scolaires d'éthique et culture religieuse au Québec contribue-t-il à un meilleur vivre-ensemble? *McGill Journal of Education/Revue des sciences de l'éducation de McGill*, 48(1), 99–114.

Lowry, L. (1989). *Number the stars*. Boston, MA: Houghton Mifflin.

Matas, C. (1993). *Daniel's story*. New York, NY: Scholastic Paperbacks.

Nash, M. (2014). Enlarging the circle of students' self-understanding through stories. In R. J. Nash & S. Viray (Eds.), *How stories heal: Writing our way to meaning & wholeness in the academy* (pp. 161–175). New York, NY: Peter Lang.

Seidman, K. (2014, April 2). Holocaust education lacking in Quebec textbooks. *The Gazette*. Available at: ezproxy.library.ubc.ca/login?url=https://search-proquest-com.ezproxy.library.ubc.ca/docview/1512493323?accountid=14656

B5

A Response to *Still Dancing: My Bubby's Story*

Bruce G. Hill

"When is the teacher?" Intrigued by this question, I chose to attend the session with this title at the Provoking Curriculum Studies Conference held at UBC early in 2015. As a preliminary reflection, I suggest it is necessary for the teacher to avoid the trap of abstraction and "be" both in the present and in the past. Nowhere is this more difficult to do than in the study of historical wrongs, which are often hidden from view in a tangle of taken-for-granted personal, family, national, and world histories. Oral histories are a means to call into question these histories and, at the same time, offer access to the truth of these wrongs.

In her presentation at the session, Shauna Rak dealt with the Holocaust, perhaps the most grievous of all historical wrongs. In her opening remarks, she said that her Bubby, or grandmother, Elka Rak, was from an Orthodox Jewish family who up until the war had been well established in Warsaw. Elka, she went on to say, was a Holocaust survivor. The word *Holocaust* for me begs the so-far unanswerable question: why? I leaned forward to listen.

In her performance of "My Bubby's Story," she spoke in her grandmother's voice, walked in her shoes, exuded her positive energy, and, accompanied by images and sound, evoked memories of her past. Up there, on stage as it were, with all eyes on her, she morphed into the spunky and vibrant Elka Mezinska, born in 1920, about the same time, I figured, as my mother. As if by some conjurer's hand, Elka came dancing across time into the classroom, transforming herself from stranger to acquaintance to neighbour, making her family's struggle for survival on the eastern front during World War II all too real, all too personal, all too daunting. I watched and I listened, enthralled.

Post-conference, I downloaded and read a copy of Shauna's MA thesis, entitled *Still Dancing: My Bubby's Story: How Family Histories Can Inform Multi-sensory Learning in Art Education* (Rak, 2015). The thesis included a chapter entitled "My Bubby's Story" and six other chapters. In my reading of the thesis, I paid particular attention to the story, and the story of the story, and was able to move beyond my first impressions of Shauna's performance of the story.

In her story of the story, several points stood out for me. Her interest in stories of the Holocaust arose in part out of her family background and in part out of her critique of her high-school experience with Holocaust history. The gist of this critique was that the history of the Holocaust as presented to her in school was all about facts and dates and did not engage her in a meaningful way (Rak, 2015, pp. 5–6). Drawing on her strengths as a teacher, artist, and storyteller, she conceived a project based on Elka's life story that sought to improve student engagement in Holocaust history through "the strategies of storytelling, multi-sensory embodiment and experience, and artmaking" (pp. 23–24).

Her research posed difficulties worth noting. In the early days of her interviews with Elka, she and her father had difficulty dealing with Elka's fading memories of time and place and her insistence on taking the lead in the interview. They made a decision to "let her go" and just listen (p. 45). From that moment on, Shauna says, "the interview came alive" (p. 46). In her Bubby's "passionate and wild storytelling style," Shauna "felt a sense of purpose—to honour her vision" (p. 46). Elka's vision was to tell the story of her life in her own way.

To honour Elka's vision, Shauna had to surpass mere transcription. In writing up the literary story of her Bubby's life, Shauna pieced together verbatim excerpts from the transcripts of the interviews and used an embodied approach to "[bring] the finely textured experience of the body to the art of [her] writing" (p. 31). To this end, she visited Poland, retraced part of Elka's journey, walked miles in her shoes, and embodied what Elka must have felt, seen, heard, and smelled long ago in those far away places. For me, the final version of the story has the power and energy of a novel.

Shauna holds that, even with its omissions and contradictions, Elka's life story carries weight, not only as oral history but also as a part of history (p. 74). She holds also that this oral history, conceived and developed as a multi-sensory learning opportunity, may afford students an engaging point of entry into a study of the Holocaust. She anticipates that multi-sensory learning in conjunction with family history will be used in the study of the historical wrongs of other nations, especially, one presumes, those of Canada (p. 23). I think this last point is important, and I will return to it.

In my reading and re-reading of Elka's story, I noticed her penchant for understatement, for open-endedness, provoking in me a desire to complete her story. I mean this as a positive comment. Her poignant story of survival stands on its own as a literary creation. But, for the reader, it raises questions, invites dialogue, and summons history.

"I survive a lot of things," Elka says (p. 66). Did she ever! She survived the German invasion of Poland, seven years of virulent anti-Semitism, and seven years of exile in hostile surroundings. She survived a 12-year flight from terror in many forms, hopping from one place to the next, from Warsaw to Minsk, from Minsk to Archangelsk, from Archangelsk to Osh, from Osh to Bremen, and from Bremen to Montreal. She survived the loss of her home in Warsaw, the loss of most of her family, and the loss of the two men she fell in love with. She survived the trauma of witnessing the murder of two of her brothers and the sudden deaths of her father, nephew, and mother. She survived 16 months in a work camp in Archangelsk, approximately two years on a trek in the wild to Osh, and several more months in a women's prison in Osh. She survived the privations of hunger, cold, overcrowding, and disease, and, most soul destroying of all, the terror of strangers calling her names: *verfluchte Juden, verfluchte Juden*; cursed Jew, cursed Jew (pp. 47–67). The bare facts of Elka's story suggest her survival was a miracle, and many of her actions were heroic.

In naming all the stops in her pre-war, wartime, and post-war travels from Warsaw to Montreal, Elka understates details of the distances and dangers involved. I did some mapwork. By my count, Elka travelled some 20,000 kilometres during and after the war, nearly half of which was through territory fought over by Germans or Russians. While in Poland, at, between, or behind the front lines, the family had to be wary, not only of capture by Germans and Russians, but also of betrayal by non-Jewish Poles. In German-occupied Poland, it was against the law for Poles to harbour Jews and for Jews to possess property, creating an incentive for Poles to steal from Jews and then murder them (Lipson & Perlow, 1961). There were few safe havens in Poland for Jews on the run from the terror of the Holocaust.

In closing her account of life in a work camp in Archangelsk, Elka says, "There was amnesty," but she provides few details about it (Rak, 2015, p. 54). It is worth adding this historical footnote: the Russians offered amnesty, not out of the goodness of their hearts, but because in June 1941 the Germans invaded Russia, and the Allies, as a condition for Allied support for Russia, required that Russia declare an amnesty for their Polish prisoners of war. Free to leave the work camp, the family made their way south through the forest to Kuibyshev and, from there, on to Osh. She says they didn't stay long in Kuibyshev because they heard the Germans were coming and were going to bomb the city. All she says about the time of the journey from Archangelsk to Osh was that it was not good. Even when pressed for details by Shauna in the interview, she said only "not good" (p. 74).

Again, I turn to mapwork for a few details. Archangelsk is in the north of Russia, Osh in the south. I estimate the journey from Archangelsk to Osh covered a distance of 4,500 kilometers and, based on the implicit timeline of Elka's story, took about two years to complete. In October 1941, the Russians moved their capital from Moscow to Kuibyshev, turning it into a place of symbolic if not strategic importance, but nonetheless a target for German bombs. For the first half of the journey to Osh, the family was well behind the frontlines of Russia's western front but possibly in the middle of the staging areas supporting the front lines. The German advance into Russian territory reached its limit in December 1941 and, from that month on to the end of the war, Russia mounted a fierce and relentless counterattack. Whatever the untold details of the Mezinskas' journey to Osh, we know this much: it was a journey fraught with danger. These facts of history and geography help provide Elka's oral history with some historical context. Like the bare facts of the story, these additional facts also suggest that Elka's survival was a miracle and her actions heroic.

In her interpretation of the story, Shauna uses Maslow's hierarchy of needs to identify the themes of survival, choice, humour, and self-actualization. According to Shauna's take on Maslow, an individual, in the course of a lifetime, will move upward through the hierarchy toward self-actualization. Shauna locates the sub-themes of luck and faith at the level of self-actualization, making the claim that "both themes [involve] personal growth, experience and fulfillment, central to developing pedagogical opportunities for emotional, spiritual and transcendent experiences" (Rak, 2015, p. 108). Was it luck or was it faith that led to the help strangers offered Elka in her struggle to overcome difficult situations? In the context of the hierarchy, it doesn't matter. As regards Elka's status as hero, Shauna cites Hannah Arendt, who says that a person is a hero for having the courage "to insert one's self into the world and begin a story of one's own" (Arendt, 1959, as cited in Rak, 2015, p. 33). In these terms, the hero belongs at the level of self-actualization. Shauna asserts with conviction that her Bubby is "a Holocaust survivor, my hero and the foundation of my family" (p. 1). But, what are we to think of the millions of others who didn't survive and whose stories have never been told? Through their stories, Elka and other survivors of the Holocaust bear witness to what happened and speak up, not just for themselves, but also for all those who perished in silence. They are heroes, too.

In support of this insightful interpretation, though outside Maslow's frame, I point to Elka's emergence in the story as pedagogue. When Elka understates the shooting deaths of her brothers, I wondered: where's the rage? Shauna believes that the rage Elka must have felt in this situation and others like it was "channeled into a fierce determination to live a normal life" (p. 104). I concur but also believe that Elka's pedagogy accounts in part for the rechanneling of her rage and for her penchant for understatement.

Allow me to pursue this line of thinking. Elka tells the story of her life in a way that is remarkably upbeat considering all the references to tragic events woven into the story. "I believe she wanted me to leave the interview," Shauna says, "feeling inspired and empowered" (p. 114). Was a pedagogic intent driving her relationship with Shauna? I believe so.

In her story, Elka provides us with ample evidence of her pedagogic relation to the children she encounters in her life. At the age of 13, she taught children math at school. "[Sixteen] children I teach. A matter of fact at the end of the year I go to see all of them and they went through" (p. 49)! About to run from Warsaw, her sister-in-law asked her to "'take my Shmuel, the little boy, home.' And we took him," Elka says (p. 51). At the synagogue in Drohiczyn, she took children under her wing. "You see, a lot of young people there they want me to go work with them, care for them. Walk a little, talk a little, be with them" (p. 52). In Archangelsk, Elka did not follow her boyfriend to Moscow because "I was responsible for my parents and the boy" (p. 54). In Osh, Shmuel "got the measles and I took him to the hospital" (p. 55). She was the one who had to tell her mother that Shmuel had died. In 1946, she "born Lynn" and took care of her (p. 61). In 1954, she "born" David and took care of him (p. 63). In 1990 or so, she had a granddaughter and cared for her. In the story of her life, in all her encounters with children, Elka acts pedagogically out of a concern for their well-being. She acted no differently with Shauna.

Was a pedagogic intent driving the story itself? Did Elka say what she did in the way she did because she wanted Shauna, and through her, future generations, to understand the violence and injustice of the Holocaust without getting caught up in vengeance toward the perpetrators? I think so. Through her story, Elka establishes a pedagogic relation with readers, a move that increases the efficacy of the story as a prompt for a study, not only of the Holocaust, but also of other historical wrongs.

In conclusion, I would like to return to Shauna's point that multi-sensory learning in conjunction with family history may be used in the study of historical wrongs other than the Holocaust. I agree with her on this point and believe that this wider focus better fits the ethnic and multinational diversity of Canadian classrooms. I know this from personal experience.

Once, years ago, a boy in my Grade 6 class extended to me an invitation from his parents to join the family for dinner. On the night of the dinner, the boy confided in me that his father did not get along with one of the neighbours.

"Why is that?" I said.

"He's a Serb." I was perplexed.

"It's hard to explain," he added.

His family had recently immigrated to Canada from Croatia, but, at the time, I had no inkling of the future civil war in Yugoslavia or of the long-standing blood feud among Croats, Serbs, and Bosniaks. I didn't see the relevance of the boy's comment for my teaching. I didn't follow up in any way. For all intents and purposes, I lost his story.

I realize now that all students bring their stories of family history into the classroom and that all will have some connection to the historical wrongs of the nations of the world. They will have connections to the historical wrongs suffered in Canada by First Nations, Métis, Chinese Canadians, and Indo-Canadians, or to the historical wrongs suffered in other nations of the world, such as Rwanda, Egypt, Syria, Yemen, Congo, and Nigeria. In a study of historical wrongs in a social studies class, it is up to the teacher to draw out these connections, taking care to open a space for the sharing of the stories of both the descendants of perpetrators and the descendants of victims. It may be enough simply for students to listen to each other with respect and learn to pose questions of each other at the margins of what they know and understand.

I recommend the use of Elka's story as a prompt in the study of the Holocaust or as a prototype for the selection of a prompt for a study of some other historical wrong. This story has many features that commend its use as a prompt. From Shauna's performance of the story, I learned first-hand of its multidisciplinary and multi-sensory appeal and so can easily imagine the adaptation of the story into a Reader's Theatre script for students to interpret and perform in small groups. From my reading of the story, I see a connection between Elka's insistence on understatement and her pedagogy. In her story, Elka takes care to stick to the bare facts about events and doesn't play the blame game. She says that some Germans and Russians do bad things but other Germans and Russians do good things. She wants to bear witness to the truth and call out for justice without inciting vengeance. She wants to say that it is wrong to murder someone for being a Jew, wrong to murder someone for being a communist, wrong to say hateful words like "cursed Jew, cursed Jew." She wants to leave room for her readers to make up their own minds on matters of truth and justice. She wants to say, not just that she survived, but that she survived with grace. By understating events and emotions, she opens a space in which students may ask questions, participate in dialogue, and create history.

What might a Grade 10 social studies student take away from a performance or a reading of "My Bubby's Story"? I imagine students would find resonances with their own families and, likely, would not wish on others the sad and tragic fate that befell Elka's family.

In her life, even in the darkest times, Elka finds time to go dancing (p. 49). For her, dancing was a pure form of the joy of life, a requisite for survival. In the classroom, if ever things get too serious, students might take their cue from Elka. "Never forget to dance," she says (p. 164).

REFERENCES

Lipson, A., & Perlow, Y. (Eds.). (1961). *The book of Radom: The story of a Jewish community in Poland destroyed by the Nazis*. Available at: www.jewishgen.org/yizkor/radom/radom.html

Rak, S. (2015). *Still dancing: My Bubby's story: How family histories can inform multi-sensory learning in art education*. (Unpublished master's thesis). University of Concordia, Montreal, Quebec.

INVOCATION

Dear Canadian Curriculum Studies Colleagues

John J. Guiney Yallop

D ear Canadian Curriculum Studies colleagues:

When I needed an academic home, you opened a door and pulled out a chair from the table and said, "Welcome." How simple that word is with its two syllables inviting me to be well, to come sit with you, to come into a place of wellness, even to come to a well.

I did not expect to be among you, but putting a checkmark in a box on my membership application to the Canadian Society for the Study of Education meant that I now belonged to you, not in the sense of ownership but in the sense of relationship, of community. Your embrace assures and reminds, and for more than a decade I have felt that embrace, that holding in relationship, that encirclement by community.

I wonder now, as our community grows and encounters new realities, what it means to continue to be welcomed and to be welcoming. How might we continue to be well with each other and with others? How might we continue to invite each other and others to come into wellness, to come drink from this well that has met our thirst? And how might this well continue to be full if it is not filled with our own being? Indeed, what is this well if it is not me, not you, not us? We satisfy the thirst in each other and in others by remaining unsatisfied with any facsimile; we want, need, each to be real.

So, my hope is that we will remain real for ourselves and for each other and for any others who will come to this door, this table. May they find a chair pulled back and a well that is full, and a full welcome into relationship, into community.

Love,

John J. Guiney Yallop

B6

Rumi and Rhizome: The Making of a Transformative Imaginal Curriculum

Soudeh Oladi

INTRODUCTION

To deconstruct neoliberalism's domineering narrative, it is imperative to incorporate a curriculum development model that espouses an *intersubjectivist* paradigm that is continuously evolving. Instead of revealing the complex and fluid nature of social phenomena, the neoliberal narrative, and by extension free-market logic, situates individuals in non-negotiating spaces. Hence, what is needed is a curriculum that cultivates a socially just teaching and learning environment, encourages moral and ethical conduct, and ultimately sows the seeds of transformation both at an individual level and in the external world. To this end, I explore evolving discourses in Rumi's philosophies through the lens offered by Gilles Deleuze's *nomadic identity* (Deleuze & Guattari, 1987). Invoking the Deleuzian dialectic, I explore the exciting possibilities that Rumi's focus on collective and spiritual identities offers the field of curriculum studies. In this respect, a curriculum that embodies a nomadic component is celebrated for its *placelessness* and ability to function on alternate playing fields.

THE RHIZOMATIC CURRICULUM

The Deleuzian concept of rhizome allows for a greater role for a dialectic construction of knowledge in the context of curriculum design. In a rhizomatic curriculum, learning experiences take on personal as well as social dimensions and knowledge is creatively co-constructed. The rhizome, as a way of *becoming*, contrasts static thinking as it constantly redirects and morphs into new beings. Rhizomatic thought desires a *becoming* existence and extends a discourse of multiplicity that "makes random, proliferating and decentred connections" (Colebrook, 2002, p. xxvii).

Rhizomatic thought is deeply embedded in the postmodern curriculum due to its ability to function outside the confines of divisional structures. A rhizomatic curriculum embraces chaos and creativity as it breaks with binary structures and adopts a pluralistic discourse. Possessing a dynamic quality, this curriculum is not content to settle and is always changing and moving. A curriculum inspired by Deleuze's conceptual creation, the rhizome, is generative and has a desire to create. What distinguishes this curriculum from others is the lack of a beginning or an end and the existence of a middle milieu where moving in a linear line is nearly impossible. This curriculum is a collective creation considering that "the rhizome is always an acentered, non-hierarchical, invasive, and chaotic mass" (Deleuze & Guattari, 1987, p. 21). In this curriculum, there is a shift of focus from the static body of knowledge to the dynamic process of knowing (Wallin, 2010).

The unpredictability of the rhizomatic curriculum can slow down the march toward conformity as the disruption of social practices viewed as stable forces (Livingston, 2000) allows the learner to become part of the experience and engender change in a space where the "curriculum does not exist, it just happens" (Pinar, Reynolds, Slattery, & Taubman, 1995, p. 483). As co-constructors of knowledge, learners and educators create lines of flight that allow them to escape the structure imposed by the central power (Deleuze & Guattari, 1987). The rhizomatic curriculum does not seek to replace as much as it is interested in rupture and undoing fixed binaries and frameworks.

A rhizomatic curriculum takes on a critical and participative role where it becomes "intensely historical, political, racial, gendered, phenomenological, autobiographical, aesthetic, theological, and international. Curriculum becomes the site on which the generations struggle to define themselves and the world" (Pinar et al., 1995, p. 848). The rhizomatic curriculum creates a space of constant wandering that disrupts sedentary behaviour since "the rhizome is not a journey toward a fixed end, as denoted by the standards, but wanderings along a 'moving horizon'" (Deleuze & Guattari, 2004, p. xix). This is a curriculum that resists a dystopian future with a system of values insensitive to the neoliberal impact on the homogenization of culture and exacerbation of inequalities.

THE IMAGINAL CURRICULUM

To disrupt the increasing influence of the neoliberal discourse on educational spaces, there is a need to embrace curriculum models that help reinvigorate education as a beacon of hope and possibility and unleash the nomadic potential in learners. Nomadic potential is a form of belonging that rejects an individualized notion of identity (Deleuze & Guattari, 1987) and instead views learners as *beings* capable of taking collective action with and for others. This contrasts the neoliberal curriculum, where safe spaces for criticism continue to erode and where principles of social justice do not prevail. In the meantime, Rumi pulls the conceptual rug out from under us and replaces it with an emphasis on a transformed state of consciousness. Rumi's writings have the potential to eschew pre-established ways of thinking and, as Deleuze would have it, find a way through the cracks to resist the striations imposed by domineering power structures. Rumi's stories ratify a form of knowledge construction that is particularly effective for learners who have lost their sense of wonder and awe.

Rumi's philosophies are critical for an imaginal curriculum that endorses compassion toward others, while at the same time laying emphasis on concepts such as ethics, courage, and justice, and the necessity for learners to explore their inner selves. I understand *imaginal* as developed by Henry Corbin (1976), who derived the term from the Latin *mundus imaginalis* (the intermediary level of reality) and the Persian *na-koja-abad* (the land of nowhere). In advancing the imaginal curriculum, I tap into Rumi's seven stages of enlightenment in an effort to unfold the potential insights they may offer the field of curriculum development. My objective is to promote a curriculum that has the ability to endlessly connect to any point and always function in a middle milieu without a beginning or an end; like a *na-koja-abad*, it is in a place that is nowhere. This curriculum resists settled patterns of activities and exclusionary visions of the future. The imaginal curriculum expands on Rumi's views on learning through an exploration of wisdom and imagination in hopes of reaching an alternative transformative paradigm. This is where imagination takes on a life of its own as it mediates between the worlds of sensibility and understanding. In search of a curriculum that advances critical thinking and in-depth self-reflection, I have segmented the discussion of the imaginal curriculum into seven sections inspired by Rumi's seven stages of enlightenment.

This is where imagination as rooted in *im-ago*, or "I act from within" (Armitage, 2012, p. 2), becomes a space within which the individual reveals her/his creative potential through the language of symbols and metaphors. In a curriculum that

Rumi's seven stages of enlightenment (Oladi, 2016)

Farsi	Translation	My Interpretation
Talab	The desire to know/Thirst/ Search	Seek/ Problematize
Eshgh	Love/Devotion	Passion
Ma'refat	Knowledge of all/Science & wisdom/Ethics	Experience/ Insight
Esteghna	Content/Equanimity	Independent/ Empowered
Tohid	Unity/Oneness	Identity
Heyrat	Wonder/Questioning	Awe/Imagination
Faghr & Fana	Poverty & annihilation/ Nothing-ness	Becoming at one with a cause/ Fully immersed activism

values *becoming* over *being*, creativity is required to imagine a disruption of the status quo and the possibility of alternative futures. A curriculum informed by Rumi's philosophies challenges neoliberal discourses by illuminating reality for what it is and endorsing a culture where learners have the power to confront untruths. The creative and imaginative nature of this kind of curriculum incorporates a never-ending process of *becoming*. This helps develop the learners' sense of agency and of self along with a desire for knowledge creation.

To embrace a curricular reform that incorporates the narrative concurrent with an imaginal curriculum, important questions need to be asked. For one, how can curriculum scholars incorporate aspects of Deleuze's nomadic identity into an imaginal curriculum? Additionally, how can the imaginal curriculum promote a desire for knowledge, ethics of care, wisdom, and social and spiritual activism within learners?

The imaginal curriculum's ontology is one of practice that unmasks an illusory vision of reality in favour of a conscious and undetermined reality. The transformation that is sought through an imaginal curriculum "is clearly a tension-filled process that necessarily entails discomfort and disruption" (Maistry, 2011, p. 130). The imaginal curriculum encourages learners to engage in the construction of conscious thought that is transformative in nature. In this context, an imaginal curriculum based on Rumi's seven stages of enlightenment can inform the field of curriculum inquiry.

One of the imaginal curriculum's primary quests is to rekindle a sense of wanting and seeking in learners. This can be accomplished by espousing a critical discourse that seeks to disrupt the learners' ideological and pedagogical stances. A sense of wanting can be ignited by complicating stable structures in hopes of creating a greater sense of agency through a series of problematizations, including the unsettling of traditional paradigms in education, problematizing the relationship between self and *other*, and disrupting the dominant culture of power. Moreover, problematizing common sense assumptions, unsettling established binaries and hegemonic discourses, as well as questioning the lack of pluralism in educational spaces can contribute to such dynamic spaces. Rumi views education as an inquiry and believes the *sa'lek*, or seeker, of knowledge should walk toward knowledge. He advocates lifelong learning as opposed to an education that prepares students for the immediate future. Even as educational systems are intent on preparing learners for the future, Rumi offers moral education as a supplement to educational praxes that focus solely on logic and instead encourages learners to be seekers of the knowledge of the self, society, and the universe.

An imaginal curriculum strives to instil different passions in students: passion for learning, living, and making a difference. Educators and curriculum developers are encouraged to explore different ways to cultivate conscious and creative passions in learners and practice trading predictability for a space of unpredictability. Educators can engender a sense of passion for learning by including in the curriculum stories that impact the lives of students.

In this respect, the fusion of passion and activism through storytelling can awaken a strong sense of justice in the learners' consciousness and lead to a desire to go beyond oneself. Rumi (1995) is of the belief that a story has the ability to illuminate the truth and can help individuals transcend the difficult barrier between intellect and intuition, which is necessary for the transition from knowledge to action to occur. Rumi aspires, through stories and poems, to disrupt any sense of certainty toward a culture of difference and *otherness*. The central theme running through Rumi's poems and stories is a disdain toward opaque realities and a desire to "lay bare" what is unknown. Exploring the tapestry of identities in Rumi's stories reveals a continuous struggle between various forces that swing the pendulum of opposites in the direction of the "field of possibilities" (Barks, 2003, n.p.).

In an imaginal curriculum, fostering creativity and curiosity is a driving force of passion as students practice loving something for its own sake. In such a curriculum, learners and educators are involved in the co-construction of knowledge that leads to insight. Learning experiences through community engagement, mentorship, and apprenticeship can help students develop insight and clarity as they learn to connect to deeper sources of knowledge. Students can also become insightful and participative as opposed to consistent and predictable through activities such as reflective reading and exploring the biographies of exceptional individuals.

Rumi also urges his readers to be involved in a process of ongoing self-reflection and evaluation of multidimensional discourses. Through the purification of the heart, a moral identity that identifies with justice and liberty is formed. For Rumi, love never loses its rhizomatic quality because, "[l]ike Adam and Eve, Love gives birth to a thousand forms; the world is full of its paintings but it has no form" (Rumi, Divan, 5057, as cited in Chittick, 1983). Rumi is confident that crossing the threshold of love leads to transformation and transcendence. With its potential to energize everything, love as a life-force that animates is in fact "the Sea of Non-being: there the foot of the intellect is shattered" (Rumi, 1995). Like a rhizomatic existence, a being enveloped in love is indeed a "Non-being, that which is not (absent), that which is yet to be (come into being)" (D'Souza, 2014, p. 13). The love Rumi describes possesses the power to motivate and transform individuals and lead to the development of the person's character.

In addition to love, the pursuit and practice of wisdom is vital to the educational experience in the imaginal curriculum. Here, teachers can partake in a continual process of co-construction of knowledge by opening themselves up to learners in an authentic way. Seeking wisdom is both an individual and a collective endeavour and is guided by values, ethics, and a strong sense of care and compassion for oneself and others. Fostering wisdom and a multidimensional expansion of consciousness can be attained by adopting practices that enhance self-awareness and counter the decline of moral standards.

Furthermore, an imaginal curriculum works to empower learners by giving voice to local, global, and personal concerns. Through empowerment, learners embrace dissension and difference and engage in a transformative dialectic of change and acceptance. Through in-depth reflection, learners are empowered with voice and agency and, along with the teachers, they practice decoding discourses that disconnect them from their fellow citizens and transcend beyond their own struggles in order to bring substantive change to the present. To encourage independence, educational objectives can be aimed at rejuvenating communities and empowering local citizens and institutions to address issues pertaining to injustice and inequality.

The role of identity is another central premise in the imaginal curriculum. Students are encouraged to imagine a realm beyond the narrow confines of the classroom, which prevents them from constructing a sense of shared identity. By endorsing a culture of unity, learners practice coexisting with others in different discourses, and this informs a sense of identity and value that leads to meaningful interaction. The learners' desire to develop and negotiate their own identities in educational spaces is a central concern for the imaginal curriculum. Educators need to include activities that permeate the consciousness of learners at both the individual and societal level by urging students to reflect upon their sense of identity. While the learners' sense of identity is partly socially constructed, the interface of individual agency with social constraints and opposition allows students to create and recreate their identities within new categories that include citizen and activist. The learners' search for new identities can become a site of struggle by practicing inclusion and honouring diversity.

The imaginal curriculum also works to revive a sense of wonder and imagination in learners and teachers. This curriculum aspires to excite the deepest levels of human curiosity, cultivate the power of imagination, and encourage the pursuit of lifelong learning. By encouraging inquiry, learners will relish in the joy of consciously discovering the mysteries of their inner selves and the universe. An imaginal curriculum invokes the desire to engage with the world and rekindles a sense of wonder in educational spaces. The invigorating potential of imagination creates a space for learners to transform their emotions and experiences into conscious knowledge and transformative empathy. Imagination is the link that helps learners reach for creative solutions to seemingly inflexible problems. Imagination as action taps into the learners' capacity to create and function as portals that link the unlimited world of possibilities to the *now*. The imaginal curriculum tackles the disconnect between imagination and knowledge where imagination can also be used as an exercise of personal growth with dynamic possibilities that challenge striated modes of thinking.

In Rumi's world, the individual is on a quest to reach the supreme stage of nothingness, or *fana*. Marks (2010) argues that even though Deleuze's philosophical goal is creativity, there is a *fana*-like element in his philosophy as well:

> I must be clear that Deleuze's philosophical goal is not *fana'*: it is creativity—the capacity for new perceptions, affects, and thoughts. Nevertheless, something rather like *fana'* takes place in the hoped-for dispersion, which Deleuze and Guattari emphasized again and again, of the usual limitations of the individual. (p. 17)

An individual, whom Rumi encourages to enter into a space of non-existence, is similar to the individual that Braidotti (2006) depicts as "suspended between the no longer and the not yet." This provides a potential point of contact with the Deleuzian perception of the subject who does not arrive. This non-arrival is also evident in Rumi's Sufi-based practices where the individual is in a perpetual state of motion, moving toward nothingness, since "annihilation is the negation of something that never truly was" (Chittick, 2007, p. 44). It is in this space of non-existence that the *other* is seen and an impetus for action that is rooted in the learners' willingness to engage in intense self-reflection unfolds.

For the imaginal curriculum to be implemented successfully, it is essential that educators and learners engage in various personal, social, political, economic, and cultural forms of activism. Raising activist voices in traditional academic settings helps learners merge their academic work with their personal, spiritual, political, or social ideals. The imaginal curriculum resists, raises awareness, creates, and turns the learning space into a site of production. The activism that plays out against the backdrop of educated risk can help build bridges with the larger community.

The different stages of the imaginal curriculum inspired by Rumi's seven stages of enlightenment advance a subjective consciousness in pursuit of inner wisdom and challenge static discourses by advancing a culture where learners are empowered to confront untruths. The imaginal curriculum encourages learners to engage in the construction of conscious thought that is transformative in nature. It is a reinvention of the learners' subjectivities and a reflection of the *beings* both teachers and learners aspire to *become*. This curriculum, as a site for transformation, incorporates constant acts of reconstruction where new stories emerge as the learners and teachers transition from *beings* to *becomings*. The imaginal curriculum is unique in that it breaks down boundaries and creates spaces where metamorphosis can include completeness, unity, fracture, and multiplicity all at the same time. Its invitation to imagine the impossible creates an opportune moment to envision realities that have yet to be created.

REFERENCES

Armitage, A. (2012). A methodology of the imagination. *Journal of Business Administration Research, 1*(1), 1–12.

Barks, C. (2003). *Rumi: The book of love: Poems of ecstasy and longing.* New York, NY: Harper Collins.

Braidotti, R. (2006). The ethics of becoming imperceptible. In C. V. Boundas (Ed.), *Deleuze and philosophy* (pp. 133–159). Edinburgh, Scotland: Edinburgh University Press.

Chittick, W. (2007). *Sufism: A beginner's guide.* Oxford, England: Oneworld Publications.

Colebrook, C. (2002). *Understanding Deleuze.* Crows Nest, Australia: Allen & Unwin.

Corbin, H. (1976). *Mundus imaginalis, or, the imaginary and the imaginal.* (R. Horine, Trans.). Ipswich, Australia: Golgonooza Press.

Deleuze, G., & Guattari, F. (1987). *A thousand plateaus: Capitalism and schizophrenia.* (B. Massumi, Trans.). Minneapolis: University of Minnesota Press.

Deleuze, G., & Guattari, F. (2004). *Anti-Oedipus.* (R. Hurley, M. Seem, & H. R. Lane, Trans.). London, England: Continuum.

D'Souza, R. (2014). What can activist scholars learn from Rumi? *Philosophy East and West, 64*(1), 1–24.

Livingston, D. (2000). *Wondering about a future generation: A Deleuzian perspective on curriculum* (Unpublished doctoral dissertation). Georgia Southern University, Statesboro, Georgia, USA.

Maistry, S. M. (2011). Transformation through the curriculum: Engaging a process of unlearning in economics education pedagogy. *Alternation, 18*(2), 115–134.

Marks, L. U. (2010). *Enfoldment and infinity: An Islamic genealogy of new media art.* Cambridge, MA: MIT Press.

Oladi, S. (2016). *Disrupting the instrumentalization of education: Unleashing the nomadic potential in learners through Freire and Rumi* (Unpublished doctoral dissertation). University of New Brunswick, Fredericton, New Brunswick.

Pinar, W. F., Reynolds, W., Slattery, P., & Taubman, P. (1995). *Understanding curriculum.* New York, NY: Peter Lang.

Rumi, J. (1995). *The essential Rumi.* (C. Barks, with J. Moyne, A. J. Arberry, & R. Nicholson, Trans.). San Francisco, CA: HarperSanFrancisco.

Wallin, J. J. (2010). *A Deleuzian approach to curriculum: Essays on a pedagogical life.* New York, NY: Palgrave Macmillan.

INVOCATION

To Enchanted Lands

David Lewkowich

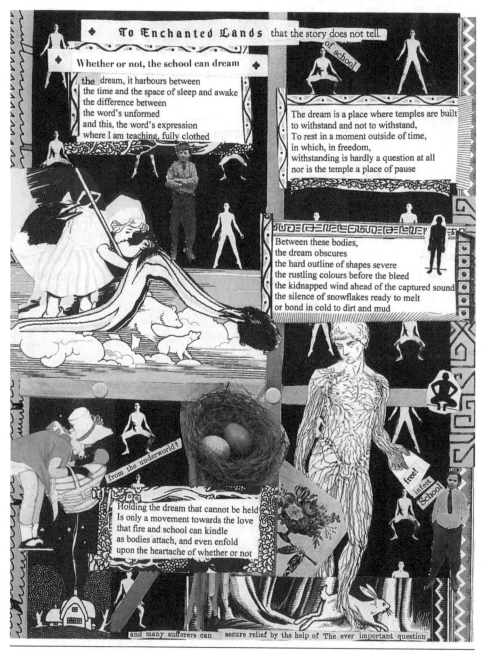

David Lewkowich (2017). *To enchanted lands that the story (of school) does not tell.* Collage

B7

Theorizing as Poetic Dwelling: An Intellectual Link between Ted Aoki and Martin Heidegger

Patricia Liu Baergen

The intellectual odyssey of a scholar is complex and dynamic, especially when such an odyssey was lived in the juxtaposition of linguistic cultural dynamics and intellectual traditions. Dr. Ted Tetsuo Aoki (1919–2012) was a pivotal Canadian curriculum theorist and a public pedagogue. His publications and public lectures since the late 1960s "shaped the field of curriculum studies and the discipline of education in significant ways in Canada, North America, and international contexts" (Hurren & Hasebe-Ludt, 2014, p. xiii). He was a scholar, a dear lifelong mentor to many students, and a strong critic of the division between theory and practice and the binary between East and West.

The interwoven, complex, dynamic, and poetic style that underscored Aoki's intellectual formation and scholarly works, especially as influenced by the writings of prominent continental philosopher Martin Heidegger (1889–1976), lacks attention. This chapter is engaged with the question: *In what ways does Aoki draw upon Heidegger's writings in forming his critical, reflective, and poetic style of theorizing?*

INSTRUMENTALISM OF CURRICULUM-AS-PLAN

[I]n the field of curriculum we have come under the sway of discourse that is replete with performative words such as goals and objectives ... achievement and assessment—words reflective of instrumentalism in modernity.... [U]nder the hold of technological rationality, we have become so production

oriented that the ends-means paradigm, *a* way to do, has become *the* way
to do, indifferent to differences in the lived world of teachers and students.
(Aoki, 1990/2005, p. 368)

Aoki's critical concern about Ralph Tyler's (1949) rationale, cast in the technical
power of instrumental procedure, was that it had become the dominant, pervasive
way of understanding curriculum. In 1974, Aoki suggested "A basic problem in
implementation of programs may be found in the producer-consumer paradigm"
(p. 37). This linear view perceives curriculum as the pre-chosen ends of goals. This
speaks of education as a technical ends-means where instructing students "becomes
in-structuring students in the image of the given" (Aoki, 1996a/2005, p. 418). In
so understanding, students become objects, rather than subjects who speak the
language of humanness and diversity. Although the array of curricular disciplines
may appear as diverse and plural, it is ultimately "an illusion," manifesting "a singular meaning of curriculum: curriculum-as-plan" (Aoki, 1996a/2005, p. 417). This
ends-means paradigm ignores the possibility of human potential and this provision
of universal education comes at a cost to humanity and its cultural diversity. Aoki
(1996a/2005) was concerned about this mono-vision of curriculum, and he pointed
out that "we seem to be caught up in a singular meaning of the word *curriculum*" (p.
417) and that such "instrumentalism reasoning based on scientism and technology"
amounts to "a crisis in Western reasoning" (1983/2005, p. 113). This is "an internal
crisis" (1983/2005, p. 114) in understanding curriculum.

This crisis is a "fundamental contradiction between ... [the] commitment to
technological progress and ... [the] commitment to the improvement of personal
and situational life" (1983/2005, pp. 113–114). The crisis of curriculum development in North America is the obsessive pursuit of growth (development) in science
and technology, and such curriculum development in instrumental reasoning replaces substantive reasoning. Modern scientists claim that researchers must speak
this language of science to communicate. Therefore, supposedly, for researchers in
the field of curriculum to unlock the secret of the social system, they need only
take the time to follow the instructions in a manual with data analysis. However,
the sophistication of data analysis cannot compensate for the lack of the subjective
human dimension. The results derived from turning people into things through a
process of reduction cannot escape the trap of assimilating people into the discourse
of power, class, and gender.

In such an instrumentalist educational system, teachers and educators perhaps
feel an unconscious tendency to *produce*. Their efforts to translate theories into
applications to produce a *successful* and *rightful* teaching/learning experience are

relentless. Consequently, the role of teaching manifests itself as being *technical* in nature—attending to the *doing*. The ministry of education or the school district office *enframe* the worldview of curriculum into curriculum-as-plan, where the roles of teachers and pupils and the subjects are prescribed and assumed far ahead, outside the classroom. The language spoken in this world, like "goals," "aims," and "objectives," is arbitrary to "statements of intent and interest" (Aoki, 1986/1991/2005, p. 160). According to Aoki's critique, teachers in this scheme of things are regarded as "installers of the curriculum, where implementing assumes an instrumental flavour" (p. 160). The curriculum becomes a tool. The problem with the singular, technological rationale in thinking curriculum is the fundamental separation of *human* and *world*, *theory* and *practice*. Instead of seeing a problem as seeking a particular solution, Aoki took an etymological and phenomenological approach toward curriculum as possibilities of *opening* up. Aoki returned to the live(d) ground of students and teachers—the *is-ness* of curriculum.

THE QUESTIONING CONCERNING TECHNOLOGY

> Questioning builds a way. We would be advised, therefore, above all to pay heed to the way, and not to fix our attention on isolated sentences and topics. The way is a way of thinking. All ways of thinking, more or less perceptible, lead through language in a manner that is extraordinary. We shall be questioning concerning technology, and in so doing we should like to prepare a free relationship to it. The relationship will be free if it *opens* our human existence to the *essence* of technology. When we can respond to this essence, we shall be able to experience the technological within its own bounds. (Heidegger, 1977, pp. 3–4)

For Martin Heidegger (1977), "*Technology* is not equivalent to the *essence* of technology" (p. 4) in modern times. In his 1953 essay "The Question Concerning Technology," Heidegger began with the everyday account of technology in modern time—the vast array of instruments, machines, artifacts, and devices that humans invent, build, and ultimately exploit. In so understanding, technology is merely a tool that humans control. Heidegger (1977) depicted this everyday account of technology as providing only a limited, over-exercised "*instrumental* and *anthropological* definition" (p. 44).

He also wrote that the "revealing [of technology] that holds sway throughout modern technology ... [is] challenging ... which puts to nature the unreasonable demand that it supply energy which can be extracted and stored as such" (p. 14). Per se, modern technology *reveals* its essence, which is *concealed* in nature, by placing, ordering, hunting—which in one way or another are all a sense of the "German verb *stellen*" (p. 15)—in order to reform, store, distribute, and redistribute. Through this mode of revealing, resources are exploited as means to ends, instrumental, and a product of human activity. In his later writing, "What Are Poets For?," Heidegger (1971b) stated that "man becomes the subject and the world the object" (p. 110) and "life is supposed to yield itself to technical production" (p. 109).

Heidegger's primary concern was about the discernment of the *essence* of technology that is established in a deeply embedded instrumentalist worldview in modern science. Also, by revealing the *essence* only through the mode of the measurable and the manipulable, ultimately it reduces beings to no-beings. For Heidegger (1977), such essence of technology defines and manipulates the modern way of living in the West as dangerous—a power that humans themselves do not control. Therefore, he warns that "as long as we represent technology as an instrument, we remain held fast in the will to master it" (p. 32). Ultimately, Heidegger turned to the Greek and brought *technē* into presence:

> There was a time when it was not technology alone that bore the name *technē*. Once that revealing that brings forth truth into the splendor of radiant appearing also was called *technē*. Once there was a time when the bringing-forth of the true into the beautiful was called *technē*. And the *poiesis* of the fine arts also was called *technē*. (p. 34)

To respond to the calling of *technē*, Heidegger turned to the poetic realm of Friedrich Hölderlin and dwelt on an old wooden bridge that spanned the Rhine river for hundreds of years. Later a "monstrousness" (Heidegger, 1977, p. 16) of technological production, a hydroelectric plant, was set beside it. This poetic thinking and dwelling of humans in the world as openness to the *being-ness* of being is what both Heidegger and Aoki expounded.

THE *IS-NESS* OF CURRICULUM-AS-LIVED

Aoki (1978/1980/2005) wrote:

> I find it important to center curriculum thought on a broader frame, that of "man/world relationships," for it permits probing of the deeper meaning of what it is for persons (teachers and students) to be human, to become more human, and to act humanly in educational situations. (p. 95)

He also challenged us: "If living on earth as humans, experiencing being and becoming, matters in education, it behooves us to transform the language of school life such that multiple meanings of the word *curriculum* can prevail" (Aoki, 1996a/2005, p. 420).

Aoki's phenomenological approach toward curriculum revealed the *is-ness* of curriculum-as-lived. To expound the *is-ness* of curriculum is to move away from the dominant instrumental understanding of the word *curriculum-as-plan* that fundamentally separated *human* and *world*, *theory*, and *practice*. By juxtaposing the lived moments that happen inside/outside the classroom, professional/personal, tensional/open, Aoki spoke the word *curriculum* in multiple Heideggerian and poetic ways.

Sharing his phenomenological understanding, Aoki suggested that the teachers' and students' lived experiences become part of a curriculum, interconnected and not separable, "a lived situation, pregnantly alive in the presence of people" (Aoki, 1986/1991/2005, p. 159), a pedagogic situation. Aoki revealed what has been concealed in the habitation of the scientific rationale—the privilege of ideology.

For Aoki (1990/2005), the *essence* of curriculum also resonates much in the *auditory*, such as music. By asking a jazz trumpeter, Bobby Shew from California, to play, speak, and sing to the question "When does an instrument cease to be an instrument?" (p. 367), Aoki attuned us to the sounds of curriculum. The language in the Western world has come to "overly rely upon visuality, thereby diminishing the place for other ways of being in the world" (Aoki, 1990/2005, p. 373).

To further open up this foreclosing horizon, Aoki etymologically, metaphorically, and phenomenologically dwelt in the wor(l)d of poetry. Calling upon the metaphors of *sonare* (to hear) from the "sound of the beat and rhythm of the earth" in ancient Greek's *geo-metron* to dwell juxtaposedly with *videre* (to see) in the Chinese character of poetry 詩 (p. 373), Aoki (1990/2005) sought space for "a way of *composing* curriculum that allows for polyphony" (p. 375). Heeding what Heidegger (1971b) described as the "mirror-play of the simple onefold of earth and sky, divinities and mortals" (p. 177), Aoki (1990/2005) dwelled poetically in "an Occidental reading of an Oriental word" (p. 375) of "earth, measure, temple, mouth, echoes" (p. 375) as a human being in the world.

POETIC THINKING

For Heidegger, genuine thinking is never a pursuit achieved through man-made assembling of abstraction from reality, it is humanity's most essential manner of *being* human. Genuine thinking is rarely attained through demanding. It manifests in the relation in between humanity and Being. For Heidegger, when poetic thinking takes place, Being and thinking are one. As Heidegger wrote in his 1959 essay "On the Way to Language," "We might perhaps prepare a little for change in our relations to words. Perhaps this experience might awaken: all reflective thinking is poetic and all poetry in turn is a kind of thinking" (Heidegger, 1971a, p. 136).

Ultimately, poetry was Heidegger's inquiry into the essential *being* of language that carries layered cultural and historical influences, which has not "lost its magic potency by being used up and abused" (Heidegger, 1977, p. xii). Thus thinking through *enframed* language, like in metaphysics, has limitations. Poetry is the way to return to the nature of language, the house of Being where the reciprocal relation between Being and human is fulfilled through language.

Here, Heidegger's (1971b) call for "*unconcealedness*" (p. 51) is a call for the *is-ness* of experience itself—a portal for opening into the process of making and creating. An opening allures us to dwell deeper in the relation between poetry and thinking, more so, in *poiesis* as ways of being, knowing, and understanding.

In Heidegger's 1947 essay, "The Thinker as Poet: *Aus der Erfahrung des Denkens*," which translates directly as "From the Experience of Thinking," he uses a traditional cabinetmaker apprentice to illustrate *poiesis*. He writes:

> If he is to become a true cabinetmaker, he makes himself answer and respond above all to the different kinds of wood and to the shapes slumbering within wood—to wood as it enters into man's dwelling with all the hidden riches of its essence. In fact, this relatedness to wood is what maintains the whole craft. Without that relatedness, the craft will never be anything but empty busywork, any occupation with it will be determined exclusively by business concerns. Every handicraft, all human dealings, are constantly in that danger. (Heidegger, 1977, p. 379)

It is this ancient *attunement* with the experience itself where the artist hears and feels the essence of nature. Heidegger (1977) suggested that we should not "push on blindly with technology" nor "curse it as the work of the devil" (p. 330). The way forward, as Heidegger suggested, is not to end technology, but to dwell in it differently, poetically. More so, what is in need in the modern age is to transform a calculative way of thinking into poetic ways of being, being with, being-in-the-world.

DWELLING IN-BETWEEN

In Aoki's (1990/2005) theorizing, he writes:

[H]aving opened ourselves to the Occidental tonality of "geometron," allow me to in-tone an Oriental counterpoint for whatever sound it may reveal. I begin with the Chinese character for "poetry," a character that refuses linearity.... In the presence of this word, I ask: "What does it mean to dwell poetically?" (p. 374)

When curriculum returns to the ambivalent ground of human being, essentially the *is-ness* of curriculum-as-lived, then what might these juxtaposed voices, locations, cultures, and languages, these mixed and multiple identities, be like in thinking curriculum? In each classroom there is another world, a world that is filled with the names of pupils, and behind each name is an array of different cultures and life stories. In this world, the language is abstract and linguistic, filled with surprises and frustrations—a world that is constructed by unplanned or unplannable curricula.

Curriculum-as-plan, formalized by the ministry, provides a legitimate institutional tool for teachers, who are accountable for *what* and *how* they teach. However, at the core of the curriculum-as-plan lies the assumption of sameness and the ignorance of the uniqueness of the pupils and the teachers. In so thinking, doing, and speaking, the curriculum-as-plan reduces their live(d) experiences as pedagogical possibilities.

Moving away from the rigidity of instrumentalism, the over-reification of curriculum, and the binary of dualism, Aoki (2000/2005) was particularly attuned to the place in-between, whether inside or outside the classrooms, Western or Eastern knowledge. Instead of focusing on the "apparent" differences culturally and linguistically, Aoki (2000/2005) pointed to the profound spaces in between. He suggested "indwelling in the zone between curriculum-as-plan and curriculum-as-lived" (1986/1991/2005, p. 163). To attune to the possibilities of the in-between place, Aoki (1996b/2005), heeding Heidegger's "ontological essentialism," metaphorically built a bridge "as a site of being" (p. 317). Instead of rushing to cross over the bridge to "overcome the tensionality," Aoki imagined, pondered, dwelled, and lingered on the bridge, the space in between, "dwelling aright within it" (Aoki, 1986/1991/2005, p. 163). How might this bridge, this in-between space, lead toward understanding curriculum cross-culturally?

Aoki (1991/2005) spoke poetically to shift the attention to the crossing in-between cultures:

Now I slide away from the crossing, and sink into the lived space of between—in the midst of many cultures, into the *inter* of interculturalism.

Indwelling here is a dwelling in the midst of differences, often trying and difficult. It is a place alive with tension. In dwelling here, the quest is not so much to rid ourselves of tension ... but more so to seek appropriately attuned tension, such that the sound of the tensioned string resounds well. (p. 382)

Aoki, a second of seven children, born to a Japanese immigrant family in a coal-mining town, Cumberland, Canada, in 1919, knows well the dwelling in the midst of differences. His childhood experiences of double schooling (public school and Japanese language school) "positioned" him in the midst of "twofold Pacific languages and histories" (Aoki, 1995/2005, p. 304). Growing up in this small but diverse community, Aoki (1995/2005) described himself, "since very early, a mixed-up hybrid kid" (p. 304). As a second-generation Japanese *nisei* (二世), Aoki (1979/1995/2005) shared the lived curricular of his *being-ness* in 1941, during the World War II years. Either *being* confined in the internment sites of his birth land, Canada, or being a *stranger* in his heritage land in Tokyo, Japan, Aoki knew the dwelling difficulties of *homelessness* first-hand. It is the generosity of Aoki's offering by reflecting on his own injuries that opens the door for me to hear the polyphonic sounds of pedagogy that he spoke of. I can step outside of the confined way of thinking, speak the language of curriculum in its multiple meanings, and then begin to see and appreciate the hybrid nature of the curriculum landscape.

POETIC DWELLING

For Heidegger (1971b), "To be a human being means to be on the earth as a mortal. It means to dwell" (p. 145). His emphasis was on building as "letting-dwell" (p. 156)—the true nature of building. Thus, the bridge in this sense is a space of gathering, as building, as letting-dwell. For Heidegger (1971b), dwelling is the "basic character of Being in keeping with which mortals exist" (p. 158). What is pressing to think about in our precarious postmodern times where the essence of human being is *enframed*, claimed, and challenged by technological thinking, is Heidegger's suggestion that man can only cease his misery by responding to the calling of mortals, by "giving thought to his *homelessness*" (p. 159). In Heidegger's 1934–1935 lectures about Hölderlin's hymn "The Ister," he further expounded on the homelessness of humankind. Heidegger pointed out that humans are historical beings. Through the passage of Hölderlin's discussions about the different renderings of the choral ode from Sophocles to his own "Ister" hymn, from Greek to German, Heidegger (1984/1996) recognized that the "historicality of these two humankinds is intrinsically different" (p. 124). For Heidegger, the historicality of any humankind resides in being homely. Becoming homely can only be from experiencing *unhomely*. In order to understand humankind's journey through such a poetic passage, he writes:

> The law of being homely as a becoming homely consists in the fact that historical human beings, at the beginning of their history, are not intimate with what is homely, and indeed must even become unhomely with respect to the latter in order to learn the proper appropriation of what is their own in venturing to the foreign, and to first become homely in the return from the foreign. (p. 125)

For Heidegger, poetic dwelling in between the sky, earth, mortals, and divinity is the antidote to modern technology.

A LINGERING NOTE

In questioning and provoking the instrumental rationale in thinking, Aoki, in his writings, reflected much of Heidegger's critical position of constantly pointing out the conceptual assumptions and philosophical blind spots in the wor(l)d of metaphysics. By returning to the ambivalent ground of humanness, dwelling poetically, Aoki persistently broke down walls to loosen the grids in instrumentalist thinking. There is no elevating moment toward the goal of a comprehensive rationale absolute in understanding curriculum for Aoki. Rather, there is the lived ground of curriculum that calls for the self-identified subjectivity, theorizing as poetic dwelling, as human-in-the-world.

REFERENCES

Aoki, T. T. (1974). Pin-pointing issues in curriculum decision-making. In C. D. Ledgerwood (Ed.), *Curriculum decision making in Alberta: A Janus look.* Edmonton, AB: Alberta Department of Education.

Aoki, T. T. (1978/1980/2005). Toward curriculum inquiry in a new key. In W. F. Pinar & R. L. Irwin (Eds.), *Curriculum in a new key: The collected works of Ted T. Aoki* (pp. 89–110). Mahwah, NJ: Erlbaum.

Aoki, T. T. (1979/1995/2005). Reflections of a Japanese Canadian teacher experiencing ethnicity. In W. F. Pinar & R. L. Irwin (Eds.), *Curriculum in a new key: The collected works of Ted T. Aoki* (pp. 333–348). Mahwah, NJ: Erlbaum.

Aoki, T. T. (1983/2005). Curriculum implementation as instrumental action and as situational praxis. In W. F. Pinar & R. L. Irwin (Eds.), *Curriculum in a new key: The collected works of Ted T. Aoki* (pp. 111–123). Mahwah, NJ: Erlbaum.

Aoki, T. T. (1986/1991/2005). Teaching as indwelling between two curriculum worlds. In W. F. Pinar & R. L. Irwin (Eds.), *Curriculum in a new key: The collected works of Ted T. Aoki* (pp. 159–165). Mahwah, NJ: Erlbaum.

Aoki, T. T. (1990/2005). *Sonare* and *videre*: A story, three echoes and a lingering note. In W. F. Pinar & R. L. Irwin (Eds.), *Curriculum in a new key: The collected works of Ted T. Aoki* (pp. 367–376). Mahwah, NJ: Erlbaum.

Aoki, T. T. (1991/2005). Taiko drums and sushi, perogies and sauerkraut: Mirroring a half-life in multicultural curriculum. In W. F. Pinar & R. L. Irwin (Eds.), *Curriculum in a new key: The collected works of Ted T. Aoki* (pp. 377–387). Mahwah, NJ: Erlbaum.

Aoki, T. T. (1995/2005). In the midst of doubled imaginaries: The Pacific community as diversity and as difference. In W. F. Pinar & R. L. Irwin (Eds.), *Curriculum in a new key: The collected works of Ted T. Aoki* (pp. 303–312). Mahwah, NJ: Erlbaum.

Aoki, T. T. (1996a/2005). Spinning inspirited images in the midst of planned and live(d) curricula. In W. F. Pinar & R. L. Irwin (Eds.), *Curriculum in a new key: The collected works of Ted T. Aoki* (pp. 413–423). Mahwah, NJ: Erlbaum.

Aoki, T. T. (1996b/2005). Imaginaries of "east and west": Slippery curricular signifiers in education. In W. F. Pinar & R. L. Irwin (Eds.), *Curriculum in a new key: The collected works of Ted T. Aoki* (pp. 313–320). Mahwah, NJ: Erlbaum.

Aoki, T. T. (2000/2005). Language, culture and curriculum. In W. F. Pinar & R. L. Irwin (Eds.), *Curriculum in a new key: The collected works of Ted T. Aoki* (pp. 321–329). Mahwah, NJ: Erlbaum.

Heidegger, M. (1971a). *On the way to language.* (P. D. Hertz, Trans.). New York, NY: Harper & Row.

Heidegger, M. (1971b). *Poetry, language, thought.* (A. Hofstadter, Trans.). New York, NY: Harper & Row.

Heidegger, M. (1977). *The question concerning technology and other essays.* (W. Lovitt, Trans.). New York, NY: Harper & Row.

Heidegger, M. (1984/1996). *Hölderlin's hymn "The Ister."* (W. McNeil & J. Davis, Trans.). Bloomington, IN: Indiana University Press.

Hurren, W., & Hasebe-Ludt, E. (2014). Preface: An invitation to contemplate the topos and humus of curriculum on genealogical grounds: A Festschrift/Gedenkschrift for Ted Tetsuo Aoki. In W. Hurren & E. Hasebe-Ludt (Eds.), *Contemplating curriculum: Genealogies/times/places* (pp. xiii–xvii). New York, NY: Routledge.

Tyler, R. W. (1949). *Basic principles of curriculum and instruction.* Chicago, IL: The University of Chicago Press.

INVOCATION

Lane Muses

Kent den Heyer

I live in Edmonton, Treaty 6 land. Like many prairie city houses, mine has a back lane thoroughfare. This block is magpie territory.

When some misguided other bird sits on a tree here, magpies begin unceasing harassment. They leap from branch to branch, one in front of the trespasser, one behind, one usually a branch above, and one seemingly a rover, flying in and out as required. What I have witnessed time and again is intelligence equal to wolves and other pack animals, like humans. They even have our neighbourhood cats trained. Magpies walk around like they own the place. My friend Dwayne Donald tells a story about this he heard from his Elders.

Long ago, the four- and two-legged creatures organized a foot race to finally determine which should be able to eat the other. After much deliberation, the four-legged sent their fastest buffalo, while the two-legged sent their fastest human. From the beginning, the race was not going well for the two-legged. Just as the buffalo was about to cross the finish line well ahead of the human, a magpie came out from the mane of the buffalo and flew first across the finish line. The issue was thus decided. That does explain a lot about magpies.

I delight at watching magpies from my back deck as they hop from branch to branch or along the lane. They are deliberate, graceful, and precise when they hop. To date I have seen only one one-legged magpie, a bird that showed up occasionally to eat from my bird feeder. I have not seen that bird in some time.

It is difficult to hop with grace like a magpie on one leg, don't take my word and try. To be graceful on one leg while pretending to have two is what many Canadians have been trying to do with half a history about who we were, are, and hope to be. Here, now, we are, but how do we do so gracefully if we can only try to hop forward on one leg?

B8

Transitional Spaces and Displaced Truths of the Early-Years Teacher

Sandra Chang-Kredl

INTRODUCTION

In interviewing early-years teachers about their subjective experiences and personal constructions of childhood, I have heard accounts, often traced back to
a therapist's suggestion, that the early-years teacher heals herself/himself—or
rather, "the child within"—through working with children. I respond with an-
noyance to this proposition and the simplistic logic that underlies it: that one's
childhood is accessible in this manner, and that one's aspirations can be framed
unproblematically in terms of self-restoration.

I focus on the distinctive position of the early-years teacher, an adult who—
like all of us—was once a child. The need for the adult to distinguish between
nostalgic versions of childhood and children today has been addressed (e.g.,
Nodelman, 2008); however, the space within which to examine this distinction, if indeed it exists as stated, is far from clear. Indeed, our understandings
of childhood are often constructed in the murky spaces of the unconscious.
I offer musings on the experience of the early-years teacher, a provocation of
early-care curriculum, through posing the question: "What does it mean to live
truthfully with one's self and others as an adult who cares for children?" The
early-years teacher, and to an extent, the parent, live in complex and, at times,
illusory spaces of childhood.

In this chapter, I offer a composite portrait of Megan, an early-years teacher, inspired by the voices of 12 childcare educators who were interviewed in

Montreal, Quebec, in 2015 as part of a study on memory, childhood, and teaching.[1] Portrait segments are interspersed with discussion on care, motivational displacement (Noddings, 1984), and transitional spaces, in particular (Winnicott, 1986).

PORTRAIT OF AN EARLY-YEARS TEACHER

Megan ended up studying in a teacher-education program by default. She flitted from program to program until her internalized parent voice decided for her: "At least get a degree that will secure you a job." So she graduated with a university teaching degree and an assumption that she would be an elementary-school teacher. She doesn't recall being particularly drawn to children at the time.

Megan's first teaching job was in a preschool, assisting the head teacher of the four-year-old group in the mornings, and then taking responsibility of the three- and four-year-old combined group in the afternoons. She fell in love with the work and the children, never questioning the relevance of reading an illustrated book to children sitting in front of her, consoling a three-year-old who was sad, helping children learn how to flip on their coats the "magic" way, getting wrapped up in Lego building, listening to preschoolers' stories, or telling parents about what their children did during the day. Megan's interest in children was established. During these teaching years, Megan also had her own babies, promptly falling in love with them as well.

What Megan hadn't anticipated during these busy years of teaching and parenting was that her students (and children) would grow up. She became aware of the transitory nature of working with children, and a sense of listlessness returned, as it had in her undergraduate years. A therapist suggested to Megan that she had chosen to work with children to heal the child within. Understandably, Megan was hurt when she heard this interpretation, which she understood as implying that, all these years, she had, unbeknownst to her, used children as a form of self-therapy. Another therapist suggested that she gave her students and her children what she wished she'd had herself. She realized that these ideas unveiled a certain truth, but not a version of the truth that was beneficial.

Megan asked herself, "Why does working with children, as a teacher or as a parent, stave away the hopelessness?" and "How would giving a child something that you wish you'd had as a child make things better for you?" There was something about being with children—caring for, listening to, taking seriously, giving space to—that gave Megan a sense of purpose. But it was temporary; it didn't stay with her. It was like a band-aid.

Of motivational displacements and transitional spaces

What the therapists' statements about self-healing suggest is a curious form of reversal. If the adult teacher is, in fact, giving children what she wishes she'd had, then she would be identifying herself *in* the children, that is, projecting her own needs onto the children under her care. Nel Noddings (1984) seems to address this dilemma by pointing out that care requires the "one-caring" to develop an "engrossment" (that is, understanding) for the "cared-for," as well as a "motivational displacement" to act with the purpose of meeting the needs of the other. Many feminists object, however, to Noddings' claims, arguing that this definition of other-directed care valorizes a traditional model in which women are expected to give, with little expectation of receiving. The concern is that it merely reinforces in some women a "false consciousness that equates moral maturity with self-sacrifice and self-effacement" (Sander-Staudt, 2009, n.p.).

The early-years teacher's work revolves around the protection, nurturance, and education of young children, which has been framed as the care work that mothers traditionally provided (Mullins, 2009; Ruddick, 1995). Given that, through history, mothers were expected to provide this caring labour voluntarily, naturally, and out of love (Ruddick, 1995), the extension into the paid workforce is that early-years teachers should be altruistic, self-sacrificing, and endlessly loving. A common-sense moral imperative became attached to this assumption, such that if women naturally possess these emotional and caring abilities, they are expected to be engrossed in the other and the other's needs with no desire for anything in return. Writing about her experiences as a teacher and mother, Madeleine Grumet (1988) describes how "even though we secretly respect this maternal pedagogy of ours, it seems personal to us, not quite defensible in this public place, and we provide this nurturant labour without demanding the recompense it deserves" (pp. 86–87). The child grows up. The students grow up. In referring to other-directed care, Sarah Hoagland (1990) writes that "the very purpose of parenting, as well as teaching and theraping ... is to wean the cared-for of dependency" (p. 110). What then is the mother figure/teacher left with? Motivational displacement, when taken to its furthest point, can be reflected in bell hooks' disturbing example of a completed caring relationship, using Noddings' framework, of the slave master's son who "grows up under the one-caring of the mammy to be a master" (hooks, as cited in Hoagland, 1990, p. 112).

Megan spent much of her childhood and young adulthood trying to be what she believed others around her wanted or "needed" her to be for them: the reliable, responsible, acquiescent, loving, and other-directed daughter, teacher, and mother.

The ideal of the "good enough mother/teacher" demands that "women split themselves from their own needs and desires to serve the needs and desires of children" (Boldt, Salvio, & Taubman, 2006, p. 7). Megan *did* fall in love with the work and "the activities of nurturing, comforting, encouraging" children (Daniels, 1987, p. 408). When interviewed, she described this turning point as one of having found her place, an emotional fitting-in that gave her a sense of unquestioned purpose—but not necessarily a reflection of a natural proclivity. Taubman (2006) refers to the fantasies of "loving and being loved [that] swirl in the psychic life of teachers" (p. 21), and the impossible pressure that a stance of "It's all about the kids" puts on a teacher's subjectivity. Indeed, this ideal of motivational displacement may be what provokes the opposite response in a teacher: aggressive and hateful urges (Taubman, 2006). In women, however, these destructive impulses are often directed back toward the self. Where else would a caring (*child*-caring), other-directed adult be able to direct her aggression in societally acceptable ways? In an inversion of Winnicott's (1965) infant who learns to have "a limiting membrane, so that what is not-he or not-she is repudiated, and is external" (p. 148), the caring adult must urge the repudiated not-she back inside. As far as solutions go, this one is not ideal. Motivational displacement is a difficult and questionable feat to achieve. We all struggle with the demands of an unsettled subjective and social existence. According to Winnicott (1986), "relief from this strain is provided by an intermediate area of experience" (p. 268).

Of transitional spaces and band-aids

Megan considered all the learning taking place amidst the children in her classroom: it was about love, self-respect, and shared ideas. It was about creating a caring space to really—somatically even—learn what you needed to be healthy despite whatever you were born into. It was about education, but it had to be in a caring environment for that learning to be possible.

Why would giving a child something that one wishes one had had as a child make things better for the adult? When the parent/teacher adapts to the child's needs, to give the child "the *illusion* that there is an external reality that corresponds" to the child's internal needs (Winnicott, 1986, p. 267), the parent/teacher too is able to experience that intermediate phenomenon. In this illusory space, the adult directs care toward others (children), yet the space exists "as a resting-place for the individual engaged in the perpetual human task of keeping inner and outer reality separate yet interrelated" (p. 268). Perhaps this is the kind of relief that can be found for the adult whose ethical identity is defined through being other-directed (Hoagland, 1990). How can we recognize the resistance that psychic life carries, including the presumption of natural qualities? Boldt et al. (2006) write about "how using love as a defense against undesired knowledge plays out and in many ways structures life in classrooms" (p. 5).

The illusion of the transitional space "is one which belongs inherently to human beings and which no individual finally solves for himself or herself, although a *theoretical* understanding of it may provide a *theoretical* solution" (Winnicott, 1986, p. 268). If we consider Winnicott's transitional object (think teddy bears, warm blankets—objects imbued with security and attachment), we can expand our understanding of care to Fisher and Tronto's (1990) notion of care as "a species activity that includes everything we do to maintain, contain, and repair our 'world' so that we can live in it as well as possible" (p. 41). The space becomes less a symbol of the band-aid, the temporary fix—a "neutral area of experience which will not be challenged" (Winnicott, 1986, p. 265)—and more a space of play, creativity, art, and inspiration, for the adult and the child. The illusion (in its most positive sense) is that by being in this caring space, one can experience the warmth and vitality of the transitional object.

Megan grew up in a big farmhouse in a rural community, and when her friends visited, their game of choice was hide-and-go-seek tag. The house was set up with this long hallway, and there were two rooms on either side that were connected with doors. It was like a square with two rooms on each side. Megan could literally run around in circles. The staircase banister that finished in a little twirl was always "home." The children had to hit that to be safe. The kitchen was the biggest room of Megan's house and there was an island—as a child, her head wouldn't even reach the top of the island—so it was a perfect place to hide. Megan could look out on either side and run out when the person was coming, and the door was really really big and squeaky. There were so many great hiding spots. They weren't allowed to go upstairs because it was too much; there were too many places.

In hiding and chasing games, children experience the back-and-forth movement between fear of being caught and relief of being "safe" or "home."

CONCLUSION

More and more, Megan felt that she could be herself, not feel so afraid. Initially, she felt confused, but now she brings herself to the places she is in. She directs herself to places where she can bring her whole self. As a teacher, Megan feels different, but not in the sense of being wholly transformed, nor has her behaviour with the children changed.

The strain of existing as both a subjective and a social being is a human quandary that has no solution (Winnicott, 1986). Rather than conceiving of the early-years teacher as healing herself or the "child within" through her chosen work, perhaps she can be understood anew as having found a theoretical solution that is indeed nearer to a truthful existence.

NOTE

1.   The original study, titled "Memories and Constructions of Childhood in Early Childhood Education," was supported with funding from Fonds de recherché du Québec–Société et culture (FRQSC). Permission was provided to use excerpts from the participants' interviews.

REFERENCES

Boldt, G. M., Salvio, P. M., & Taubman, P. M. (2006). Introduction. In G. M. Boldt & P. M. Salvio (Eds.), *Love's return: Psychoanalytic essays on childhood, teaching, and learning* (pp. 1–8). New York, NY: Routledge.

Daniels, A. K. (1987). Invisible work. *Social Problems, 34*(5), 403–415.

Fisher, B., & Tronto, J. (1990). Toward a feminist theory of caring. In E. Abel & M. Nelson (Eds.), *Circles of care: Work and identity in women's lives* (pp. 35–62). Albany: State University of New York Press.

Grumet, M. (1988). *Bitter milk: Women and teaching.* Amherst: The University of Massachusetts Press.

Hoagland, S. L. (1990). Some concerns about Nel Noddings' *Caring. Hypatia, (5)*1, 109–114.

Mullins, A. (2009). Paid childcare: Responsibility and trust. In A. O'Reilly (Ed.), *Maternal thinking: Philosophy, politics, practice* (pp. 52–63). Bradford, ON: Demeter Press.

Noddings, N. (1984). *Caring: A feminine approach to ethics and moral education.* Berkeley, CA: University of California Press.

Nodelman, P. (2008). *The hidden adult: Defining children's literature.* Baltimore, MD: Johns Hopkins University Press.

Ruddick, S. (1995). *Maternal thinking: Toward a politics of peace.* Boston, MA: Beacon Press.

Sander-Staudt, M. (2009). Care ethics. *Internet encyclopedia of philosophy.* Available at: www.iep.utm.edu/care-eth/

Taubman, P. (2006). I love them to death. In G. M. Boldt & P. M. Salvio (Eds.), *Love's return: Psychoanalytic essays on childhood, teaching, and learning* (pp. 13–18). New York, NY: Routledge.

Winnicott, D. W. (1965). *Group influences and the maladjusted child in the family and individual development.* London, England: Tavistock.

Winnicott, D. W. (1986). Transitional objects and transitional phenomena. In P. Buckley (Ed.), *Essential papers on object relations* (pp. 254–271). New York: New York University Press.

B9

Be/long/ing and Be/com/ing in the Hy-phens

Veena Balsawer

INTRODUCTION

As an immigrant woman, a diasporic Indo-Canadian, I feel as if I live in the hy-phens, or the liminal *third space* straddling boundaries, cultures, homelands, and languages. People here ask me: "Where are you from?" My friends in India tell me I have changed. Thus, I have started to believe that no matter where I go, I will always exist amongst strangers, be/com/ing a stranger even to myself. I am, there-fore, in search of this elusive place called home. Here are some of my ruminations on home/not home and belonging/not belonging.

"But where are you really from?"[1]
Stumbling upon Adrienne Clarkson's book
Belonging: The Paradox of Citizenship[2]
a diasporic Indo-Canadian
visible minority
(in)visible
the Other
in the hy-phens
liminal Third Space[3]
lost
between and betwixt

cultures, home-lands, identities, languages,
and silences
walking amongst strangers
all (im)migrants
crisscrossing borderlands[4]
between a here, there, and an elsewhere[5]
be/com/ing[6] a stranger to myself
Bombay/Mumbai
name/re-name[7]
home/not home
existential dilemma
I never really left home | carried it away with me[8]
Imaginary Homelands[9]
nostalgia
Trishanku's curse[10]
uneasy p__u__l__l between two cultures,
between (s)p(l)aces,
between wor(l)ds
fielding quest/ions:
"Where are you from?"
"Did you come here and learn to speak English?"
"Are you going back home after your studies?"
Where is ho[me]?
Citizen/native/non native
speaker
e-stranged visitor
visitor's visa
always the other?
How am I to live?
What does it mean to be Indian outside India?[11]
Complicated conversations with self and others[12]
yû-mu[13]
presence/absence
absent presence
and | not or
hyphe-nations
hy-phenated curri | culum
live(d) curriculum

currere[14]
course of life
a quest for home
finding me
so/journ/ing
journeys of the sel(f)ves
traversing the (un)familiar (un)known
walking the labyrinth
praying for the strength of Dhruva[15]
education
re/search
live(d) stories
diverse
multi-cultural
How to be an Indo-Canadian in a (multi)cultural Canada?
perhaps more Indian in Canada
be/come an educator, researcher, children's storyteller
Storycatcher [16]
invoke/provoke
readers/listeners
What does it mean to be/long?
find ho[me]
find me
Who gets to decide?
Who gets to re-present?
Whose life?
Whose stories?
Coming ho[me] through re/search

NOTES

1. This question forms the first part of the title of Hazelle Palmer's (1997) book on *Stories of Identity and Assimilation in Canada.*

2. Adrienne Clarkson's publication is based on her 2014 Massey Lectures "Belonging: the Paradox of Citizenship," which were broadcast as part of CBC Radio's *Ideas* series.

3. Homi Bhabha (1987) explains how people like himself who are anglicized, postcolonial (im)migrants are often caught between nations and cultures, and this in-between place that they inhabit is what he terms the "Third Space."

4. In *Borderlands*, Gloria Anzaldúa (1987) talks of the physical and the invisible borderlands that separate people, and how people have to learn to live within/amidst different cultures at the same time.

5. Trinh Min-ha (2011) says that as immigrants we are constantly negotiating or travelling, literally or metaphorically, between home and not-home.

6. I first encountered "be/com/ing" in Carl Leggo's 1995 article "Storying the Word/Storying the World." I have used it ever since because it encompasses both the act of becoming and the way of being in the world.

7. In 1995, Bombay was renamed Mumbai.

8. Sujata Bhatt's (2010) poem "The One Who Goes Away" reminds me that we can't really let go of things that we are attached to.

9. In his essay "Imaginary Homelands," Salman Rushdie (1991) casts a nostalgic glance toward Bombay and laments the fact that it now lives only in his (our) imagination.

10. Uma Parameswaran (2003) says: "People who move away from their native countries occupy (not only inherit but also bequeath to subsequent generations, actually) a liminality, an uneasy pull between two cultures. In my poetry I call this Trishanku's curse" (p. xlx). Trishanku was a mythological sage who wanted to ascend to heaven in his physical form. So he prayed to the gods and was granted his wish. But as he started to ascend to the heaven, he was denied entry because he was still living. When he started to descend to earth, the people on earth didn't want him either because of his attitude, and so he stayed suspended between heaven and earth. As an Indo-Canadian, sometimes I feel like Trishanku, existing in the hy-phens somewhere between India and Canada (and the world).

11. Rushdie (1991) also ponders over this question in his essay "Imaginary Homelands."

12. According to Erika Hasebe-Ludt, Cynthia Chambers, & Carl Leggo (2009), "Curriculum understood as *currere* (Pinar & Grumet, 1976), as autobiographical text (Pinar, 1994) and a complicated conversation with self and others (Pinar, 2000), is always a process of questing, questioning, and sojourning in words and worlds" (pp. 1–2).

13. Ted T. Aoki (2000/2005) writes: "Yû-mu as both 'presence' and 'absence' marks the space of ambivalence in the midst of which humans dwell" (p. 323), and it is a space/site of possibilities and hope.

14. See Endnote 12 for how the notion of *currere* is understood.

15. The mythological story of Dhruva, or the North Star, tells us about the dedication and the perseverance of a young boy-prince who went in search of a place to call his own, a place/home from where no one would oust him.

16. Christina Baldwin (2005) says that *storycatchers* are essential to help us to reconnect with each other through our stories.

REFERENCES

Anzaldúa, G. (1987). *Borderlands/La frontera: The new mestiza*. San Francisco, CA: Aunt Lute Books.

Aoki, T. T. (2000/2005). Language, culture, and curriculum. In W. F. Pinar & R. L. Irwin (Eds.), *Curriculum in a new key: The collected works of Ted T. Aoki* (pp. 321–333). Mahwah, NJ: Erlbaum.

Baldwin, C. (2005). *Storycatcher: Making sense of our lives through the power and practice of story*. Novato, CA: New World Library.

Bhabha, H. (1987). Interrogating identity. In L. Appignanesi (Ed.), *ICA Documents 6* (pp. 5–11). London, England: Institute of Contemporary Arts.

Bhatt, S. (2010). *The one who goes away*. Available at: www.acercarse.wordpress.com/2010/11/15/the-one-who-goes-away/

Clarkson, A. (2014). *Belonging: The paradox of citizenship*. Toronto, ON: House of Anansi Press.

Hasebe-Ludt, E., Chambers, C., & Leggo, C. (2009). *Life writing and literary métissage as an ethos for our times*. New York, NY: Peter Lang.

Leggo, C. (1995). Storing the word/storying the world. *English Quarterly, 28*(1), 5–11.

Minh-ha, T. T. (2011). *Elsewhere, within here: Immigration, refugeeism and the boundary event*. New York, NY: Routledge.

Palmer, H. (1997). *"... But where are you really from?" Stories of identity and assimilation in Canada*. Toronto, ON: Sister Vision.

Parameswaran, U. (2003). Dispelling the spells of memory: Another approach to reading our yesterdays. In M. Fludernik (Ed.), *Diaspora and multiculturalism: Common traditions and new developments* (pp. xxxix–lxv). New York, NY: Rodopi.

Pinar, W. F. (1994). *Autobiography, politics and sexuality: Essays in curriculum theory 1972–1992*. New York, NY: Peter Lang.

Pinar, W. F. (2000). Strange fruit: Race, sex, and an autographics in alterity. In P. Trifonas (Ed.), *Revolutionary pedagogies: Cultural politics instituting education and the discourse of theory* (pp. 30–46). New York, NY: Routledge.

Rushdie, S. (1991). *Imaginary homelands: Essays and criticism 1981–1991*. London, England: Granta Books.

INVOCATION

Space for "Thinging" about Ineffable Things

Wanda Hurren

aes•thet•ic

It is a thing that has something to do with thinking and spaces. It is not something that dulls the senses, like the anaesthetic administered by your dentist. It is something that enlivens the senses, creates a feeling (positive, negative, neutral, ineffable), causes you to wonder and even wander. It is something in the early morning light coming through a window and landing on a steaming cup of coffee. It is something in the moment of entering a quiet hallway and in the red of the stoplight surrounded by late-afternoon dusk. Sometimes it can be seen on the cover of a favourite book, or on the walls of a colleague's office. It is in the shine of the spoon on your table. And it is something that, if we notice it in our everyday spaces, can enhance our sense of well-being and how we think and do our work. What do you think about that? *n.*

cur•ric•u•lum

It is a thing that has something to do with thinking and spaces. Some think it is in a document developed by the government of the day; something to be covered. Or in a document developed by a parent committee that outlines what students can wear to school. Some think it is hiding in the hallways of schooling, among the lines of photographs of white men, among the trophies in the glass case outside the principal's office, or in the messages that come over the loudspeaker about textbook fees or volleyball practice after class for the senior team. Some think it is a course of study that unfolds in classrooms. Some think it is something that happens outside of classrooms; maybe even something like life itself. What do you think? *n.*

B10

Religion, Curriculum, and Ideology: A Duoethnographic Dialogue

Saeed Nazari and Joel Heng Hartse

INTRODUCTION

Five years back, when we started a scholarly collaboration on our inter-faith dialogue on Christianity and Islam (Heng Hartse & Nazari, in press), we could not have imagined how our conversation would lead us forward to this new path in curriculum. We came to the discussion table with different objectives, perspectives, educational backgrounds, and narratives. Our narratives were shaped by our previous and existing contexts of residence. During our dialogic conversations, we noticed the degree to which our ideology was a product of the religious curricula in our different contexts. After three years of face-to-face dialogue and over 80 pages of email exchanges, we shifted our focus from socio-political aspects of religion and ideology embedded in curriculum toward interpersonal perspectives. Through this new lens, we looked closely at our interpersonal faith. This turning point contributed to our deeper understanding of how our religious faith transformed into our personal ideas, thoughts, beliefs, and characters. In our new approach, we became more receptive than expressive, more descriptive than prescriptive, more similar than different, and more human than individual.

In search of an appropriate method through which we were able to individually get engaged in a collaborative and transformative conversation, we came across *duoethnography* (Norris, Sawyer, & Lund, 2012), a liberal and liberating qualitative method. Duoethnography is a dual autoethnography through which the researchers exchange their ideas, thoughts, and values to come to new understandings of concepts and interests. We prefer this method for our transformative dialogue as its semi-structured framework gives adequate space to our individual voices in a collective conversation. Our shared interest in interpersonal dialogue has been religious ideology, a topic we can discuss for hours in our de facto secular North American context. In this chapter, we move on from our earlier discussion of religion in English-language teaching to a broader discussion of ideology, religion, and curriculum. Before we start the dialogue, in the following section the tenets of duoethnography and how it is founded on the method of *currere* will be briefly discussed.

DUOETHNOGRAPHY AND *CURRERE* IN TANDEM

There are four basic principles of duoethnography as Norris (2008) has identified, including the nature of the method, the objective, the scope, and the voice of the interlocutors. Considering the nature of the method, it should stay open to help the interlocutors continue their natural and authentic dialogue. Regarding the objective, duoethnography does not intend to uncover meaning; rather it is a transformative dialogue through which meaning is created and changed. The scope of the method is not limited to similarities or universals. Differences in the researchers' ideas, thoughts, and perspectives are regarded as strengths. Finally, duoethnographers explicitly express their voices without necessarily agreeing on something as the final product.

The inspiration for the method is William F. Pinar's notion of *currere*, which is an autobiographical method of curriculum to understand one's educational lived experience (Pinar, 1975a, 1975b). Pinar's "Currere: Toward Reconceptualization" (1975a), "The Method of Currere" (1975b), and Pinar and Madeleine Grumet's *Toward a Poor Curriculum* (1976, 2015) introduced this method. *Currere*, from the same Latin root as that of *curriculum*, means "to run the course" or "the running of the course" (Pinar & Grumet, 1976, p. 18). Pinar's concept of *currere* (Norris et al., 2012) views "a person's life as curriculum" (p. 12) and involves "an act of self-interrogation in which one reclaims one's self" (p. 13) when one analyzes and synthesizes the meanings of life. *Currere* challenges the traditional understandings of curriculum by drawing on phenomenological and existential traditions of thought. It seeks "an architecture of self, a self we create and embody as we read, write, speak and listen" (Pinar, 1985/1994, p. 220), and through which we can "reconnect the minimalized, psychological self to the public, political sphere" (p. 219). *Currere* employs the Freudian psychoanalytic technique of free association to generate data about one's lived experience. With this technique, one studies one's educational experience employing the four phases of *currere*—regressive, progressive, analytic, and synthetic—and records observations. The method, as both a concept of curriculum and a form of inquiry, interrogates the students' and teachers' "inner experiences and perceptions" rather than external learning objectives and subject content (Miller, 2010, p. 62).

We use duoethnography and *currere* in tandem, as *currere* facilitates a self-exploratory dialogue by generating data on our lived experience, and duoethnography connects this private and personal sphere to our public and collective sphere. Considering the four phases of *currere*, this method will give us access to our past, present, and future educational experiences, and facilitate construction of self-knowledge. The method's self-interrogation helps us create our existential data in curriculum. We will reflect on this data that will support our transformative duoethnographic dialogue. In the next section, we introduce a theoretical framework that defines the scope of our dialogue in curriculum.

LEGITIMIZED KNOWLEDGE IN CURRICULUM

Michael W. Apple is an educational theorist specializing in education and power, curriculum theory and research, and the development of democratic schools. Apple's social, economic, and political views in his book *Ideology and Curriculum* (2004) will provide us with a critical framework for this dialogue. He believes that schools control people and the process of meaning making, that these powerful institutions distribute perceived legitimized knowledge and structure cultural legitimacy on the knowledge of particular groups. He assumes that it is possible to "interrupt new-liberal and new-conservative policies and ideologies ... and create schools that are closely connected to a larger project of social transformation" (p. xii). This has implications for both of us vis-à-vis our own experiences involving religious faith and education.

Drawing upon this theoretical framework, we discuss questions about our lived experience that will shed light on our past and present educational experiences and academic achievements in the United States, Iran, and Canada. Of note, this inter-curricular dialogue has been possible for us because we live in Canada and are detached from our previous contexts. Living in our Canadian context has made both of us conscious about our former and current curricula and enabled us to consider our lived experience in education as a reliable source of data. In the following sections we will engage in an actual dialogue on our educational experiences in our previous and current contexts.

OUR DUOETHNOGRAPHIC DIALOGUE

Saeed: I am grateful to have an opportunity to observe my educational experience through the autobiographical method of *currere* (Pinar & Grumet, 2015) and ponder on the nature of knowledge I received in my school. As an "amateur intellectual" (Said, 1994) who is critical of educational institutions, I can never overlook my schooling experience and am always busy answering the following questions with regard to the nature of knowledge at school: What knowledge was taught in my school? Why was that specific knowledge considered legitimate? How did politics inform the legitimacy of knowledge? Who decided what knowledge to include and what knowledge to exclude? Who designed the curriculum? Was it a democratic process? Whose democracy was followed? Who benefited from the curriculum and who became marginalized? What was the language of instruction? How about other heritage languages? How were they systematically minoritized? What religion was included in the curriculum? How about the other religions? What hegemonic ideology dominated education? Whose ideology was preferred? How were power and politics embedded in the ideological knowledge of curriculum? Whose power was considered legitimate? Was the knowledge of self included in curriculum? Did I learn enough about my own self, feelings, talents, dreams, and values? Was it a self-exploratory educational system? Did I learn about self-regulation and self-talk? These are some questions I am posing here and invite you as well to think about. I do not know why I feel uncomfortable to answer them. Perhaps as our conversation develops naturally, I will feel ready.

Joel: There is so much to explore! I am a neophyte when it comes to theoretical explorations of curriculum, yet I also believe that our chosen methodology affords us a way into insights on whatever topic we happen to be discussing (in this case, curriculum) that might not be available if we simply attempted to approach the topic in a more traditional scholarly paper.

Our last collaboration had quite a bit to do with the role of religion and whether it influenced our own practices as English-language teachers. Interestingly, our career paths have both since deviated from being "ESL teachers," but I think we both maintain some interest in issues involving religion, spirituality, and secularity when it comes to education.

Ideologically, the idea of a split between either "public" or "religious" schooling seems to loom large in my imagination when I consider some of your questions. When I was in the job market, I was interested in working for a religious university, but I now work at a public university in Canada, and

I find myself wondering what implications that has for my own identity as someone who has seen Christian values as paramount to my work and life. At Christian institutions, a notion that "we're all in this together" feels easier to come by for me; I am never sure what exactly the purpose is of public education, of whether there are truly shared values I can point to in order to encourage my students. A few weeks ago I asked my class what they thought the purpose of university was: every single one of them said some version of "to get a job." I'm sure that isn't what I would have said at my Christian liberal-arts university, but maybe those were different times.

Saeed: These are all liberal and liberating thoughts regarding religious ideology for me. I am in favour of all religions and belief systems when they improve our positive perspectives of life and inspire us but am more open to Abrahamic religions, perhaps because I am familiar with them from an early schooling experience. Religious ideology is my light of life and I proactively practice my faith as a Muslim academician in a de facto secular Vancouver context. For instance, I pray five times a day, fast in the month of Ramadan, contribute to charitable organizations, and so on. No matter how my social field (Bourdieu, 1991) and institutions in my new context would endeavour to work on my subjectivity, I consider myself a religious individual. I personally believe, regardless of which context we live in, an individual like myself will follow a certain religious system due to his or her mental perception of life. However, one difference I perceive in our approaches to this topic is that you have positive feelings about your school curriculum, while I critique the curriculum. One reason I am critical, perhaps, is that religious ideology, politics, and power can form a solid control system to legitimatize certain knowledge in curriculum. I am not in favour of excluding religious faith from the curriculum; however, I consider it more important to take care of all individual voices in the school curriculum. We should be wary of the harm particular knowledge, including religious knowledge, might inflict on our children. In designing curriculum, each individual's needs should be considered. Instead of following a top-down process in which the content of materials is prescribed in an ideological curriculum, we should follow a bottom-up curriculum in which each individual voice has sufficient space to be heard, respected, and valued. You might question the possibility of designing such a curriculum? At this point, I am not certain how, but I am theorizing my philosophy.

Joel: I have to ask you what you mean by "school curriculum" here. Public school? Private school (and if so, what kind)? Some other option, like homeschooling? I find myself in the interesting position of ostensibly being a scholar of education but being confused and having a lot of mixed feelings about, for example, the schooling of my own children, when I think about the options available to me in our local context. I went to a mixture of public and private institutions in my own schooling (private Montessori Kindergarten, public elementary and middle school, Catholic high school, evangelical college, and public universities for my graduate training), and each one seemed to have very different ideological orientations to curriculum, religious or not. My older son is currently in a Montessori preschool—whose philosophy, despite some of the criticisms that could be levelled at it, strikes me as very purposefully a "bottom-up" curriculum—and soon we will be faced with the question of what kind of school he'll go to when he's older. Will our decision have an impact on his ability to flourish? Would Catholic schooling provide, as I perceive it, a more holistic "whole-person" education than our local public school, or is this just my personal bias?

Saeed: Those are provocative questions for me. And surprisingly, you have options in your new context. You not only have the luxury of cherry picking from among those, but you can think of which curriculum will follow a holistic approach for your son. What if you were a Muslim in our Vancouver context? Would you like to place yourself in my shoes for a moment and see how the power dynamics will disempower and at some point cripple you in a cosmopolitan city like Vancouver? The closest Muslim school I can register my son in is a half-hour drive away in Richmond. And as informed academic parents, my wife and I are not sure how our son's attendance in an Islamic curriculum will affect his future employment opportunities in Vancouver. Once schooled, will he consider himself an integrated member of his secular society or be prone to seeing himself as a marginalized citizen? Will the Vancouver job market consider his religious schooling an asset or a defect, especially considering the aftermath of September 11? And you know how the media is inundated with propaganda intended for Muslims' systematic marginalization (Said, 2003). As our decision on choosing the right curriculum would affect our son's future resources, we are still wondering which school we should register him in. Regarding an alternative education, I understand homeschooling is an option. I have noticed how religious families in my neighbourhood and in academia may pick that option, but it is not practical for us as immigrant working parents. And we are not sure how homeschooling will give our son a chance for his proper socialization. I have found my religious teachings at home the most effective and practicable ones. He observes my prayers five times a day and my fasting in Ramadan. I also teach him Farsi and Arabic languages, read Islamic stories for his bedtime, and show him related video clips.

Joel: I also wonder about the interplay between "religious education" and simply "education." From a philosophical standpoint I assume there is no difference; all learning is learning. Yet we may live in a basically secular culture in cosmopolitan Vancouver, and certainly as academics we are aware that religious perspectives are not as welcome as some others in academia. I remember hearing about a new Catholic Montessori Kindergarten in my neighbourhood; it has a catechism (that is, Christian religious teaching) area, but parents can decide whether their kids will actually go into that area and participate with those materials. It's a striking example of literally delimiting the boundaries of religious education. I admit I feel uncomfortable with this line drawn between different kinds of education. I would rather it be more holistic—but perhaps that is a curriculum that can only be modelled by individuals and not by schools. Maybe you can only look at the life of an engaged religious believer who is active in a secular context as a kind of embodied curriculum.

Saeed: From a globalized perspective, one of the reasons that secular policies in the curriculum are dictated is perhaps to maintain the ranking of Vancouver among other cities in the world. The Vancouver context is kept secular perhaps because many immigrants, including those who are investors, will not move to a place dominated by a certain religious ideology. From a capitalistic view, if we regard this city as a profitable market, any options that might threaten the profit margins should be excluded. So which religion do you think might threaten these margins, Islam or Christianity?

Joel: I would hope that any religion would threaten profit margins. I think that most faith traditions offer a principled alternative to unbridled capitalism. Ultimately my hope is that any religious education schools us in alternative and more authentic ways of being human apart from solely biological or economic or other secular narratives. The question I am left ruminating on after all our discussion is whether we are going to be living and working—being scholars of education, and raising/educating our own children—in a *pluralist* context or a *secular* one. It seems to me there is a difference between a society that has a genuine, robust respect for differing traditions, and one which demands secular orthodoxies. My hope is that we live in the former, but I sometimes fear it is the latter.

A FINAL NOTE

In this chapter, we briefly discussed how schools legitimize knowledge in curriculum. We used two methods in tandem to generate data in our dialogic discussions, duoethnography and *currere*. We employed the former to facilitate a liberating transformative dialogue and the latter to form narratives on our educational lived experiences. Apple's (2004) theoretical framework opened a window to our discussions of "legitimized knowledge" at school. We discussed how schools might exclude religious education from curriculum to maintain and control "particular forms of ideology" in their hidden curriculum (p. 77). It has occurred to us that throughout the whole dialogue, we have concentrated on our current context and discussed religious ideology as our main topic and concern. One reason might be that our previous contexts were less secular than Vancouver, and we would prefer a non-secular cosmopolitan context and educational experience for ourselves, and more importantly for our children. Another reason might be that the context of our transformative dialogue is Vancouver and as informed parents, we want to resist the hegemony created by school knowledge for our children. The shared consciousness gained throughout this dialogic conversation between a Muslim educator and a Christian educator has strengthened us in our mutually (in)formed thoughts, beliefs, and perspectives.

REFERENCES

Apple, M. W. (2004). *Ideology and curriculum* (3rd ed.). New York, NY: RoutledgeFalmer.

Bourdieu, P. (1991). *Language and symbolic power.* J. B. Thompson (Ed.). Cambridge, MA: Harvard University Press.

Heng Hartse, J., & Nazari, S. (in press). Duoethnography: An interfaith dialogue on lived experiences in TESOL. In M. S. Wong & A. Muhboob (Eds.), *Spirituality & language teaching: Religious explorations of teacher identity, pedagogy, context, and content.* Bristol, England: Multilingual Matters.

Miller, J. L. (2010). Curriculum as a consciousness of possibilities. *Curriculum Inquiry, 40*(1), 125–141.

Norris, J. (2008). Duoethnography. In L. M. Given (Ed.), *The Sage encyclopedia of qualitative research methods* (Vol. 1) (pp. 233–236). Los Angeles, CA: Sage.

Norris, J., Sawyer, R. D., & Lund, D. (Eds.). (2012). *Duoethnography: Dialogic methods for social, health, and educational research.* Walnut Creek, CA: Left Coast Publications.

Pinar, W. F. (1975a). Currere: Toward reconceptualization. In *Curriculum theorizing: The reconceptualists* (pp. 396–414). Berkeley, CA: McCutchan Publishing.

Pinar, W. F. (1975b). The method of currere. In *Autobiography, politics, and sexuality: Essays in curriculum theory 1972–1992* (pp. 19–27). New York, NY: Peter Lang.

Pinar, W. F. (1985/1994). Autobiography and an architecture of self. *Counterpoints, 2,* 201–222.

Pinar, W. F., & Grumet, M. R. (1976). *Toward a poor curriculum*. Dubuque, IA: Kendall/ Hunt.

Pinar, W. F., & Grumet, M. R. (2015). *Toward a poor curriculum* (3rd. ed.). Kingston, NY: Educator's International Press.

Said, E. W. (1994). *Representations of the intellectual: The 1993 Reith lectures*. London, England: Vintage.

Said, E. W. (2003). *Orientalism*. London, England: Penguin.

INVOCATION

Living with Generosity: A Rumination

Anita Sinner

I offer this invocation to living with generosity in the academy as a construct of interconnections, a rumination on the *métissaging* of openness as an aesthetic encounter. Generosity is defined as the nobility of conduct, to have courage, magnanimity (Brown, 1993, p. 1074). And if we choose to live with love for our scholarship, then perhaps generosity is also a state of vulnerability, where we give over to another, in our courses, conversations, articles, and the moments in between that define how and why we abide by the notion of *what if*, in both our networks of relations and the conditions of intellectual exchange that compose the politics of this space.

And yet I question, can generosity, and indeed love, be found in critique? In a sea of red ink on the page recommending revisions? In the tears of students? In my own tears? Is generosity found in silence? Or is generosity a kind of reciprocation, as in the Ridley (1996) context, a form of academic ritualization that is beneficial to both sides by creating an obligation? Though I hope not quite as parasitic as Ridley claims. But, what if Ridley's hypothesis is correct, and generosity is really an act of selfishness, and at the same time, part of the ethics of empathy, embracing those who do not fit in the neat boxes of curriculum studies?

Bringing generosity to the fore serves as an ideological disruption of the conversation, freeing the scholarly self for the opportunity to "sensually communicate" (Darder, 2011, p. 1), while begging the question: What is the moral responsibility we hold when living with generosity, with the messy and contested values that are the basis of trust in the research relationship? Or simply, do we not bother, and so ease our thinking-burden?

REFERENCES

Brown, L. (Ed.). (1993). *The new shorter Oxford English dictionary on historical principles.* New York, NY: Oxford University Press.

Darder, A. (2011). Embodiments of public pedagogy: The art of soulful resistance. *Policy Futures in Education, 9*, 6. Available at: www.wwwords.co.uk/PFIE

Ridley, M. (1996). *The origin of virtue: Human instincts and the evolution of cooperation.* New York, NY: Penguin.

B11

Agency and the Social Contract: Algorithms as an Interpretive Key to Modernity

Sean Wiebe

ALGORITHMS AND THE SOCIAL IMAGINARY

On December 8, 2014, Barack Obama became the first US president to write a computer program. True, he learned nothing more than how to write a simple code that reproduced a square on the computer screen, but what is significant is the rhetoric pushing the learn-to-code movement in school curriculum, itself a phenomenon of how algorithms have become predominant in modern life. Whether it is a patented Netflix algorithm that leverages "big data to produce hit shows" (Hoffman, 2016) or Pearson's automated grading algorithms for introductory math and psychology courses, the growing social and economic significance of algorithms deserves theoretical attention from curriculum scholars, particularly since the algorithm appears to have had a significant effect on what Charles Taylor (1989, 2004) has called "the social imaginary."

Taylor's social imaginary is an extension of Locke's ideas of the social contract: similar to agreements that individuals might make to form a civil society, the social imaginary comprises ideas that are strongly valued in society. Just as institutions arise from social contracts, Taylor (2004) argues that institutions and ideas are also mutually determined. Historical consideration of social imaginaries is a possible refocusing of the orienting question for curriculum studies, where more significant than a study of "what knowledge is of most worth" (Spencer, 1861; Pinar, 2007) would be a study of the complementarity of ideas and social institutions. While the former binds curriculum pursuits to the localities and historicities of knowledge communities, the latter considers how ideas are arranged to form processes that are visibly and invisibly valued as social contracts.

For scholars familiar with William F. Pinar's notion of *currere* (Pinar, 2004; Pinar & Grumet, 1976), consideration of a social contract of strong valuations would also be a consideration of the nature of the individual's relation to the social order(s) that arise from the valuation processes of contract making. So while *regression, progression, analysis,* and *synthesis* have become familiar terms to guide curriculum work that employs *currere*, perhaps less familiar is that the instigation of *currere* is a consideration of the individual's relation to the social order. Using Taylor's terminology, this order would comprise the social contracts, the institutions that arise from these contracts, and the ideas that are mutually constitutive of both. If we follow Pinar's (2010) reasoning that an individual's acquiescence to the social order is "submersion in the banal" (p. 1), then an individual's agency is the work of *currere*, wherein lies the possibility of "emancipatory reaggregation" (p. 3). There is clearly a tension here, pitting the collective and the individual against one another, but there is an important complementarity as well. Breaking free "of one's socially determined subject location" (p. 1), says Pinar (2010), "implies self-shattering" but also "presses us into the world" (p. 1).

For Pinar (2010), agency is a kind of psychoanalytic self-shattering where the ego, submerged in the banal (in the predetermined social order), must be shattered, and, in so doing, the reaggregated or renewed self experiences eman-cipation. For Taylor (2004), agency is direct access to the social contract, and he categorizes the individual's relationship to the social order as either premodern or modern. A premodern order is hierarchical in that it limits an individual's access to the privileges and responsibilities of the social contract. Premodern orders are also transcendental, meaning that while an individual's position in the hierarchy limits access, some access is still possible through an intermediary, such as a god or a king. Modernity, by contrast, is characterized by a social order where the individual has equal and direct access, where each member is "immediate to the whole" (p. 157). Taylor's distinction of premodern and modern orders is a useful way of thinking about the instigating moments of *currere* where an individual's access to the social order is a central question. This creates the theoretical space to consider the multiple and interrelated spheres of politics, economics, and edu-cation as social contracts that are constituted in the realm of ideas, what Taylor has called "social imaginaries."

CONTROLLING FOR THE HUMAN VARIANT

The term *imaginary* recalls Plato's allegory of the cave, where social behaviour cannot be verified as real, since the constraints of existence are limited to what can be perceived. Similarly, Taylor's (1989, 2004) concept of the social imaginary is moral, that is, obligations implied by the social contract are regulated through normative ideals rather than through any legal or empirical means. It is an important distinction for curriculum studies, for if beliefs motivate actions, and in some cases justify them, there is a strong social benefit for attending to the ideals that drive social contracts and the institutions that protect and realize them. Gert Biesta (2010) makes just this point when he describes the limits of social-science research for education. Outlining a knowledge deficit, an efficacy deficit, and an application deficit, he cautions against basing practices on educational research (p. 491), noting that to restrict teachers to only those actions that are based on evidence not only threatens professional judgment but is, quite rightly, "a form of totalitarianism" (p. 492). The issue, says Biesta, is not so much "whether there should be a role for evidence ... but what kind of role" (p. 492). Problematic, especially in the domain of policy making, is the idea that evidence determines knowledge, or stands in for knowledge, for such a "mechanistic" view leads to "expectations about evidence that are impossible to achieve" (p. 492). Instead, Biesta proposes a "value-based education" that evidence might serve in providing justifications. Biesta's reasoning that "it is not evidence itself to which the question of truth or falsity applies" (p. 492) is similar to Pinar's (1988, 2004) basis for insisting that faculties of education ought to chiefly concern themselves with the study of curriculum rather than pedagogy. Both scholars are concerned with the complexity reduction implied in studying practices, which includes—necessarily—the reduction of teachers' professional autonomy.

A study of values returns us to the centrality of ideals that are resident in social imaginaries. Biesta (2010) aptly describes the idealism that drives educational research. If we are able to conduct "sufficient research in order to be able to encapsulate all factors, aspects and dimensions that make up the reality of education, [and if] we are able to coordinate our research efforts and channel available resources all in the same direction then, so the argument goes ... we will, at some point in time, have a perfect evidence-base for educational practice" (p. 494).

The social idealism of a body of educational research to account for every situation is a complexity reduction, one that demands conditions where important aspects of reality (such as race, class, gender, ability, age, and historical context) are rendered invisible—not because they don't exist, but because in the controlled conditions of the school (which ideally functions like the medical laboratory) the point is to create conditions that optimize learning. The ideal school with optimal teaching practices will have learned to control for the human variant and remove the confounding conditions of place, time, or being. In a substantial literature review of 1,648 studies, Arnold Dodge and Ruth Silverberg (2015) found clear evidence of a normalizing discourse in educational research that has been propagating the social ideal that what is needed in education is further top-town, large-scale, instrumental processes that can be verified through assessment. The obsession, they say, is reductive, "inhibiting the public goals of education and nurturing corporate interests" (p. 2). Ben Williamson (2013), too, reminds us of the research politics influencing curriculum. The control of teachers through the control of information through the control of the kinds of data that matter has a long history of devaluing personal knowledge creation (McKnight, 2006). However, there is another twist to this story, what Williamson (2013) calls the "CompPsy" phenomenon, where programs (in the language of computer science) become programmatic and where learning (in the language of psychology) becomes a literacy, a descriptive and discrete outcome to be classified, then made calculable for its measured social utility.

Over the last decade, increases in class size, student diversity, learning needs, testing, and administrative duties have corresponded with decreases in support, budgets, and autonomy. Positioned as a new hope, advances in educational technology are supposedly a research-based response to these increasing demands and complexities in education. Obama's learning-to-code media event indicates the strength of the social fantasy, and school districts across North America mandating that students learn to code demonstrates the extent. Douglas Aoki (2002), a Lacanian scholar, argues that human beings are culturally and psychologically invested in their beliefs and practices, so to understand the social imaginary we must look to society's fantasies. I thus ask: What fantasies drive the wider social, economic, and cultural changes that demand best-practices movements, what-works research, or outcomes-based curriculum? How are these produced as social ideals, and how might we understand these fantasy ideals as betrayals to humanity, that is, as complexity reductions of human differences?

FROM CONCEPT TO FUNCTION IN VALUING THE HUMAN BEING

To pursue these questions, I draw on Paolo Totaro and Domenico Ninno's (2014) recent essay that traces the history of the relationship between human beings and the recursive function. Using money as an analogy, they note a shift in thinking from concept to function where, like money, the value of a human being is no longer in itself but in what it can be exchanged for. Just like a gold coin is no longer worth the amount of gold that it is made out of, so the value of a human life is no longer its existential condition. It is exactly here that I suggest we can find the fantasy of instrumental approaches to education that, in the ideal, imagine the value of the student as a function of the competencies that can be exchanged in the economic system. Williamson's (2013) neologism, *CompPsy*, is part of a larger social imaginary where through the combination of computer science and educational psychology, students will be shaped into "workers for the competitive pressures of economic globalization" (p. 89). With a focus on "personal choice, personal projects, and self-enterprise" (p. 88), "self-entrepreneurial behavior," he says, "is the globalized cultural expression of a set of Silicon Valley cyber libertarian values" (p. 89). Graduates of this school system are imagined as

> portfolio people who think and act in terms of their résumé, and who define their own personal projects in entrepreneurial terms as businesses or enterprises ... [who are] flexible, interactive, and constructivist learners able to continue learning and adapting, based on constant reflexive self-analysis, right through the life cycle. (p. 96)

CompPsy is an apt descriptive term. With the algorithm, once the variables are defined, and once the relationships among them are mapped, computers then make the decisions, that is, they calculate probabilities. In this metaphor, *teaching* and *programming* are synonymous terms. The teacher designs a lesson in the same way a programmer designs a game. The students are players, and intuiting the system is what is called learning. Returning to Taylor's (2004) argument that a key distinction between modern and premodern social imaginaries is an individual's access to the social contract, we see that in the idealism of algorithms individuals express their agency through operations, that is, through functions that are of social value, namely, their competencies or literacies. Because the acquisition of literacies is a means by which an individual gains access to the privileges and responsibilities of the social contract, it is my contention that when literacies are operations that resemble the hierarchical structure of an algorithm, the individual's relationship to the social contract is premodern in such a way that access is denied unless via an intermediary.

Outlining the trends of an increasingly globalized knowledge economy, Phillip Brown, Hugh Lauder, and David Ashton (2008) make a significant case for today's intermediaries being employers. They warn of a digital Taylorism that will reduce "autonomy and discretion" and "segment talent in ways *that reserve the permission to think* to a small proportion of employees [i.e., intermediaries] responsible for driving the business forward" (p. 139, emphasis added). Through the logic of the algorithm, human skills are standardized to reduce labour costs. Brown et al. (2008) write:

> The communication technologies that we have today ... have created the realistic possibility of developing global standards that reduce technical complexity and diversity. Business processes ... can be broken down into their component parts, which include the unbundling of occupational roles so that job tasks can be simplified and sourced in different ways. (p. 138)

The literacies movement in education is linked to the ways human labour has been divided into discrete functions to increase the profitability of companies. Whether the literacies in vogue are reading, coding, or something yet to be determined, the knowledge that is of most worth will be that which gives students employment, and while employment is socially desirable, a significant struggle for individuals today is their restricted access to the social contract, access that is controlled through their employer. Brown et al. (2008) are particularly critical of the "education gospel" that ascribes continuous economic development to better education (p. 31). What should give curriculum scholars pause is the common oversimplification that a student's increased expertise in the use of a particular tool will lead to better social or economic prospects.

ALGORITHMS AS AN INTERPRETIVE KEY IN CURRICULUM STUDIES

Technocratic models of human advancement depend on the faulty assumption that high skills equal high wages. But, as a historical view of human labour shows, market competition drives down wages, regardless of whether they are high or low skill (Lazonick, 2003). In today's global economy, governments no longer have the power to protect the wages of their domestic labourers, so it is a red herring to blame employment challenges on lacks in the education system. And it is just as distracting to suppose that improvements in the education system will lead to rising incomes. As Brown et al. (2008) argue, "If knowledge is the key asset of the new economy, the task of business is not to pay more for it but less.... At a time where human knowledge is being taught, certified, and applied on a scale unprecedented in human history, the overall value of human knowledge is likely to decline rather than increase" (p. 134).

What literacies education and labour standardization share is the logic of the algorithm that breaks down knowledge processes into isolated tasks that can be recombined in technical and automated ways. The potential to reduce the complexity of work (and pay less for it) is only limited by the ability to articulate creative and complex thinking processes into knowledge sets and/or technical skills. Thomas Wolsey and Dana Grisham (2007) argue that a focus on literacies "conveys a different set of values about what is important and who the architects of learning should be or can be" (p. 31). With employers acting as intermediaries to the social contract, significant curriculum attention should be brought to the market systems and processes that are part of the capitalization of human labour, including soaring corporate profits, income inequality, employment precarity, wage reduction, weakening labour law, and knowledge commodification.

If *currere* can be a means of emancipatory reaggregation (Pinar, 2010), with respect to the individual's relation to the social order, what if teachers' and students' lives became the site for study, and a classroom vibrant with their needs became the motivating activity for understanding teaching and learning? Wouldn't we arrive at the conclusion that the critical point in our being human is the existential condition of our differences, our limits, our vulnerabilities, and our failures? When difference is eliminated the point is not that there is suddenly community or equality, but that the powerful few generalize and replicate who they are across the population and become intermediaries who control access to the social contract. As argued above, in the logic of the algorithm, in human systems there is a strong profit motive for reducing difference.

Totaro and Ninno (2014) argue that exploring the social imaginary behind algorithms is an "interpretive key of modernity" and that it "has not been exploited in all its potentiality" (p. 30). Speculating as to why the concept of the algorithm is often overlooked in educational theories, they explain that it is likely because of the mistaken assumption that algorithms, recursive functions, and like operations belong exclusively in the realm of numbers (p. 31). Given the prevalence of the education gospel tying prosperity to literacies, in curriculum studies we need further theorizing of how the logic of the algorithm is deeply rooted in the social imaginary.

REFERENCES

Aoki, D. S. (2002). The price of teaching: Love, evasion and the subordination of knowledge. *JCT: Journal of Curriculum Theorizing, 18*(1), 21–39.

Biesta, G. J. J. (2010). Why "what works" still won't work: From evidence-based education to value-based education. *Studies in the Philosophy of Education, 29*(5), 491–503.

Brown, P., Lauder, H., & Ashton, D. (2008). Education, globalisation and the future of the knowledge economy. *European Educational Research Journal, 7*(2), 131–156.

Dodge, A., & Silverberg, R. P. (2015). Dominant discourse, educational research, and the hegemony of test scores. *Critical Education, 6*(1), 1–22. Available at: ojs.library.ubc. ca/index.php/criticaled/article/view/184561

Hoffman, G. (2016, February 27). Netflix: The force awakens. *Techcrunch.* Available at: techcrunch.com/2016/02/27/netflix-the-force-awakens/?ncid=rss

Lazonick, W. (2003). The theory of the market economy and the social foundations of innovative enterprise. *Economic and Industrial Democracy, 24*(1), 9–44. Available at: dx.doi.org/10.1177/0143831X03024001598

McKnight, D. (2006). The gift of curriculum method. *Curriculum and Teaching Dialogue, 8*(1–2), 171–183.

Phelan, A. M. (2011). Towards a complicated conversation: Teacher education and the curriculum turn. *Pedagogy, Culture & Society, 19*(2), 207–220. doi: 10.1080/14681366.2011/582257

Pinar, W. F. (1988). *Contemporary curriculum discourses.* Scottsdale, AZ: Gorsuch Scarisbrick.

Pinar, W. F. (2004). *What is curriculum theory?* Mahwah, NJ: Erlbaum.

Pinar, W. F. (2007). *Intellectual advancement through disciplinarity.* Rotterdam, The Netherlands: Sense Publishers.

Pinar, W. F. (2010). Notes on a blue guitar. *Journal of Educational Controversy, 5*(1). Available at: cedar.wwu.edu/jec/vol5/iss1/18

Pinar, W. F., & Grumet, M. R. (1976). *Toward a poor curriculum.* Dubuque, IA: Kendall/ Hunt.

Spencer, H. (1861). *Education: Intellectual, moral, and physical.* New York, NY: Appleton.

Taylor, C. (1989). *Sources of the self: The making of the modern identity.* Cambridge, MA: Cambridge University Press.

Taylor, C. (2004). *Modern social imaginaries.* Durham, NC: Duke University Press.

Totaro, P., & Ninno, D. (2014). The concept of algorithm as an interpretative key of modern rationality. *Theory Culture Society, 31*(29). doi: 10.1177/0263276413510051

Williamson, B. (2013). *The future of curriculum: School knowledge in a digital age.* Cambridge, MA: MIT Press.

Wolsey, T. D., & Grisham, D. L. (2007). Adolescents and the new literacies: Writing engagement. *Action in Teacher Education, 29*(2), 29–38.

INVOCATION

Nocturne, Curriculum, and Building a Bench

Hans Smits

Recent and ongoing events across the world invoke darkness, a failure to form words and understanding. Darkness suggests the failure of reason and "universal knowability" (Berkowitz, Katz, & Keenan, 2010, p. 5); but yet, as Hannah Arendt urged, we must think. That kind of thinking suggests curriculum as *nocturne*: while nocturne is evocative of the dark, nocturne as in music represents the creative urge to make sense of our feelings of loss and the precarious nature of our lives. Curriculum as nocturne suggests that we are aware of the dark and the unknown, but still guided by dreams that represent a "radical hope": where we "are directed to a future goodness that transcends the current ability to understand what it is" (Lear, 2006, p. 103).

Recently some colleagues and I turned to Arendt's work and her concern about how in modern times, "work" has supplanted contemplation (Panayoditis, Lund, Towers, & Smits, 2016). Arendt's concern was also, however, the pervasive and lingering privileging of ideas and concepts over action, that what we *do* is a subordinate form of engagement. Yet the privileging of ideas is not contemplation but, as she suggests, an exercise in manipulating "empty shells that have lost their connection to their 'underlying phenomenal reality'" (Schwartz, 2016, p. 93).

Such ideas came to mind this past summer, when I built an outdoor bench from a rescued old timber. Perhaps the bench and its making represent the loss of a tree and a neglected piece of wood once alive, and yet something that can be renewed through our imaginations and the work of our hands: a nocturne, in other words; a way to serenade possibility even when there is dark. My bench was not a chair, but it was, nonetheless, in the words of Pablo Neruda (1994), an invitation to contemplation:

> *Bring me a chair*
> *in the midst of*
> *thunder,*
> *a chair for me*
> *and for everyone*
> *not only*
> *to relieve*
> *an exhausted body*

but
for every purpose
for squandered strength
and for meditation. (pp. 25–27)

REFERENCES

Berkowitz, R., Katz, J., & Keenan, T. (Eds.). (2010). Introduction: Thinking in dark times. In *Thinking in dark times: Hannah Arendt on ethics and politics* (pp. 3–14). New York, NY: Fordham University Press.

Lear, J. (2006). *Radical hope: Ethics in the face of cultural devastation.* Cambridge, MA: Harvard University Press.

Neruda, P. (1994). *Ode to common things.* (K. Krabbenhoft, Trans.). Toronto, ON: Little, Brown and Co.

Panayotidis, L., Lund, D., Towers, J., & Smits, H. (2016). Worldlessness and wordlessness: How might we talk about teacher education in a fractured world? *Critical Education, 7*(7). Available at: ojs.library.ubc.ca/index.php/criticaled/article/view/186130

Schwartz, J. (2016). *Arendt's judgement: Freedom, responsibility, citizenship.* Philadelphia, PA: University of Pennsylvania Press.

MÉTISSAGE C

C1

"What Happened Here?": Composing a Place for Playfulness and Vulnerability in Research

Cindy Clarke and Derek Hutchinson

> *You lifting that out, lifted something out of me.*
> *And now I am playing with space.*
> * * * *
>
> *Yeah. I entered*
> *into that space thinking*
> *no one else would be there*
> *and yet, there we were.*[1]

In this chapter, we discuss our experiences as emerging narrative inquirers engaged in ongoing research conversations about the importance of vulnerability in research. We imagined how our work together might itself be the foundation for a deeper understanding of vulnerability within narrative inquiry. As we continued to share our thinking, we began to see our work in light of María Lugones' (1987) ideas of world travelling and play. We crafted narratives playfully with one another, and in doing so expressed our thoughts, feelings, and reflections. Through our play we created a new space of research, one that allowed for vulnerability and the exploration of lives in progress through experience. We begin this chapter with the role of place in narrative inquiry and move through an examination of the academic landscapes shaping our understanding of ourselves as researchers. Through the creation of a poetic research dialogue, we discover new possibilities for multiple research spaces welcoming of vulnerability and playfulness.

THE PLACE OF PLACE IN NARRATIVE INQUIRY

As we talked, we noticed common threads of experience around the places in which we engaged in research as well as the places in which we composed our stories to live by (Connelly & Clandinin, 1999). We travelled in multiple worlds together (Lugones, 1987). We began to attend to the ways our home and research spaces/ places shaped our experiences and identities as researchers. Tensions emerged as we shared experiences for which we had no common context. We realized this dissonance represented the multiple perspectives we brought into the sharing of stories of our experiences. Our contemplation of the tensioned spaces between these shared threads created a common context that added depth to our understanding of our evolving sense of ourselves as narrative inquirers and as colleagues.

REFLECTIONS ON THE ACADEMIC LANDSCAPE

Within institutional research landscapes (Clandinin & Connelly, 1995) many stories exist that shape the ways researchers understand themselves in relationship to others and their work. Laurel Richardson (1997) described one predominant academic storyline when she wrote:

> Academics are given the "storyline" that the "I" should be suppressed in their writing, that they should accept homogenization and adopt the all-knowing, all-powerful voice of the academy.... Powerfully entrenched academics, threatened by this poststructuralist turn, pressure those "beneath them" to conform to nineteenth-century notions of academic writing. (p. 2)

As researchers, we have experienced the tension Richardson (1997) described. We found ourselves navigating and recomposing our stories of what it means to be a researcher within similar research contexts. We were cognizant of the necessity to shape spaces that fit into the academic research landscape described by Richardson, but that were also inclusive of challenges to structuralist notions of research. As narrative inquirers, we intentionally lifted up stories of research that allowed for playfulness (Lugones, 1987) as a starting place for the creation of new research spaces marked by vulnerability. In so doing, we sought to "write ourselves into our texts with intellectual and spiritual integrity" (Richardson, 1997, p. 2). In light of Lugones, we wondered about the ways that research might be an act of playfulness. With this in mind, we entered into spaces between our respective research experiences to highlight the necessary tensions and complexities within experience.

As we attended to those experiences, we began to consider the spaces/places in which they occurred. Keith Basso (1996) suggested,

> In modern landscapes everywhere, people persist in asking, "What happened here?" The answers they supply ... should not be taken lightly, for what people make of their places is closely connected to what they make of themselves as members of a society. (p. 7)

Basso led us to wonder "what happened" within conventional research places we have experienced, which have shaped our stories of research. Basso helped us to recognize "we are, in a sense, the place-worlds we imagine" (p. 7). We experienced the 2015 Provoking Curriculum Studies Conference as a space that invited methodologies and perspectives transgressive to dominant stories of research. While we recognize that we must, as researchers, attend to the place-worlds imagined by the dominant stories of research, we must also intentionally develop spaces that call into question the underlying assumptions about research and researcher identity. The stories we compose about research are shaped by the people and places within a research place. As Clandinin (2013) suggested, "people, place, and stories are inextricably linked" (p. 41). By constructing meaning around the research places we have experienced together, we began intentionally to create new academic spaces that were inclusive of multiple stories of research and knowing. In this chapter, we provoke notions of vulnerability within research by co-composing our own stories of relational research spaces through poetic research dialogues.

COMPOSING MULTIPLE STORIES OF RESEARCH

Part of our composition of vulnerable research spaces included the sharing of personal, private stories with one another. This inquiry was a consequence of the vulnerability we experienced as researchers sharing private stories publicly. The poetic research dialogue that follows was generated out of our conversations together and shared in a public performance at the 2015 Provoking Curriculum Studies Conference (Clarke & Hutchinson, 2015). As we reflected on the experience of sharing our research conversations publicly, we grew into an understanding of this dialogue as a co-composed expression of our experiences. What began as a dialogue evolved into a multi-vocal, multi-layered poetic expression. At times the voices within the poetic expression of our experiences overlap and intertwine. In this way, our poetic expression of our experiences as researchers functions as both interim research texts and final research.

THE PLACE OF VULNERABILITY IN RESEARCH

She is in the middle
of transition. She feels it
the changing light
afternoon fading
full with the click of keys
the infinite feet of a thousand
fireflies, dancing.
All thoughts, all words
reflect back without anything
profound to mark their passing.
Echoes of the divine leave her
wondering, how could she,
could she make a difference?

The beauty of routine
gently fingers the growing dusk
to enter more deeply into
the ritual of life.
She thinks,
we can question the significance
of work, of play, of love, or
separation, question where the meaning
                                        lies
in any of it, in all of it
what is most important
what can pass away without
concern, without grief.

Today, she thinks,
meaning is the sacredness of each detail—
the towel hung over the shower rod to dry.
The soap arranged in a dish
placed beside a star-shaped tea light
on top of a porcelain tank.
A clean mirror.
The aging bath mat that still matches the towels.

The ankle bracelet, broken, hanging
from the spine of a journal, four round peace signs
attached at regular intervals from its silver chain.
Today, she sits at her desk and thinks
it is enough. Today, she feels
it is enough.

> *I see you*
> *riffling through things, searching*
> *digging through things.*
> *You're looking for a nugget*
> *something that's real, significant*
> *only, it's all significant. It's all*
> *experience.*
> *It's who you are.*

What makes a life important?
What is it about a life
that makes it important?
Is it what you said?
In the end, it's just that
it's a life. It starts out important.

> *This is the struggle I've had my entire life*
> *to balance the work I do against what my heart*
> *tells me to do, against all those expectations*
> *around what success is and then realizing*
> *I don't even believe that definition of success*
>
> *but when you reject it*
> *even when you reject it*
> *even when you reject that standard*
> *and you say, I'm going to live differently,*
> *my life means something different,*
> *you know what they're thinking.*
> *They're thinking, you know*
> *they're thinking that you can't do it*
> *that you're pretending you don't want to do it*
> *because you can't do it.*

Like the aging bath mats
that are still clean,
not stained, still functional,
there's no reason to get rid of them. They still match
the 30-year-old towels. They make a picture
of a home, of a life   and yet,

when I'm asked to identify the significance of things
in my research, I can't. I can't talk about the bath mats
and yet, I think I will. How will people understand?
How will they understand why the bath mats are important?

       I wonder if you are asking yourself the right question.
       I wonder if you should ask, how do I tell their story?

       You're trying to hold two things together
       that maybe don't need to be held.

       How do you,
       how do you
       ascribe importance
       or significance?
       It is,
it is
    experience.[2]

Through our research conversations, we contrasted our relational work together as narrative researchers, which allowed spaces of vulnerability to open up. These spaces of vulnerability stood in contrast to the rigid spaces of the academy that encouraged agonistic (Lugones, 1987), competitive scholarship. Through dialogue and reflection, we began to explore the idea that in order to work in relation with someone, it is necessary to be vulnerable.

As Carl Leggo (personal communication, February 20, 2015) reminded us, vulnerability in research is of the highest importance. To honour the need for vulnerability, we focused our inquiry on better understanding the complexities of research places and how we might, as researchers, compose forward-looking stories of research that value playfulness and vulnerability.

THE GEOGRAPHY OF DEVIANCE

Even though I felt sure about who I was when I was 21, there were desires that I didn't understand but desperately wanted to figure out (*read: fix*). Having grown up in a fairly conservative home and church community, I knew what was expected. For university, I attended a small Christian liberal arts school with the motto *Esse Quam Videri*, meaning "to be, rather than to seem." As the student-body president, I was fairly well known to the students, faculty, and staff from the various meetings and events we planned and attended together. So, it was to my surprise (*read: terror*) that I might see one of them in this new world that I had begun to explore. Feeling rather curious one night, I built up the courage to visit an adult bookstore in a different part of the city. Just as I entered the gay section, downstairs in the basement, I bumped into a man trying to go upstairs. This man happened to be an administrator at the university. We knew one another, having met several times at student-government association events—I knew that he had children and had even met his wife.

I remember seeing his eyes widen and his face cringe; I am sure that my reaction was something similar. I remember a feeling of panic, thinking that if I kept walking, perhaps he wouldn't know who I was, but I know now, that was ridiculous. I could see in his eyes that he was as scared as I was and that fear could only come from the understanding that our identities, as we knew them, were in danger. The stories we held up around ourselves that allowed us to have jobs and go to school in that context may have come to an end. Perhaps feeling similarly, saying nothing and refusing to give a second glance, we stepped aside, continued walking, and left the store immediately. The next Monday, I saw him again in the cafeteria. He kindly waved and nodded as I passed. We never spoke to one another again.

> *I wondered, did you know then*
> *who you were? You say*

> This is my cover story
> stuck between the fear of finding out
> who I really was and an identity
> I was not ready to accept.

> *So, I thought, did you know*
> *who you were or did you feel*
> *things did not quite mesh*
> *but you weren't sure why?*

So many layers, all the ways
we carry these cover stories.
Sometimes we can't figure out
where the cover story ends
and we begin.

What is the origin of shame?

You say

> On the other hand, there were these desires
> I didn't understand, desperately wanted
> to figure out (to fix).

The idea that somehow you're damaged
or somehow having these desires makes you
like you have to fix, you have to fix, it's like
it's like you have to be
repaired.   So, to me, that's not a bracket.
That's big   and it makes me think

there's a noticeable silence
in this piece
about who you love
and who turns you on.

> That liminal space was protective in some ways, too.
> Because if I had to choose, I had to define ...

The silence of those things fits
with the silence in your life at the time.
This is the moment   just before
you break the silence.
Not the moment when you speak but
the moment before.

> This was just the reality of my life at the time.
> It wasn't this crux or the denouement of my story.

It wasn't the turning point. It was just
reality.

I've had those moments.
Everyone has had those moments.
You think,   I can live anonymously
               I can live my cover story
               and no one will ever find out.
Then, who you are will not be denied. It will
               it will surface.

        The reality of who you are emerges at some point.

        If we were in a place, a space
        that was safe, not a borderland,
        we might, we would
        make different choices.

That's my bias. I shouldn't interpret your experience.
But, how do you acquire the experience to explore the possibilities
if the context surrounding you is a space
where this is something we don't talk about?

        That's the purpose, I think, of silence.
        Because if we can silence it
        then it's not a choice.

What you are describing is how
the embodied experience you had
had no context
for you to make sense of it
and the social context
did not allow
did not even invite
a conversation
around it.

You lifting that out, lifted something out of me.

And now I am playing with space.
Look at me, going to that cordoned-off section
of the bookstore

in the basement

yeah

the geography of deviance.

Yeah, I entered
into that space thinking
no one else would be there
and yet, there we were.

Someone that you thought you knew
who was married and had kids,
married to a woman, with kids
who has a life   or a piece of a life
that doesn't make sense, or isn't making sense
to you, that makes you wonder, well ...
what about me?

It creates a question almost too big even to articulate.

Why can I inquire into this now?
Why couldn't I inquire into it then?

I'm playing with it.

The connection between context and experience.
Context there was terror.
Now I think it's hilarious,
like reading a story that's not yours.
The feelings are so real,
but the context is different.

That's the complexity of experience.
Temporality
moving backward and forward
at the same time
moving inward and outward
at the same time.
Never a static moment.

> I don't feel that way.
> When you reflected back to me,
> I don't feel that way.
> Taken back to the initial feelings,
> started playing ...
> actually, that's not it.

Both are expressions of your experience.
Context then.
Context now.

> A bridge from what I experienced then, to what I am experiencing now.
> Living in the closet
> thinking I am still in the closet,
> pretending, but
> I am not in the closet anymore.
> I interpret my experience in terms of context.
> Identity shifting
> before the closet
> in the closet
> on the other side of the closet.

An intensely powerful metaphor.
It's iconic.
Everyone knows what we mean when we say
coming out of the closet.
A phrase that has taken on its own life—
a way to make sense of the world that's individual.
What does it mean for you to move through the closet?
Not generalized experience.

Intensely personal.
Bumping into somebody that you never expected to see there.
The complexity of narrative.

> The meaning I ascribe to that experience shifts,
> shifts my past also.

Shifts your sense making of the past.

> Shifts my interpretation of the event.
> My relationship with that moment has changed.

And you'll never go back to that.
Never go back to the same relationship
because nothing is static
can't reproduce exactly that context
can't produce exactly that moment

> Then, my closet is protective.
> Then, my closet is restrictive.
> Now, my closet is hopeful.
> Now, my closet is like a gateway to freedom.

and you'll never go back
never go back
to the same relationship.[3]

CONTINUING THE CONVERSATION

The work we have shared in this chapter represents the beginning of an inquiry that is ongoing. Our engagement together in spaces of vulnerability lifts out research moments that are rich and valuable to sustaining future possibilities of multiple research places and researcher identities. We wonder about the many silent stories researchers bring to academic spaces that have not yet found a welcoming place for expression. From our own experience, we understand these stories not only as shaping influences in our perspectives but also as constituting knowledge itself. We hope our conversations about vulnerability will begin to compose places for once silent stories to find expression. In a methodology that emphasizes being in relationship with our participants, understanding the place of vulnerability within research is crucial. By sharing our poetic research dialogues, we open up new opportunities for the recognized value of vulnerability in research.

NOTES

1.   The epigraph at the beginning of this chapter is an example of the narratives we co-composed through our methodology as interim research texts (January 4, 2015).

2.   This research text was co-composed from Clarke's (2015) unpublished poem and subsequent research conversations between Clarke and Hutchinson in January 2015.

3.   Like the previous research text, this research text was also co-composed from Hutchinson's autobiographical narrative and subsequent research conversations between Clarke and Hutchinson in January 2015.

REFERENCES

Basso, K. (1996). *Wisdom sits in places: Landscape and language among the Western Apache.* Albuquerque, NM: University of New Mexico Press.

Clandinin, D. J. (2013). *Engaging in narrative inquiry.* Walnut Creek, CA: Left Coast Press.

Clandinin, D. J., & Connelly, F. M. (1995). *Teachers' professional knowledge landscapes.* New York, NY: Teachers College Press.

Clarke, C., & Hutchinson, D. (2015, February). *From the edge and in between: Exploring liminal spaces evoked by representations of identity making and curriculum making in two narrative inquiries.* Presentation at the 7th Biennial Provoking Curriculum Studies Conference, Vancouver, British Columbia.

Connelly, F. M., & Clandinin, D. J. (1999). *Shaping a professional identity: Stories of educational practice.* New York, NY: Teachers College Press.

Lugones, M. (1987). Playfulness, "world"-travelling, and loving perception. *Hypatia, 2*(2), 3–19.

Richardson, L. (1997). *Fields of play: Constructing an academic life.* New Brunswick, NJ: Rutgers University Press.

INVOCATION
Viscera

Celeste Snowber and Tamar Haytayan

Tamar Haytayan (2016). *Photo taken in the UBC Botanical Garden.* Digital photograph

What if our hands
were our feet, touching
bare naked the moss
which welcomes us home
as a creature among
many micro-organisms?
What would the world
look like if we knew
in the viscera, our place
among the plant beings
and they too
were our teachers calling us
not only to take care but be care.

C2

Conversations in a Curriculum of Tension

Stephanie J. Bartlett and Erin L. Quinn

It is unlikely that a Kindergarten teacher and a middle-school teacher-turned-school-board-specialist would find common ground. We met through a graduate course focusing on creativity in the classroom. We thought this desire to design learning that emphasizes creativity was what bonded us so deeply and closely together. Although we didn't know it at the time, our real common ground was a desire to live in the space between a lived and a planned curriculum (Aoki, 1986/2005).

I. RUMINATION: A REFLEXIVE REFLECTION

Four years into our critical friendship, we are learning that the action of pausing and reflecting is what pushes us, and our work, forward. In our pauses, we read the work of influential curriculum theorists. Together, we revisited our questions, consulted the work of these curriculum theorists, affectionately known as "our relations," such as David Jardine (2014), Ted Aoki (1989/2005), William Doll (2012), David Smith (2014), and Jackie Seidel (2014). We had lengthy, meandering conversations, and began to truly feel a physical "sudden, short intake of breath" as our questions began to make sense (Hillman, 1999, p. 201). We wondered how we could define and describe those moments when we *know* learning is happening on a deeper level and students are absorbed in their learning. Where is the place of curriculum within this? What is the role of relationship in these moments? Each relation affirmed our right to ask these questions and they revealed to us the questions we needed to ask. We offer this "reflexive reflection" (Doll, 2012, p. 166) as an attempt to make sense of not only the topic of teaching but also our "own method of studying, or indeed … way of being" (Doll, 2012, p. 166). We hope these reflections serve to propel us even further into our need to understand our own work.

This reflection takes the form of a poetic inquiry, an interplay between prose and conversation. Our sense making has taken the form of a text-message conversation between us over the past four years. Our text messages have often leaned toward a deeper and more philosophical conversation than a usual text-message thread, and we recognize them as a form of poetry. Writing ourselves as people and educators *into* this article became a key component to our journey. Laurel Richardson and Elizabeth St. Pierre affirm writing as a *method of inquiry*, a condition of possibility for "producing different knowledge and producing knowledge differently" (St. Pierre, as cited in Richardson & St. Pierre, 2005, p. 969). The very act of writing is what enabled us to make sense of our questions and follow Hans-Georg Gadamer's advice to start to find out "what is the question for which *this* (event, text, saying) is the answer?" (Smith, 2014, p. 178). Two parallel conversations take form here: the conversation between the two authors (the text messages, identified by author name) and the conversation with the theory we consult as inspiration and validation for our work (the text in paragraph form). The interplay of these two parallel conversations is what allows us to find clarity and understanding.

Ours is a story of relationship, discomfort, questioning, and messy joy. It is only through the combined text messages, conversation, writing as inquiry, and reading of curriculum studies theory that we have been able to arrive at the topic, and indeed find clarity in the question: Why do we seek tension in our practice?

II. TENSION

Ted Aoki (1987/2005) wrote that "to be alive is to be appropriately tensioned and … to be tensionless, like a limp violin string, is to be dead" (p. 360). He also wrote of the tension between the curriculum-as-plan and the curriculum-as-lived (Aoki, 1986/2005, p. 159). Curriculum-as-plan has a clear endpoint. Curriculum-as-lived embraces ambiguity, question seeking, and a personal connection with a worthy topic. Curriculum-as-lived requires a personal truth. Curriculum-as-lived requires you to make a connection. This causes an uncomfortable tension in many. Many would propose that it is desirable to overcome this tension. Many of our colleagues would be happy delivering a curriculum-as-plan.

Erin: I think it is difficult to understand when we use the word *tension* because people don't want to be more stressed and overworked than they already are.

Steph: Being tense is not something anyone wants to be.

Erin: Except we do. We seek those situations where things are ambiguous, and we don't know the answer.

Steph: The idea of tension can be softened, I think, when put in the context of a violin string that needs to be appropriately tensioned in order to function at its best.

Erin: Maybe the perfect amount of tension, the kind that makes the violin string taut but not too tight or too loose, is what we aim for.

Steph: When something starts to feel like it's going smoothly, I feel like something's wrong.

Erin: Sometimes that's exhausting, always pushing toward the edge. But I don't think I would be happy teaching, or living, any other way.

Steph: If we keep going with Aoki's metaphor, if the violin string is too loose, it's dead. But if it's too tight, it snaps. In both scenarios, you can't play the violin.

Erin: If it's work worth doing, it's going to be disruptive. But then how do we tune the violin appropriately?

When thinking of worthwhile learning experiences as a perfectly tuned violin, it is important to think of how to achieve balance. Balance in the moment comes from building and nurturing a sense of community and curiosity in students and using this mindset as a foundation for learning experiences. Gadamer (2004) suggests that *sensus communis* is about being prepared for the unexpected. *Sensus communis* offers the knowledge to respond to unknown events or discussions that might arise. We are preparing our students to be ready for the unexpected in life. Gadamer (2004) also writes about the importance of the topic. Achieving appropriate tension is about teaching students to be prepared for learning and to be prepared to meet the topic with an open and curious mind. We don't need or want students to be complacent in their learning, expecting the teacher to deliver the content. We want students to practice this mindset of creative thinking so that they can react to and embrace the unexpected.

Erin: In my work with many different classes and students, I can often tell quite quickly which classes have practiced creative thinking a lot and which ones have not.

Steph: Can you describe the essence of how you know?

Erin: Those who aren't practiced are often perplexed when something is presented to them that they don't expect. They don't know how to react to something unexpected.

Steph: So, if you could teach creative thinking as a mindset from the beginning of the year to build *sensus communis*, would that make a difference?

Erin: Yes, I think so. If the teacher deliberately engages students in these mindsets, they become practiced in what is required of them by the unexpected.

Steph: So appropriate tension, then, is being curious about the topic and knowing how to proceed within that field of inquiry. Students would be familiar with the practice of generating ideas, documenting their learning, discussing possibilities and asking questions.

Erin: That's it, I think. They develop a *sensus communis* for curiosity.

Steph: Sensus communis implies a community. Can we define this as a specific mindset created within the community of learners that enables a close investigation of a topic, pulling in curriculum-as-plan within a curriculum-as-lived?

We are arriving at a place of understanding or recognition that to be "appropriately tensioned" (Aoki, 1987/2005) is about finding the place of the curriculum-as-plan within the curiosity and the disciplines of curriculum-as-lived (p. 360). There is no recipe or formula for how "a curriculum-as-plan [can] be so built that it has the potential for a curriculum-as-lived that is charged with life" (Aoki, 1987/2005, p. 362). By telling these stories and sharing our conversations, we reflect on the possibilities within the parameters of our own teaching contexts. Jardine said that "creating a *sensus communis* amongst educators is to surround ourselves with stories of different possibilities" (D. Jardine, personal communication, October 27, 2015). In this way, we too can practice what it means to meet a topic together as students and educators in the field of inquiry.

III. ATTUNING

Aoki (1986/2005) understood that "indwelling in the zone between curriculum-as-plan and curriculum-as-lived experience is not so much a matter of overcoming the tensionality but more a matter of dwelling aright within it" (p. 163). The idea of equilibrium, or what we might define as successful moments of achieving this tension in the classroom, really is a dwelling in that space in between curriculum-as-plan and curriculum-as-lived. The result is "a curriculum infused with, inspirited with, 'good' or 'appropriate' tension" (Doll, 2012, p. 170). After this realization, we began to wonder how we could critically reflect on the components of a successful moment, one that creates "good" tension. Recognizing that it would be different for everyone depending on their context, how could we achieve and define a special experience and then share the essence of what we deemed to be that well-tuned violin? The appropriate tension, then, takes a positive learning experience or feeling and provokes personal reflection as well as a push forward or deeper into our journey to achieve "attunement."

Erin: Here's the thing. I actually don't believe that curriculum-as-plan and curriculum-as-lived should be equally balanced. I actually think curriculum-as-lived is more important. I couldn't care less if my students remember how osmosis works. Or the exact order of events that led to Canadian Confederation. I'd rather my kids solve real problems and be creative and be lovely, caring human beings. Actually, that's not totally true. I do care that my students learn about osmosis and Confederation. But I want them to find the poetry of the discipline of biology and the fascination of history in these things. In doing that, they become lovely, caring human beings.

Steph: It isn't a complete balance. Just like that violin string, it needs constant adjusting to stay in tune.

Steph: It is no longer about me and my students carrying out a plan. It is about me having a plan about the curricular aspects that I want us to experience, but really, my day doesn't begin until I look into the eyes of my students. Take this a step further and include the relationships with community members and the actual field of study and my pedagogy is in constant motion as I tune and retune.

Erin: Okay. So where is the place of the program of studies in all of this?

For curriculum to "come alive in the classroom, the curriculum itself has to contain, said or unsaid, an invitation for teachers and students to enter into it. Not only that, there needs to be a reciprocal invitation" (Aoki, 1987/2005, p. 362). It's easy for teachers to get caught up in planning their curriculum and delivering it. When reflecting upon his own practice, Aoki (1987/2005) noticed that this approach is dehumanizing: "[W]as I not understanding people, teachers, and children not as *beings* who are *human* but rather as *thing beings*? Is this not 'education' reduced to a half-life of what it could be?" (p. 358). Jardine (2014) agrees: this "requires that we understand the topics entrusted to teachers and students in school as constituted, not by lifeless fragments and bits and pieces, but by living disciplines, live inheritances and fabrics into which our lives are already woven" (p. 85). Where we should begin, then, is with our students as human beings, not with our outcomes or skills.

Steph: So it's a relationship between the topic and the people. The children, the teacher, the community. Not the teacher and the program of studies.

Erin: It's not the people. It's not the topic. It's how they relate to one another, on that day, in that space. Each experience leads to another, and builds upon what came before. This is practice. This is experience. That's how we figure out how to find our balance between curriculum-as-lived and curriculum-as-plan.

Steph: I saw that today with my class. We headed outside to explore and develop our French language and conversations. We were in the midst of checking in with each other when we noticed all of the ice chunks. Exclamations of delight led us into learning how to say "Je cherche des formes" and "J'ai trouvé un cercle, un triangle, un rectangle, ou un carré." Students were naturally finding examples of those shapes, but also learning about octagons, parallelograms, and the properties of each shape. One student proudly showed me a series of triangles moulded within mud where the ice had been removed. Another marked a circle of grass surrounded by icy, lingering snow. My own heart tripped when one showed me a heart that he had found. If we think about a perfectly tuned instrument, that was it. Groups of students staying close and yet very obviously all searching for shapes.

Erin: So they were absorbed by shapes.

Steph: Then the tension became too tight. It was when I asked them to make piles and sort the shapes! All of a sudden, their deep learning experience became a bit disjointed and the mood was instantly altered.

Erin: Because you interrupted them? Did it become untuned because you asked something of them that they weren't ready for?

Steph: Now that I think back, they were busy exploring. Perhaps the directed teaching or guidance comes after that. It takes skill, then, to listen carefully for the right moment.

Dwelling within the tension between curriculum-as-lived and curriculum-as-plan, or finding attunement, becomes a knowing and understanding of one's self and the others in the community as well as an active and conscious weaving of living disciplines throughout. Seidel (2014) describes attunement to mean that we as educators need to yield to the possibility of giving "more time [to] the delicate balances, intimacies, and complexities of this space to emerge" (p. 176). Referring again to Gadamer's (2004) idea that practice helps us become experienced, once we recognize this appropriate tension in our teaching practice, we will continue to seek other moments of attunement, always recognizing the key role that relationship plays within a curriculum-as-lived.

Through this writing, this conversation, this consultation of our relations, we found that our own violin string tightened and loosened while we tuned our thinking. Had we waited to write "until [we] knew what [we] wanted to say, that is, until [our] points were organized and outlined," we may not have arrived at this interpretation (Richardson & St. Pierre, 2005, p. 960). The process of writing permitted us to find a place of balance within the curriculum-as-plan and the curriculum-as-lived. Taking the time for our "reflexive reflections" has, as we hoped, pushed us forward in our own journey. We can hold this process as another layer of the conversation and the messy joy that lives within this tension.

REFERENCES

Aoki, T. T. (1986/2005). Teaching as indwelling between two curriculum worlds. In W. F. Pinar & R. L. Irwin (Eds.), *Curriculum in a new key: The collected works of Ted T. Aoki* (pp. 159–165). Mahwah, NJ: Erlbaum.

Aoki, T. T. (1987/2005). Inspiriting the curriculum. In W. F. Pinar & R. L. Irwin (Eds.), *Curriculum in a new key: The collected works of Ted T. Aoki* (pp. 357–365). Mahwah, NJ: Erlbaum.

Aoki, T. T. (1989/2005). The dialectic of mother language and second language: A curriculum exploration. In W. F. Pinar & R. L. Irwin (Eds.), *Curriculum in a new key: The collected works of Ted T. Aoki* (pp. 235–245). Mahwah, NJ: Erlbaum.

Doll, W. E. Jr. (2012). Revisiting Aoki's "inspiriting the curriculum." In N. Ng-A-Fook & J. Rottman (Eds.), *Reconsidering Canadian curriculum studies: Provoking historical, present, and future perspectives* (pp. 165–174). New York, NY: Palgrave Macmillan.

Gadamer, H.-G. (2004). *Truth and method.* (J. Weinsheimer & D. Marshall, Trans.) London, England: Bloomsbury Academic. (Original work published 1975)

Hillman, J. (1999). *The force of character and the lasting life.* New York, NY: Random House.

Jardine, D. W. (2014). Lessons from a dog named Fideles. In J. Seidel & D. W. Jardine (Eds.), *Ecological pedagogy, Buddhist pedagogy, hermeneutic pedagogy: Experiments in a curriculum for miracles* (pp. 57–90). New York, NY: Peter Lang.

Richardson, L., & St. Pierre, E. A. (2005). Writing: A method of inquiry. In N. K. Denzin & Y. S. Lincoln (Eds.), *The Sage handbook of qualitative research* (3rd ed.) (pp. 959–978). Thousand Oaks, CA: Sage.

Seidel, J. (2014). Some thoughts on teaching as contemplative practice. In J. Seidel & D. W. Jardine (Eds.), *Ecological pedagogy, Buddhist pedagogy, hermeneutic pedagogy: Experiments in a curriculum for miracles* (pp. 172–183). New York, NY: Peter Lang.

Smith, D. G. (2014). *Teaching as the practice of wisdom.* New York, NY: Bloomsbury Academic.

C3

Dwelling in Poiesis

Shirley Turner

This collection of poems and art represents an exploration of my developing perspective as a teacher-researcher during the course of my doctoral journey. The poems that I have included in this chapter embody my personal reflections on a school garden's potential to co-teach and my participation in ongoing garden practices. The use of figurative language allows me to *return anew* (Jardine, 1998) to my feelings about my research experience in a hermeneutic way, providing insights that sometimes remain hidden around the corner of formal prose. The juxtaposition of image and language reflects the ambiguity of representing my learning in a way that addresses Maurice Merleau-Ponty's idea of a structural correspondence between lived experience and the expressive power of words (Langer, 1989). My use of poetic and visual representation is an attempt to liberate myself from the tyranny of the academic prose in order to transform my knowledge into holistic multi-faceted representations of the understandings I gained from my research process (Meyer, 2008).

During my doctoral journey, I quickly came to realize that the research process involved all aspects of my being—emotional, physical, social, and spiritual as well as intellectual. It also became apparent that coming to know this particular place in which I live and work was a large part of my burgeoning understanding, which led me toward the notion of *dwelling* as an enablement for growth. My life had been largely transient until coming to Vancouver, and cultivating my own growth depended on the fundamental task of firmly locating myself within the web of creation in a specific locale. This implies that the process of education needs to be relational—connecting students and teachers not only to human interactions but also to interactions with other living beings. Wendell Berry (1987) suggests that one way to enact such relationality is to view education as "an enablement to *serve* ... the living community in its natural household or neighbourhood" (p. 52). To be of service, we need to observe and act on opportunities to interact with our community. Work in a schoolyard garden allows us to interact with the living world in a purposeful role that assigns us both accountability and agency, incorporating us into the body of the garden community. Our attentiveness to what enables plants, compost organisms, and schoolyard chickens to flourish can create opportunities for us to reflect on the interdependency of the web of life, then identify and act on what we have to offer others. As David Abram (1996) has noted, "Humans are tuned for relationship ... we are human only in contact, and conviviality, with what is not human" (p. ix). To this end I have capitalized *Other* in certain poems to emphasize the centrality of our relationship with the more-than-human world and embeddedness within that world.

A relational approach to education values the prior experience of all participants. Everyone brings something to the table so that each person as well as the garden inhabitants and seasonal opportunities influence our collective understanding. My personal experience with embodied ways of knowing through Iyengar-yoga teacher training supplements my more traditional academic studies. The practice of yoga provides one aspect of my recovery from addiction by creating opportunities to dwell in my body after years of drug use that allowed me to dissociate from it. The holistic nature of this personal awakening further convinced me of the value of embodied ways of knowing that reconnect learners with the living world. A yogic philosophical approach to the world, combined with my use of experiential methods, suggests that learning can be characterized in terms of participation and experience within a supportive environment. I envisage this as an ongoing co-arising enactment within the living web around us. The opportunity to integrate my passion for yoga and gardening into my educational work has led to self-care being front and centre in the face I present to my students.

Moving into the cultural space that has been created between producers and consumers, especially in urban settings, offers a chance "to understand and to mistrust *and to change* our wasteful economy, which markets not just the produce of the earth, but also the earth's ability to produce" (Berry, 1972, p. 81). There is a political dimension to focusing on process-oriented learning that creates a kind of countercultural space through collaborating with Other living beings in a garden. My ever-awakening realization of the cyclical nature of life has informed my use of recursive teaching strategies that seek to engage my students with curricular content in ways that allow them to find their own meanings. Similarly, my investigation of ecologically based, process-oriented approaches to education has helped me find more ways to accommodate my students as individual learners while fostering community building in my classes. Through these practices, I have developed a deep respect for the ways my students find to overcome their life challenges, and I have been encouraged to continue experimenting with curricular spaces that cultivate "the ability to dwell openly in that which can not be named but within which we live and move and have our being" (Smith, 1999, p. 23).

Dwelling
Willing to learn
from life
perceiving my experience
without unhooking it
from the tapestry of creation
myriad fleeting impressions
a synergistic symbiosis
sourced by interaction
myself
my community
Other living beings
my ecological environment
cultivated and wild
making sense by
rooting myself in grounding vitality
dwelling here and now
Earthbound
enfolded by flourishing
embodied wisdom
be-coming re-connected
re-membering a place
where I belong
coming home to myself.

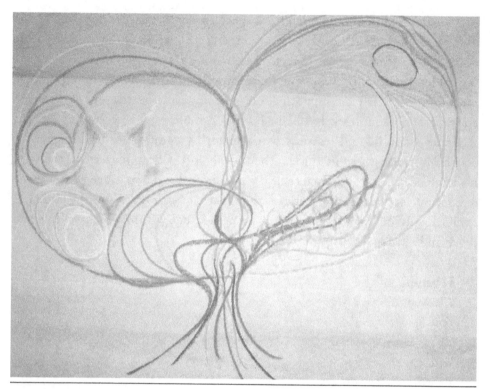

Shirley Turner (November 2012). *Tapestry of creation.* Pastel drawing

Structural Correspondence [1]

Back to basics
prune away the clutter of contrivances
hindering access to the natural world
our own nature
intertwined in structural correspondence.

Daily exposure to a living garden
urban opportunity to interact with Others
observe the simplicity within complex systems
reap and sow
expand and extend sensibilities.

Learn to see anew
re-cycle through decomposition

fertilize and mulch
formulate and assess strategies
evaluate growth.

Foster direct scrutiny of specifics
embedded in concentric contextual circles
intersecting epistemologies
inform action
shift gears beyond
(all too common) mediated encounters.
Plant seeds for the future
who knows upon what ground they fall
whether they will survive technological pounding
to germinate
substantiating coming to know this enveloping Earth.

Previous experience with outdoor wilderness education
suggests conceptual comprehension
digestion a slow process
uptake uneven
emotional engagement a determinant.

So encouraged I continue to share
my alfresco enthusiasm
keep the faith
that living environments
can enliven anaesthetized senses.

Reach out to one student at a time
gradually assess individual topography
play to strengths
cultivate a willingness to bear witness
as potential unfurls
educationally envisage enlivening
a felt awareness of our shared world.

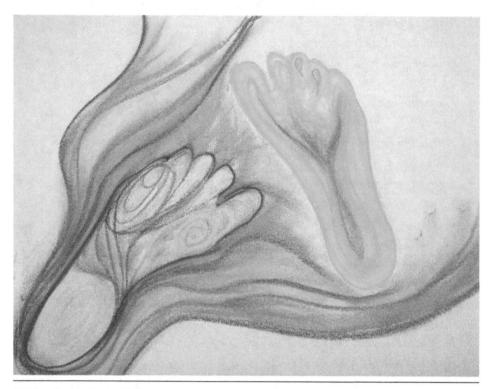

Shirley Turner (July 2013). *Dancing in the dirt.* Pastel drawing

Sustenance

I bring to the table
experience of my own healing process
connecting with a yogic culture of breath
exploring contemplation, revitalization, rejuvenation
with air as my teacher; my body as my guide
tempered by healing interaction
the power of a supportive group
to catalyze individual transformation
moving beyond Cartesian compartmentalization
into wider integration
finding commonality in food wisdom
a many-faceted field
creating a broad context for personal connection
a weighty matter for all living beings
webbed together by our common need for sustenance.

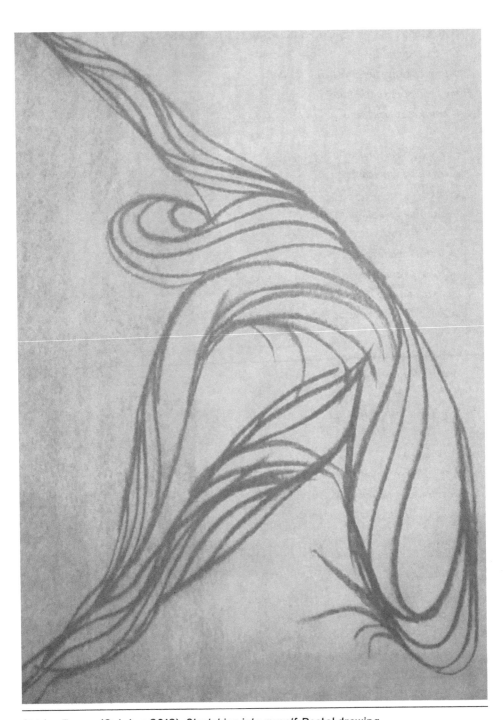

Shirley Turner (October 2012). *Stretching into myself*. Pastel drawing

Knowledge Is Power, Understanding Is Liberation[2]

Do we even notice
your propensity for connecting the dots
my tendency to path-find?
What is the background for all this activity?

Can we look beyond securing
curricular frameworks
topos
—claiming ground to defend?

Is there a broader perspective
a field of possibility
that might allow us to move
within and without these spaces?

Grow through them ...
towards the source of all life
the living soil
bringing schools to life and life to schools.

If education is
an enablement to serve
the full living community
ecology in the service of economics.[3]

What lies on the other side
of institutionalized structures?
Can we move down a level of abstraction
forget the future to enter the present?

Free space to commune with the fullness of learning space
outside addressing the dimension of place
each living thing's inter-relatedness to every other
an underlying reciprocity within the natural world.

Can we ease into our surroundings
embody our understandings

sense the ongoing flux
find field and foci?

Is it possible to sense a need for structure
without be-coming caught
trapped in a web of knowing
that limits rather than liberates?

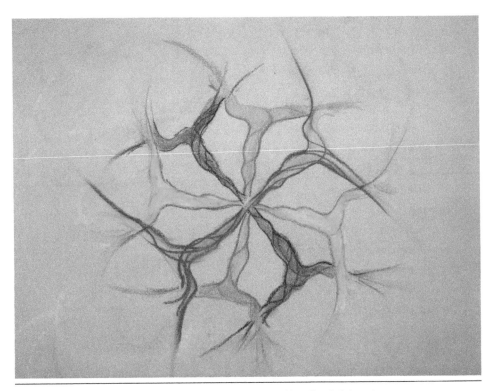

Shirley Turner (August 2013). *Stretching into each other.* Pastel drawing

Opening

Releasing my endeavours
in the school garden
to the constraints of time
and a sprinkler system
I leave the city
for the solace
of my island retreat ...

I refocus on my lowly plot
carved from an alder bottom
learning from a different place
cultivating vigorous soil
with local elements
seaweed, grass clippings, horse manure.

Opening
to another environment
a subterranean fungal ecosystem
cultivation in a different tone
a new melody
dancing seeds to life
where the rainforest rules.

Returning to the city
I visit the flourishing schoolyard garden
thriving tomato thickets
towering sunflowers
semaphoring jubilation
celebrating a break in the summer drought.

Water regulations demand
sprinkler off despite the downpour
I prune back vivacious tomatoes
to give the basil airspace
reap garlic, compost borage
joyously dripping
in harmony with my green team.

Immersed in my connection
to Earthly offerings
presenced by the fecund tomato bed
I contemplate possibilities
might the garlic bed become a nursery
for volunteer kale seedlings
relying on a mere weekend's rain?

The plantlets hum in anticipation
eager for an opening
to spread their roots
reach high and wide
it might be a long shot
but nothing ventured nothing gained
the only other possibility the return of the mower.

Tuning in to two gardens
learning each rhythm
syncopated yet diverse
I open up extending my range
a sapient bud
blossoming through my own practice
learning to teach gardening
as grounds for cultivating well-being.

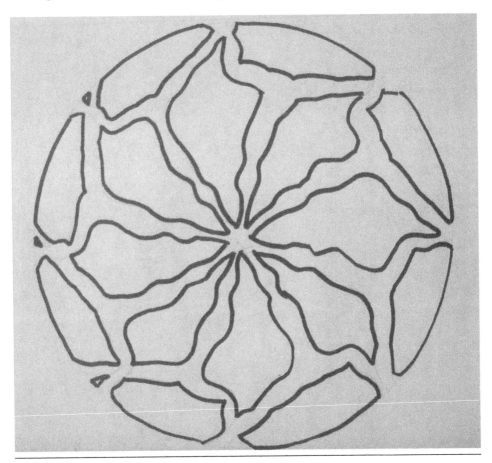

Shirley Turner (July 2013). *Stretching into each other [draft].* Pen sketch

Responsive Reciprocity

Where do "I" end and "we" start?
our mutual co-exist-ing
inter-action
dependent on our natures
not determined by them.

In your absence
I would surely perish
your fluid swirls and eddies
turning us both inside out
my gift to the world to be touched.

There is no beginning
or end
just shades of transience
all the way down to the molecular level
mutually "open incomplete entities"[4]
embracing each other
"destined for relationship."[5]
I am but
an actor on a larger stage
impoverished
when I fail
to be moved
beyond my limiting self-conceptions
forgetting my member-ship
in a greater "we."

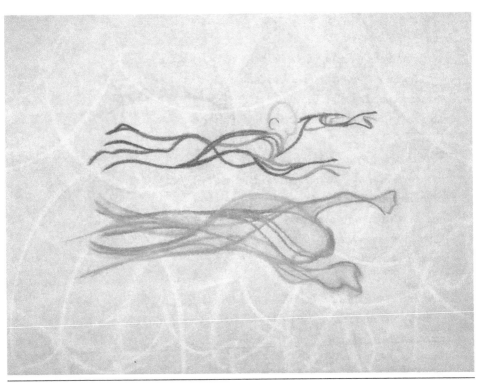

Shirley Turner (July 2014). *Acknowledging my Elders.* Pastel drawing

Waking Up the Rake

The heavens open
the clouds lift
a break in the downpour
trees enshrouded in mist prior to revelations of sacred geometry
a final brightening of the ghostly grey
lifting my eyes and spirit
like a student articulating a conceptual connection.

Leaves shed in rain shadows
drying out into multi-coloured earthbound splashes
marking the passing of the storm
language which can be interpreted by the careful eye
translation of teacher talk into learner lingo
growing season's grand finale.

Time to get out the rake
reap the fall harvest
burnished coppers, bedraggled crimsons
drifts of airborne beauty come to ground
partner to perceptual crystallization
manifest re-presentation of synthesized sensibility.

In the rhythmic scrape of tine and rustle of leaf
time to reflect as the seasonal cycle turns beneath my feet
not unlike mustering my memories
from each pass at unit planning
gleaning aha moments—successful analogies
collecting connecting successful teaching strategies.

As nights draw in, leaves float free
matured shootlings that earlier proclaimed spring's return
sheathing urban concrete in multi-hued green
sheltering us in a leafy canopy
calling forth the hoe—the rake's sibling
the need to weed—differentiation of emergent potentialities.

How many times have I raked this path?
How many times have I planted this bed?
Tended this place year about year, the round of seasons circling
returning these rakings to the prolific Earth
reviewing, revising, reworking.

Food for the worms—a diet for detritivores
winter insulation for myriad micro-organisms
tucking my garden beds up in mulch blankets
layering activities, cultivating understanding
beyond facts and figures
time for gestation, germination—time to build stories
chilly countenancing of deep digestion.

Trust in the eventual replenishment of rest
the rich loam renews its wealth
in the elemental dance
air, water, light
waxing waning in a magical life-giving synthesis
analog to my learning/teaching process
if I but heed its message in the headlong rush to "finish" the curriculum.

Next to unconditional offerings of shade and shelter
"marriage of water and green-leafed dripping"[6]
progeny oxygenating the smog
deep rooted stability
my contribution seems sparse
—my saving grace a reiterative willingness
disciplined focus—creative ecopoiesis.

So I choose to rake—to hoe
task without end—recurring repetition
mirroring my work in education
homily to interconnectedness
acknowledgement of my personal dependence on an educational community
an act of reciprocity.

As the sky purples in the west
leaves complementary flaming tracks
the respite passes and the heavens open
a downpour drumming accompaniment
another reaping in the winds
fluttering foliage tumbling in the twilight.

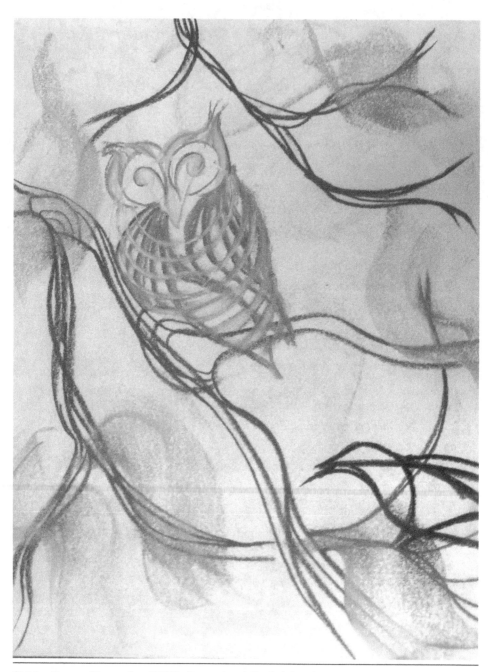

Shirley Turner (December 2012). *Harvest owl*. Pastel drawing

NOTES

1. *Structural correspondence* is a term used to describe the relationship between experience and expression. Maurice Merleau-Ponty emphasized the creative character of expressive language that arises as an echo of our experience of the interconnected web of sensorial reality (Langer, 1989).

2. *Knowledge is power, understanding is liberation* (Meyer, 2008, p. 229). This poem is based on my experience of exploring how educators might move beyond content-based teaching toward a process-based approach with an indigenous scholar.

3. As previously cited in this chapter, Wendell Berry (1987, p. 52) suggests that one way to enact a relational approach is to view education as "an enablement to *serve* … the living community in its natural household or neighbourhood." This perspective echoes Manulani Aluli Meyer's (2008) question, "What do you have to offer the world?" (p. 230).

4. *Open incomplete entity*: David Abram (1996) suggests, "We may think of the sensing body as a kind of open circuit that completes itself only in things, and in the world. The differentiation of my senses, as well as their spontaneous convergence in the world at large, ensures that I am a being *destined for relationship*: it is primarily through my engagement with what is not me that I effect the integration of my senses, and thereby experience my own unity and coherence" (p. 125).

5. *Destined for relationship*: see previous note.

6. *Marriage of water and green-leafed dripping*: A line by Linda Hogan (1996, p. 107) identifying the place our breathable air is born.

REFERENCES

Abram, D. (1996). *The spell of the sensuous: Perception and language in a more-than-human world*. New York, NY: Pantheon Books.

Berry, W. (1972). *A continuous harmony: Essays cultural and agricultural*. New York, NY: Harcourt Brace Jovanovich.

Berry, W. (1987). *Home economics: Fourteen essays*. San Francisco, CA: North Point Press.

Hogan, L. (1996). *Dwellings: A spiritual history of the living world*. New York, NY: Simon and Schuster.

Jardine, D. W. (1998). *To dwell with a boundless heart: Essays in curriculum theory, hermeneutics, and the ecological imagination*. New York, NY: Peter Lang.

Langer, M. M. (1989). *Merleau-Ponty's phenomenology of perception: A guide and commentary*. Basingstoke, England: Macmillan.

Meyer, M. A. (2008). Indigenous and authentic: Hawaiian epistemology and the triangulation of meaning. In N. K. Denzin, Y. S. Lincoln, & L. T. Smith, (Eds.), *Handbook of critical and indigenous methodologies* (pp. 217–232). Los Angeles, CA: Sage.

Smith, D. G. (1999). *Pedagon: Interdisciplinary essays in the human sciences, pedagogy, and culture*. New York, NY: Peter Lang.

INVOCATION

"To Know the World, We Have to Love It"

David W. Jardine

If one's sight is clear and if one stays on and works well, one's love gradually responds to the place as it really is, and one's visions gradually imagine possibilities that are really in it. Vision, possibility, work, and life—all have changed by mutual correction.

(Wendell Berry, 1983, p. 70)

Below the ecological crisis lies a deeper crisis of love. For love to return to the world, beauty must ... return, else we love the world only as a moral duty.

(James Hillman, 2006, p. 175)

I don't know of any topic in any Canadian curriculum guide that is not worthy of love, devotion, and study. I've never seen any topography, treated with affection, that cannot become an open and rich and living field of good work, good questions, and thrilling, often humiliating and painful and worthwhile discoveries and lessons. Loved, such places begin to glow and shed their light on us.

"Sometimes it is necessary to reteach a thing its loveliness" (Kinnell, 2002, n.p.). This is our central task as teachers, not just with students, but also with all the knowledge entrusted to us in schools. *All of it:*

> This can't be hurried; this is the dreadful situation that young people are in, and I think of them and I say, well, the situation you're in is a situation that is going to call for a lot of patience, and to be patient in an emergency is a terrible trial. (Berry & Moyers, 2013)

In times of embattlement, I tend to panic, and panic belies patience and patience belies affection. Cultivating love and affection for the ways and runs and paths of things (*currere*) is a terrible trial in times of terrible trial.

We are being asked, as teachers, as scholars and writers and readers, to not join in the fray of spellbinding, distracting, affliction-arousing, manipulated, real and imagined urgencies. We don't need urgent cures for urgency. Urgency changes territories and landscapes and eco-surrounds into battlegrounds where love and studious affection have no chance.

Be ready, talking and thinking and acting like this, for the ridicule that will surely come from a fraught world. It is part of the terrible trial. Know full well that you are not alone in such readiness.

Listen: "To know the world, we have to love it" (Berry & Moyers, 2013).

If I can? When I'm able? Should the circumstances allow? If I have the time? The permission? The funding? The right school? The right kids?

No. Love is not an outcome of the right circumstances but a cause of right circumstance.

REFERENCES

Berry, W. (1983). *Standing by words*. San Francisco, CA: North Point Press.

Berry, W., & Moyers, B. (2013, October 11). Writer and farmer Wendell Berry on hope, direct action, and the "resettling" of the American countryside [Video interview]. *Yes! Magazine*. Available at: www.yesmagazine.org/planet/mad-farmer-wendell-berry-gets-madder-in-defense-of-earth

Hillman, J. (2006). The repression of beauty. In R. J. Leaver (Ed.), *City and soul* (pp. 172–186). Putnam, CT: Spring Publications.

Kinnell, G. (2002). *Saint Francis and the sow*. Retrieved October 30, 2014, from: www.poetryfoundation.org/poem/171395

C4

Provoking "Difficult Knowledge": A Pedagogical Memoir

Mary J. Harrison

Recently, I was a member of a team instructing teacher candidates in a large section of a core Models and Foundations of Education course. For the first time, the course was taught online. To facilitate engagement in the new online setting, the course was designed so that students joined one of 10 thematic groups. Each teaching assistant took responsibility for a theme—my tutorials were organized around gender and education, for instance—and we were then tasked with delivering a short lecture about our topic as a way to attract students to our tutorial groups.

I began my talk on gender and education with a personal anecdote. I told the 300 teacher candidates assembled that I had recently become a mother, and I described a dilemma I'd grappled with pertaining to my daughter's education in gender. When my daughter was born I began collecting artifacts to archive her new life. I had planned to keep a newspaper from the day she was born so that, as she grows up, she can know about what else was going on in the world that day. I recounted my hesitation when the cover story of one of Canada's national newspapers on the day my daughter was born memorialized a young woman who raised national attention when she died in the wake of gendered and sexual violence and bullying by her high-school classmates. My hesitation to save the newspaper reflects my wish—a maternal fantasy—that my daughter will never need to confront discrimination and violence associated with any of the ways in which she might express her gender identity throughout her life, and that there will be no need for her to witness or even think about violence, tragedy, hate, or injustice at all. In the end, though, I did save the newspaper for my daughter. As a parent and an educator, I know that I can't prevent my child from learning difficult things about this world, but what I can do is help her to think about those things in smart and critical ways, and recognize that her questions will help me in my own learning. My daughter, like all of us, is and will be a gendered person and, also like the rest of us, will be schooled in gender all her life: we all experience ways in which our gender identities are under surveillance, policed, celebrated; feel frustrating and pleasurable; and, sometimes, are punished or persecuted. When my daughter is old enough to have questions about the memorialized young woman's story, her education in gender will already be well under way, and she will need to know that she can ask me all of her difficult questions.

Following my talk to the students about gender and education, many teacher candidates were enthusiastic to work with me and to develop and expand their own sets of interest about the topic. My year with the students was successful. Many students asked provocative questions, several risked reflecting on their own entanglement in the discourses we explored together, and most seemed genuinely interested in learning more and differently about how, why, and where questions and issues of gender erupt in schools and culture more broadly. Yet, when the course drew to a close, I felt curiously dissatisfied about my work with the students.

Because the course was online, and because online pedagogy was new to most of the instructional team, including me, we weren't entirely sure what to expect in terms of our communication with the students throughout the year. Twitter became an important tool for keeping in touch with the students, sharing extracurricular resources that might interest them, and generally demonstrating that I held them in my mind even though we didn't meet face to face. New to the platform, I soon noticed a pattern in how I used Twitter. I almost never tweeted or retweeted stories or news items about violence, gross injustice, hate, or discrimination, opting instead to share items that were about empowerment, equality, or, generally, wins for social justice. For instance, as our course began in September 2013, stories were breaking about blatantly sexist frosh-week activities at various universities across Canada. These stories—one was about the inclusion of a frosh chant that advocated date rape, for instance—made it clear that rape culture is alive and well in Canadian higher education. This interested me very much as a woman who has a right to be and to feel safe at my place of work, and as a scholar who researches women's roles and experiences of belonging in the academy. The stories captured women's otherness in the context of an institution that has been built around the normative experience of men, and conveyed a requirement that women weather an ongoing threat of gendered and sexual violence as a condition of occupying space in the public world. Although these stories extended my own thinking about women in higher education, I declined to share any news items about them with the students who had just signed up to study gender and education with me.

At the end of the school year, while thinking about the vague dissatisfaction I felt about my work as an online instructor, I kept returning to my resistance to share "bad news" stories with the students. Now that the course was over, I could begin to articulate the worry at the heart of that resistance: What if I had shared an article about rape culture and it had reminded one of the students about her own experience of being raped? This question now seems preposterous, and highlights my fantasies of omnipotence as a teacher: the students' awareness of rape—whether their own or others'—did not depend on whether I clicked "retweet" one afternoon. At the time, I felt like I was protecting the students from something. Yet, through the *afterwardness of thinking* (Pitt, 2003), I can consider how my protectionist impulse did them a tremendous disservice—both as young people seeking to think and learn about the world, and as developing educators themselves.

My story contains a striking parallel. When it was my daughter's difficult knowledge at stake, I made a commitment toward our future difficult conversations; I put that newspaper in the archive as one way to signal my availability to talk with her about anything—*anything*—that she might feel curious about. Yet, with the students, I backed away from opportunities to engage them in difficult and painful conversations and to acknowledge that as gendered, raced, and sexual subjects in this world, they have each endured violence and pain in some form or another. By not holding open space for those conversations—under the auspices of protectionism, or, I told myself, kindness—I may have made myself unavailable as a resource for the students' researches in difficult knowledge.

This parallel between my maternal and teacherly pedagogies resonates with Madeleine Grumet's (1988) warning of how impersonal pedagogical conventions fail students:

> Ethics and the common culture provide the procedural form and cultural content for our current concepts of schooling. And if ethics and the common culture could gather together the concern and attention that we devote to our own children and extend this nurture to other people's children, then we might indeed find in the school the model for a just society. (p. 164)

I find in Grumet's (1988) *Bitter Milk* a vocabulary for describing and analyzing the sense of dissatisfaction I felt at the end of the term. She writes,

A curriculum designed for my child is a conversation that leaves space for her responses, that is transformed by her questions. It needn't replicate her language or mine, but it must be made accessible to our interpretation and translation. Curriculum decision making requires our participation, the active, responsive, interpreting activity of parents and children. (p. 173)

With this model of the thoughtful and open parental conversation as the backdrop, Grumet argues that curriculum must allow for action, not acquiescence; it must be possible for students to manipulate and alter it. Curriculum that responds to the student is interactive and intersubjective and "cannot be prescribed by securing agreement to a set of standing principles" (p. 174). Reading Grumet to think about how and why my pedagogy differs with my daughter and with students, I realize how deeply I have internalized a curriculum designed through the detached lens of the ethical—a curriculum ostensibly designed to fit everyone, and so not really fitting anyone. Twitter is an interesting model for Grumet's vision of curriculum: a site where students can enter into texts, modify them, analyze them, evaluate their relations to them. Yet, I failed to use Twitter as an opportunity to invite my students into difficult conversations, revealing how completely I've inherited a curricular tradition bound by abstract and impersonal ethics—an ethics that, Grumet argues, holds us apart from one another.

In her chapter on teaching other people's children, Grumet (1988) anticipates a fear that structures the impersonal curriculum and that is common among teacher candidates: the fear of the phone call from home, or the fear that a student's parents will indict the teacher for what she has taught. Although I was teaching adults, my worry about traumatizing them by sharing difficult news items is a version of this fear. Particularly as it contrasts with my willingness to be available for my daughter's difficult researches in the world, my worry about exposing the students to social horrors is a fear of stepping out of bounds, of providing curriculum that is too personal and alive for the classroom. This fear belongs to me despite my espousal of Grumet's call for a curriculum that can be dynamic and responsive.

Grumet (1988) argues that teachers' fears of parents are rooted in the historical construction of school as the child's introduction to public life, that is premised on the repudiation of the private, emotional, and domestic scene of the family. Teachers whose curriculum is static and bound by ethics—and therefore abstract and standardized—hope that the ethical design of the curriculum will protect them from parents' anger. Yet, Grumet insists that parents are angry less about the specific content of curricula, and more about the way that curricula are precisely founded on a repudiation of the private and emotional, a repudiation of the parental domain. In this way, the fear of the phone call from home is the return of the repressed.

Understanding pedagogical anxiety as a fear of the return of the repressed evokes Alice Pitt and Deborah Britzman's (2003) theory of difficult knowledge. Pitt and Britzman explain that "difficult knowledge is a concept meant to signify both representations of social traumas in curriculum and the individual's encounters with them in pedagogy" (p. 755). In my story, difficult knowledge is both the online news items representing the trauma of rape culture inherent to higher education for women, and the crisis those stories provoked in my pedagogical relation to the students. Difficulties we encounter in our attempts to represent the traumas of the social world return us to the difficult and internal conditions of our capacity to think. This reminds us of our mothers, for, as I have argued elsewhere, our capacity to think is born in an infantile conflict: we begin to think for ourselves when we can confront that we are individual subjects, separate and independent from the mother (Harrison, 2013, 2014). The trauma to our subjectivity enacted by the original difference from the mother can make us fear difference: the different others we meet in our classrooms, the different families from which they come, and the differences in their interpretations of the world from our own. To defend against the maternal loss that lurks at the origin of thinking, we banish our mothers from the classroom, the curriculum, the official pedagogical relation. But, as we see from my pedagogical memoir, read through the lens of Grumet (1988), the curriculum we construct to hold the intimate maternal relation at bay cannot do justice to our encounters with difficult knowledge.

In addition to difficult knowledge as social trauma and the unconscious or internal pedagogical crisis to which that trauma gives rise, Pitt and Britzman (2003) offer a third explanation for difficult knowledge: "For pedagogical theorists, 'difficult knowledge' also signifies the problem of learning from social breakdowns" (p. 756). At stake in this description of difficult knowledge is the breakdown that happens at the limits of the traumatic curriculum and our pedagogical attempts to address it: the breakdown *is* the learning. After all, it was the breakdown that led me to grapple with a particular pedagogical affect—that vague sense of dissatisfaction I described—and encouraged me to think about, and begin to reconceive, my work and role as an instructor.

Grumet (1988) and Pitt and Britzman (2003) each describe various crises in education: crises brought about by the detachment of the curriculum and by the breakdown that occurs between the representation of the traumatic social event and the impossibility of adequately teaching about it. For Hannah Arendt (1993), the crisis in education is an effect of the teacher's failure to rise to her authority.

Arendt argues that since the learner enters as a new subject in an old world, the teacher must usher the learner in with care:

> [I]nsofar as he is new, care must be taken that this new thing comes to fruition in relation to the world as it is.... [The] educators here stand in relation to the young as representatives of a world for which they must assume responsibility although they themselves did not make it, and even though they may, secretly or openly, wish it were other than it is. (p. 189)

In teaching what Grumet (1988) calls "the common culture," a culture divorced from the specific, we don't teach a culture in which students actually live and so we can't help them think about and better understand the world they know, a world where difficult knowledge exists. By avoiding those traumatic stories of rape culture, I did not protect the students from anything. I simply failed to take responsibility for the world as it is.

Arendt (1993) provokes me to consider that my responsibility as a pedagogical role model may be at stake in my story. The students were not new to the world in the same way my baby daughter was, but they were new to the profession of teaching. What if the students had sought my tutorial not only because of a shared interest in the curricular content I outlined but specifically because of their attraction to my purported pedagogy inherent to the story about deciding to save the newspaper for my daughter? Perhaps they expected not only that I would help them grapple with their own difficult knowledge, but that in doing so I would demonstrate how they could do the same for their students.

Just as Arendt (1993) calls on the educator to nurture the student's fruition, Grumet (1988) advocates care as the key to the teacher's ability to take responsibility for the newness of her students in the face of the sometimes traumatic social world. Like the curriculum she hopes we will cultivate, Grumet argues that care is dynamic and, importantly, that the "concept of care substitutes relation for rules" (p. 177). Moreover, Grumet suggests that if we normalize a practice of care in education, as opposed to the detachment of institutionalized rules, then care promises to reduce injustice, hate, and violence in this world, for which we must take responsibility. Engaging students' difficult knowledge—while also, with Pitt and Britzman (2003), acknowledging the inevitability of breakdown between my curricular and pedagogical interpretations and theirs—I will ultimately be engaging them in a more caring and less detached relation, meeting them in the world as it is. Taking seriously that responsibility will not only make me a more effective— and affective—teacher, but may also offer students a model for their developing pedagogies. And that possibility offers me its own great reassurance: for when the students I instruct meet other people's children in *their* classrooms, one of those children will be my daughter.

REFERENCES

Arendt, H. (1993). *Between past and future: Eight exercises in political thought.* New York, NY: Penguin Books.

Grumet, M. R. (1988). *Bitter milk: Women and teaching.* Amherst, MA: The University of Massachusetts Press.

Harrison, M. J. (2013). Violence, silence and storytelling: The dilemma of matricide in women's memoirs. *Changing English, 20*(3), 306–316.

Harrison, M. J. (2014). *Thinking through the (m)other: Reading women's memoirs of learning* (Unpublished doctoral dissertation). York University, Toronto, Ontario.

Pitt, A. J. (2003). *The play of the personal: Psychoanalytic narratives of feminist education.* New York, NY: Peter Lang.

Pitt, A., & Britzman, D. (2003). Speculations on qualities of difficult knowledge in teaching and learning: An experiment in psychoanalytic research. *International Journal of Qualitative Studies in Education, 16*, 755–776.

C5

Kizuna: Life as Art

Yoriko Gillard

My Liminal Place[1]

Standing quietly at the shore of Kesennuma,[2] *my mind floats above the Pacific Ocean reflecting my thoughts; sadness, hopes and obligations. The water keeps changing its appearances without my intention, as does my mind in my head. The silence of cold water makes me feel my cold fingers holding the camera steadily to capture my thoughts.*

A string of thoughts goes in every direction.

Living on the other side of the Pacific Ocean, Vancouver, takes me back to where I came from in my mind. Now, I am handed a blank note to fill in at the shore of Kesennuma. What should I fill in the note is still unknown yet my words move in every direction to catch my thoughts behind my eyelids.

Staring at the water of the Pacific Ocean makes my head numb. Cold ... very cold.... One after the other, waves come and go without my intention, as does the anxiety in my heart. Blood streams rushing to my heart, eyelids and hands closed tightly. I say in silence: "Please, not again."

I cry on both sides of the Pacific Ocean.

THE 3.11 DISASTER, TRAUMA, AND 心のケア (KOKORO NO KEA): TRUST

On March 11, 2011, an earthquake with a magnitude of 9.0 hit the Tohoku region of Japan. The event is now known as 3.11, the Great East Japan Earthquake. The 3.11 earthquake, followed by a tsunami (estimated at 37.9 metres at its highest point), also caused the Fukushima Daiichi Nuclear Power Plant radiation accident (Nagamatsu, Maekawa, Ujike, Hashimoto, & Fuke, 2011). Many people who experienced this event are still suffering emotionally from post-traumatic stress (Ministry of Health, Labour and Welfare, 2012).

I worry about people who have been removed from their hometown where their hearts belong and their spirits are rooted. I can easily imagine how tired are many of the Tohoku victims who are still living in temporary housing or with friends or relatives. The tsunami is not over for them. Researchers claim that people who experience difficulty sharing their childhood traumatic experiences with others over a period of time can develop disease-related health problems later in their lives (Pennebaker & Beall, 1986). The need for support of the victims' mental health is essential. It is important to have a long-term program supporting people in most need in the affected areas in Tohoku (Takeda, 2011). It is easier to observe the healing of disaster victims who suffered physically; the mental health of Tohoku victims is challenging to observe. Researchers are already aware that victims' mental health is an important issue to contend with. As a result, psychiatric services are absolutely essential for a longer term than the medical services for physical diseases (Takeda, 2011). While different types of doctors are searching for the best possible way to help the Tohoku victims, there are also many artists and educators who have been supporting the victims. These people often understand the value of community and maintaining connections between people.

On January 17, 1995, Kobe, Japan, was hit by an earthquake (magnitude 7.3; The Great Hanshin-Awaji Earthquake/Kobe Earthquake) that was considered the worst disaster in Japan since the end of World War II and killed 4,571 people (see "The Great Hanshin-Awaji Earthquake Statistics and Restoration Progress," 2012, p. 1). This report informs us that

> [Kobe] city's residents also suffered a great degree of indirect damage. The long period of residence in evacuee shelters caused mental fatigue, especially in children, disabled persons, and the elderly. The educational function of schools decreased due to shortened hours and the use of school facilities for shelters and temporary housing. (p. 3)

Following the Kobe earthquake, volunteer psychology graduate students from a nearby private university visited primary schools to ask the children to draw pictures as a therapeutic intervention in an effort to help the children express their thoughts and feelings about the disaster. This is called "心のケア: *Kokoro no Kea*" in Japanese, which when similarly translated into English means "care for the heart." This style of treatment became one of the main symbols of the earthquake response (Breslau, 2000). *Kokoro no Kea* was also witnessed often after the 3.11 at community events that included art exhibitions.

In the case of the Kobe disaster, living in tightly bonded communities demonstrated that social connection helped life-recovery of disaster victims, academic researchers, and local government (Sakamoto & Yamori, 2009). There are fundamental differences between the Kobe and Tohoku incidents. Kobe, a large city, was the most affected area of the earthquake in 1995. At that time, the Japanese economy was fairly strong. For the 3.11 earthquake, the Japanese economic downturn affected the mental health of the Tohoku victims (Procter & Crowley, 2011), many from fishing villages and offshore rural areas, including small islands where people were unable to receive immediate support due to inaccessibility. Moreover, this was a total horror for children and youth who could not go back to meet their friends in their school, were far from their home, or could not try to find information about their missing family members who were also suffering from their own trauma of not knowing what had happened to their loved ones. Nicholas Procter and Timothy Crowley (2011) explain that since children and young people of school age have a close connection to their school communities, school becomes a potential place for psychological support, resilience building, and emotional stability to help their well-being. This report reminds us that education and places that offer learning opportunities give people comfort and "community trust."

"ART" AS REFLECTIVE-SELF

Immediately after 3.11, I was in a deep depression and worried about Tohoku, Japan. I was a visual-arts student at the University of British Columbia in Vancouver when I heard the tragic news. I was in shock and felt sick to my stomach. I could not focus on my academic duties. I was contemplating the answers to my questions, "What am I doing in Canada now ... what can I do?" Then, I received an email from Linda Ohama, a Japanese Canadian filmmaker, my friend and mentor, who asked many of us to come together as a community of inquirers at Tonari Gumi, the Japanese Community Volunteers Association. A room full of people gathered immediately to put their ideas and concerns together. There were interdisciplinary communities of artists, entrepreneurs, government officials, students, and educators. We were there with the same question: What can we do for Tohoku, Japan?

As many people in the world were in disbelief and started to support Japan, we could also act fast to support Japan. We were a community of trust. "We trust others because we have something important in common; co-nationals meeting in foreign countries often extend and reciprocate trust simply by the virtue of finding themselves together as outsiders in a foreign country" (Lenard, 2012, p. 15).

We were all in tears together. I was able to connect with many people in the Japanese Canadian community in Vancouver right after 3.11. In a couple of days, many of us gathered and formed a society: the BC-Japan Earthquake Relief Fund. We organized countless fundraising events and exchanged our sincere feelings about Japan. Through this organization, I focused on talking with many people. Lenard (2012) states that "trust isn't only a feature of intimate, interpersonal relations; it is also a feature of our social and political lives" (p. 16).

In 2013, I visited Tohoku and tried to understand the situation. I wanted to see the situation for myself rather than just watching the news on TV in Canada. After the visit, I realized that I could not do anything but listen to victims' stories first-hand. I was emotional and lost. It felt wrong to be there and I felt helpless. A lady I met at Kesennuma, Tohoku, was sincere and appreciative to know that I came to visit from Canada even though my family is in Gifu, far from Tohoku. She was especially thankful that people had not forgotten about them and their hardships. Her wisdom showed in her speech and I listened carefully to her stories.

I was deeply depressed after this experience. I became more aware of my responsibility and found deeper meaning in my creative practice. This is a reflection of the reciprocal relationship I formed with the Tohoku people. Margaret Foddy and Toshio Yamagishi (2009) explain that we seek to understand others' identities and their trustworthiness by gathering information of others through our interaction and observation of strangers' uncertain behaviour. To me, trust needs to be studied during a specific time, at a specific place, and about specific people in order to come to a deeper understanding. "Many theoretical discussions [are] the role of trust in society ... but empirical investigations that clarified the specific role trust played in varied social settings were less numerous" (Levi, Hardin, & Cook, 2009, p. xi). I am one of many people who experienced indirect trauma from the 3.11 incident. I am still affected by this event. I believe this specific situation is worth examining and sharing with other people for future research. Levi et al. (2009)

Yoriko Gillard (2013). *Kizuna (1)*. Digital photograph

suggest that we as researchers should pay attention to various conditions and situations of the relationship of trust that are not clear.

Kizuna: Bond (2013). Art-based Research Process
March 11, 2011

I am shocked, hurt, and sad.
I reflect on my feelings for Tohoku.
At school, home, wherever my heart takes over my mind.
I know my body is in Canada.
But my mind is in Japan.
Time passes so quickly ...
Now, I am lonely.
I talk with many of you ... yes, you.
You hug me, cry with me, silently together.
We all rush to ride the airplane to solve our mind–body problem.
I start listening to my mind ...
Silence.

I look down on the Pacific Ocean from above where sun shines in my eyes.
There is no voice inside me.

I am arriving in the land of the rising sun.
I see the flag blowing in the air of new life.
A season of cherry blossoms.
"Oh, I love it!"
I scream.

The cherry blossoms have been the best supporters in our depression.
Probably ...
For their colour and appearance.
How they dance and sing together.
Our symbol.
I am happy.
I don't know why I am crying now ...

My first visit to Tohoku.
After arriving, I listen.
And listen more.
My camera stays in my bag for a long time.
But my eyes are wide open, so are my ears.
I say, "Oh, I am glad to hear and feel you!" without opening my mouth.
I feel all my senses are alive finally.

I visit a Mino Washi craftsman in Gifu.
He is a gentle master artist.
He does not show even a millimetre of his status.
His wise presence and sincere personality welcome me.

He talks and I listen.
I talk and he listens.
There is a slow and beautiful time in between us concerning Tohoku.
The room is cold.
He shows and explains.
Water splashes.
He gathers and pounds.
He releases and forms.
I watch and watch.

Precious Japanese paper looks soft and perfect with his care.
"Oh, how beautiful!"
I scream.

The paper travels back with me to Canada.
On the way home, I reflect about the people I met.
Darkness moving outside the plane window.
My mood inside alive with anxiety.
I am sad.
Sad to see the treasure I brought back from Japan, including Mino Washi.

I cut it.
I cut the Mino Washi *into pieces.*
I am crying ...
Each time I cut, I cry more.
The perfectly created Mino Washi *becomes random pieces on my floor.*
They don't know where they belong anymore.
There is a voice.
"You know where we belong."
I pick one by one and tie them into knots.
The last piece of the cut Washi *jumps into my hands to be connected with the others.*
They all form one long string.
My Kizuna *sculpture becomes alive.*

I travel to Steveston with the sculpture.
It is a gloomy day.
Cold, just like Kesennuma.
I stand at the edge of the Pacific Ocean for a long time.
I don't cry.
I look far away to where the grey fades into the endless horizon.
Huge driftwood lying still, don't know why he is there to welcome me.
I feel safe beside him.
I decide.

The sculpture is in my hands, secure.
My knots look organically beautiful.
I say gently, "Ok, ... don't worry ... I am holding you all."
I slowly immerse my knots in the Pacific Ocean.
My hands feel gravity getting stronger every second.

"Oh, no! No, no ... no."
I scream.

Soon my sculpture is soaked.
The sculpture is so heavy and helpless.
I pull all of the knots back slowly.

I rest them on the driftwood.
Drip, drip, drip ...
I sit beside them.
Drip, drip, drip ...
Each of them talks to me.
I listen and they talk.

"Don't you want to take our pictures?"
Here I hear voices again.
I am already documenting my process.
But the process is not in my hands.
It is given.
It is a gift.
I go close to them.
I hear each story; sad, happy, and courageous.

This process is never meant to just create an art project.
This process is meant to heal me and create dialogues with you ...

As my last part of the *Kizuna* ritual, I brought my dried *Kizuna* sculpture to the conference and displayed it with UBC tap water on the balcony of the Peter Wall Institute for Advanced Studies. The sculpture overlooked the Pacific Ocean. It was a beautiful sunny day. On the balcony, I shared my stories and concerns about Tohoku.

I explained to all the participants, "You can interact by pouring the water onto my artwork. *Kizuna* means 'Bond: reciprocal relationship between humans and na-ture.' Please, connect with Tohoku, Japanese culture/spirituality, the Pacific Ocean, Steveston, and the artist." Many people enjoyed standing in front of the artwork, and some people had courage and went right in front of the sculpture and poured water, and a few people stayed away from the sculpture and watched everyone's interaction for a long time. It was beautiful to see how each person interacted in their own way....

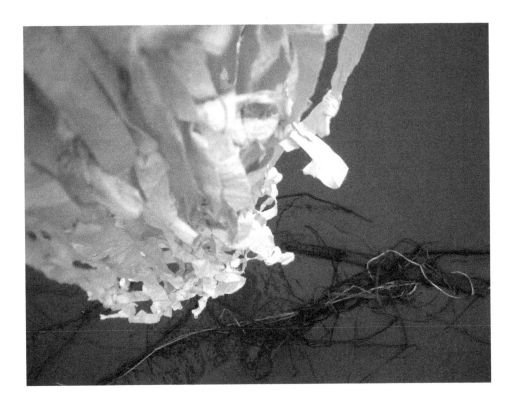

Yoriko Gillard (2013). *Kizuna (2/3)*. Digital photographs

Yoriko Gillard (2013). *Kizuna (4/5)*. Digital photographs

Yoriko Gillard (2013). *Kizuna (6/7)*. Digital photographs

Yoriko Gillard (2013). *Kizuna (8/9)*. Digital photograph

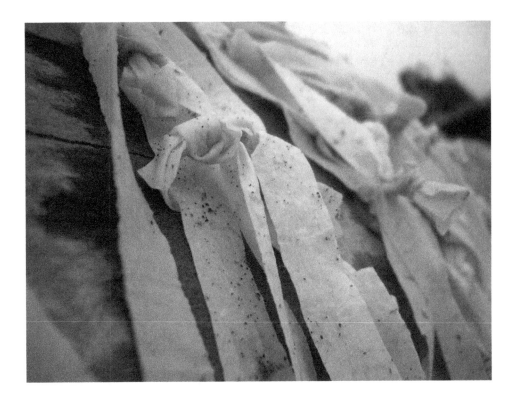

Yoriko Gillard (2013). *Kizuna (10/11)*. Digital photographs

Yoriko Gillard (2013). *Kizuna (12/13)*. Digital photographs

Yoriko Gillard (2013). *Kizuna (14).* Digital photograph

Because life and art are integrally connected, I reflect my past through creating art and writing poetry. I perform and share my feelings in public when it is appropriate. My hope is to connect with people truthfully through my creative acts. Now, my creative research continues to open dialogues with people who care for humanity. I came from the other side of the Pacific Ocean, from Japan, to reside in Vancouver, Canada. It has been over six years now since the tragedy that shocked the world, and the people of Tohoku are still suffering greatly. Many of them are still evacuated, separated from their families and living in temporary housing.

As I think of the lives of people in Tohoku, my mind floats above the Pacific Ocean creatively in the past, present, and future.

NOTES

1. "My Liminal Place" was written in 2013 after visiting Tohoku, Japan.

2. Kesennuma is the city located in Tohoku region of Japan where hundreds of houses and lives were swallowed by a tsunami after the Great East Earthquake on March 11, 2011.

REFERENCES

Breslau, J. (2000). Globalizing disaster trauma: Psychiatry, science, and culture after the Kobe earthquake. *Ethos, 28*(2), 174–197. Available at: www.jstor.org/stable/640685

Foddy, M., & Yamagishi, T. (2009). Groupbased trust. In M. Levi, R. Hardin, & K. S. Cook (Eds.), *Whom can we trust? How groups, networks, and institutions make trust possible* (pp. 17–41). New York, NY: Russell Sage Foundation.

Lenard, P. T. (2012). *Trust, democracy, and multicultural challenges.* University Park, PA: Penn State University Press.

Levi, M., Hardin, R., & Cook, K. S. (2009). Preface. In M. Levi, R. Hardin, & K. S. Cook (Eds.), *Whom can we trust? How groups, networks, and institutions make trust possible* (pp. xi–xii). New York, NY: Russell Sage Foundation.

Ministry of Health, Labour and Welfare, the Government of Japan. (2012). *Response to the Great East Japan Earthquake.* Available at: www.mhlw.go.jp/bunya/kokusaigyomu/asean/2012/dl/Introduction_Dr.Yamauchi.pdf

Nagamatsu, S., Maekawa, T., Ujike, Y., Hashimoto, S., & Fuke, N. (2011). The earthquake and tsunami—observations by Japanese physicians since the 11 March catastrophe. *Critical Care, 15*(3), 167. doi: 10.1186/cc10261

Pennebaker, J. W., & Beall, S. K. (1986). Confronting a traumatic event: Toward an understanding of inhibition and disease. *Journal of Abnormal Psychology, 95*(3), 274–281. Available at: homepage.pst.utexas.edu/HomePage/Class/Psy394V/Pennebaker/Reprints/Beall1986.pdf

Procter, N., & Crowley, T. (2011). A mental health trauma response to the Japanese earthquake and tsunami. *Holistic Nursing Practice, 25*(3), 162–164. doi: 10.1097/HNP.0b013e31821a6955

Sakamoto, M., & Yamori, K. (2009). A study of life recovery and social capital regarding disaster victims—a case study of Indian Ocean tsunami and Central Java earthquake recovery. *Journal of Natural Disaster Science, 31*(2), 49–56. Available at: www.jstage.jst.go.jp/article/jnds/31/2/31_2_49/_pdf

Takeda, M. (2011). Mental health care and East Japan Great Earthquake. *Psychiatry and Clinical Neurosciences, 65*(3), 207–212. doi: 10.1111/j.1440-1819.2011.02220.x

The City of Kobe. (2012). *The Great Hanshin-Awaji Earthquake Statistics and Restoration Progress.* Available at: www.city.kobe.lg.jp/safety/hanshinawaji/revival/promote/january.2012.pdf

INVOCATION

Detention

Elizabeth Yeoman

Postcard: Kenny was a boy I routinely kept in for detention in my first year of teaching. A sweet-faced curly-haired 12-year-old with pale, almost translucent skin, small for his age but very agile, he was utterly unable to sit still or be quiet in a classroom. The principal was still allowed to use the strap then, which shows how long ago this was. He had to have a witness and I dreaded being called in for that task. I think I would have been brave enough to refuse as I was so strongly opposed to corporal punishment, but in the end it never happened. It was the end of the era of strapping kids. Instead, detention was the main means of "classroom management." Even then, inexperienced though I was, I could see that it didn't work very well either. Not only was it not effective, it was actually counter-productive since the students who were most likely to get detention were often the ones who most desperately needed to be outside working off energy every chance they got.

One winter afternoon, after a dreary episode of marking and keeping an eye on Kenny, I told him he could go, and then took pity on him and offered to drive him home (another detail that tells you this was a long time ago—I don't think teachers can do that anymore). As we drove along the shore of the frozen Kennebecasis, he asked me to drop him off at his ice-fishing shack instead of taking him home. So I did. I will never forget watching him, like a freed bird flying across the snow-covered river. And I still regret the times I kept children like Kenny in for detention.

C6

Haunted by Real Life: Art, Fashion, and the Hungering Body

Alyson Hoy

In June 2014 the Hudson's Bay Company pulled a controversial T-shirt from its stores after a backlash ensued on social media. The shirt depicts a mock-up of a zero-calorie nutrition label with the words "Nothing tastes as good as skinny feels," a quote made popular in the press a number of years ago by British supermodel Kate Moss and considered by some to promote eating disorders.

In a public statement The Bay apologized for offending its customers, saying that while they respect the designer's art, due to the overwhelming response and sensitivity of the matter, the T-shirt was being removed from stores immediately. In wake of the controversy, designer Christopher Lee Sauvé denied allegations that the shirt celebrates the severity of eating disorders. Rather, he explained that as an artist he got his start by mocking the fashion industry and the T-shirt design is simply a continuation of that same artistic vision (Forani, 2014).

As someone who lives and breathes art and fashion and struggles simultaneously with eating disorders, my response to the T-shirt controversy has been conflicted. On the one hand I cannot help but recognize the detrimental effect the fashion industry's promotion of extreme thinness as *the* standard of beauty seems to have had on many consumers, both female and male. Eating disorders proliferate in North America and there can be little doubt that fashion images, in their sheer vastness and ubiquity, reinforce a message that ties a slender physical appearance to a sense of self-worth. As experts observe, many eating disorder sufferers already struggle with an unstable sense of self and a loss of identity and look to media images for messages about and confirmation of who they are (MacSween, 1993).

And yet, there is nothing quite so oversimplified and banal perhaps as the arguments that proliferate culturally, which draw a direct cause-and-effect relationship between the media and eating disorders as well as body-image disturbance in young women. In this view, the consumer does not exercise any kind of individual agency whereby, for example, she is imagined as actively participating in constructing and creating different meanings and messages around the image. Rather, she is seen as a passive, uncritical recipient who simply receives such images, as though she were an empty vessel to be filled.

"Nothing tastes as good as skinny feels." For the identity-less, voiceless anorexic non-agent who is quite literally consumed by dominant cultural scripts, the message seems clear. In a society where we have learned that our greatest social capital and source of self-worth as women lie in our bodily appearance, we must be thin at all costs. We must look to media images of thinness inspired by Kate Moss not merely as images to emulate, but as validation of who we are.

There is no denying that fashion imagery haunts and is haunted by the notion of the starving body. In postmodernity the image of the starving woman has found focus in the figure of "the anorexic," which has been continually re-constituted as a spectacle to be exposed to the public gaze. Images of emaciated female bodies as fashion models are routinely positioned as objects for others to gaze on. Anorexia is, in this sense, "sold." Skeletal to the point of shocking, the disease in itself becomes the brand. Within this context the consumer buys the clothing in the same moment that she purchases an idealized and feminized image of thinness, thus foretelling her own future corporeal consumption, her potential *to become* anorexic.

Yet, surely it borders on the realm of the absurd to suggest that a fashion advertisement or T-shirt, as it were, "causes" eating disorders. The very idea that a female spectator/consumer, however susceptible she is imagined to be, could embark on a course of near lethal self-starvation simply because of media images of thinness is appallingly stigmatizing and reductionist since it positions women as narcissistic and basically fatuous—what theorist Stuart Hall (1981) has famously called "cultural dopes."

Further, and more concerning, is the way in which this oversimplification obscures the reality that anorexia is a very serious condition and a mental illness, that people (mostly women) do in fact die from it. The belief that anorexia is a diet "taken to the extreme" seems to relegate probable cause to a pathological preoccupation with surface appearances while foreclosing thoughtful consideration of the kinds of psychical disturbances that are undeniably present with the disease. Personal vanity is a terrifically uncomplicated and frankly ignorant answer to questions about what causes anorexia. To that point, it does not even begin to account for the significance of voluntary self-starvation, the meanings of hunger as a per-petual mode of being, and the kinds of refusals it performs. I want to know, *what does the hunger mean?*

The position that ascribes a causative power to images of thinness by main-taining that an over-identification with such images leads to anorexia needs to be investigated not because it will offer definitive answers or bring us closer to the "truth," but because such a process, in its very undertaking, will require our grap-pling with the ever-persistent problematic of the relationship of representation to "reality." How do we understand and how might we begin to explain our desire to make reality claims about a representation? Why do we continue to deny the constructedness of the image and our own implication in the very spectacles we behold? Why, with respect to the T-shirt, were consumers seemingly so adamant in their refusal of the designer's claim that the public creates the message?

To begin to extend understandings of anorexia in ways that diverge from the commonplace notion that the "pathology" of disordered eating is triggered by cultural forces that are mostly external to the psyche requires thinking about anorexia as func-tioning beyond what it resembles and represents. The idea that there is an embodied and felt dimension of anorexia, that quite apart from the *appearance* of anorexia, there is first and foremost a reality of *being* anorexic, is evinced by the phrase "Nothing tastes as good as skinny feels," and yet, it is consistently overlooked.

It bears mentioning that the term *anorexia nervosa*, coined in the 1870s, literally denotes a neurotic loss of appetite (Brumberg, 1989). But in fact, as contemporary psychotherapists suggest (Costin, 2007), far from losing our appetites, anorexics constantly live with hunger. Speaking from my own experience, anorexic hunger is laden with various confusing and conflicting meanings that, at once, involve painful difficulties and suffering as well as a source of intense pleasure and enjoy-ment. While sick, despite the fact that I experienced constant pain and sadness, I can recall no single greater feeling than the superhuman conquering of will that led me to steadfastly deny and *not feel* my body's hunger as well as to consistently refuse food that I knew I desperately needed.

Despite the pain, I was heroic in my battle against my appetite. With time, I learned to step outside of myself and transcend my body's most basic wants and desires. I learned to take pleasure in the clean and empty feeling that anorexia gave me, and I longed for the sharp edginess and manic, buzzing hum of hunger. Like many anorexics, I devised intricate rituals around my self-inflicted hunger, which functioned paradoxically, keeping me safe and settled in the monotony of my everyday routine and diverting my attention away from the very extraordinary thing that I was accomplishing: deliberately and energetically risking my own life.

On days when I felt weak and unable to muster my resolve to stay hungry, however, I had help. "Nothing tastes as good as skinny feels," written on a piece of paper with an image of a gaunt-looking Kate Moss imprinted next to it, was my close friend and companion, my mantra and secret rallying cry. In Kate's image I saw empty, androgynous beauty and was mesmerized by it, wanting her body to be my body: the tiny breasts and sharp collarbones, the stick-thin arms and protruding hipbones, the bird-like wrists; I wished for all of it. It didn't matter that I knew the image had been digitally manipulated to make her body appear tinier than it was. I was already on a path. I needed no convincing.

On the pro-anorexia websites where I spent many of my waking hours, the image and phrase circulated constantly and were accompanied by personal anecdotes from community members about how they functioned in their day-to-day life. Some told of attaching the image to the refrigerator door as a warning to self to keep out. Others described how they routinely mobilized it as a form of "thinspiration." In my daily existence, meanwhile, the phrase assumed significance as a reminder that anorexia not only gave me an appearance of extreme thinness and an aesthetic of angularity and androgyny that I coveted, but also provided me with a *feeling*. That feeling was an intensity that I could hardly bear. Excruciating beyond any other form of suffering I had known, it was the queerest, most sadistic pleasure.

Whereas prior to anorexia, I had associated the experience of being in my body with a kind of formlessness and ephemerality, anorexia gave me a feeling of resoluteness and hardness. In a way that still feels difficult to describe, my rigidity and sharpness as an anorexic confirmed for me a sense of finally having a form. It corroborated my existence in the world. At a point in time where I was so slight and skeletal that I was physically failing and fading from view, I somehow, inexplicably, also felt strong and driven and focused, unyielding in my control and unwilling to relinquish it. I was proud of my self-discipline and the way that I was ruling my body, but pride was a slippery sensation and so hard to hold on to.

In the end, I could not escape the self-loathing. No matter what I said to the contrary or how deeply I thought I believed it, anorexia was too profound a form of antagonism toward body and self. It was ruthless, filled with so much contempt, shame, sorrow, and fear. How did "skinny" feel? It felt like I was mercilessly waging war on myself. It felt like I was a torturer brandishing a scalpel, turning the weapon against my body and etching my own despair and bad feeling onto my skin. As deep as I could cut, I wanted to cut deeper, to the bone.

I think it is important to say, however obvious it might seem, that when it comes to eating disorders, far too much emphasis is placed on what the eye believes it can see. To an undereducated public, a very thin appearance is often quickly and incorrectly interpreted as being indicative of an eating disorder. But the truth is that many individuals who suffer from eating disorders appear at an average or even an above-average weight. Outward physical appearance, particularly one's shape and body size, reveals little about what a person is experiencing on the inside, what their state of mind is, or how and with what issues they are struggling.

While it is true that a key diagnostic criterion for anorexia is the "refusal to maintain body weight at or above a minimally normal weight for age and height" (Dziegielewski, 2014, p. 185), it is also the case that weight and physical appearance vary and fluctuate within individuals, especially since other eating disorders, like bulimia, tend to coexist with anorexia. Practically speaking, one can only endure starvation for so long before other compensatory strategies must kick in. Typically it is the weight regained through cycles of bingeing and purging that keeps anorexia in play and makes it so recalcitrant.

Hunger, like nothing else, has teeth. With anorexia, however, it is not just a literal, physical hunger that takes hold and threatens to tear you apart but hunger writ large, hunger that is unnameable because it is so deep and vast and empty, hunger that overwhelms because it exceeds the organizing capacities of language. Being anorexic, I starve not because I want to be in control or because I desperately desire to be skinny or look like Kate Moss but *because I desire*. I starve to make manifest my hunger and vulnerability. I starve because after a time feeling hungry becomes my body's pulse. It is the thing that lets me know I am still alive.

Debra Ferreday (2011) argues that in Western culture the anorexic body "traditionally embodies that which cannot be represented.... It is abjected; pushed to the margins" (p. 3). Within the cultural imagination, the "size zero" models of the fashion runway are ghostly figures, "haunted by [their] own inevitable death" (p. 6). Walking skeletons that are thin to the point of barely existing, their presence is monstrous and, thus, hyper-visible, with bones jutting through skin.

At the same time, they are continually under the threat of erasure. As Ferreday (2011) notes, there has long been speculation from insiders of the fashion industry that the "too-skinny" female body has been purposely erased by designers who desire their clothes to drape as though framing a coat hanger and not a real body. "There is an age-old theory that male fashion designers design clothes for ultra-skinny women because they are secretly thinking about men" (p. 18). Yet, as much as the too-thin body wishes to get beyond the limits of flesh and is even made to disappear, it is nevertheless not absent, for its bones are constantly on display. Those bones are "the object of the gaze but also simultaneously a challenge, since they excite revulsion as well as desire" (Ferreday, 2011, p. 19).

It is this tension between the hyper-visibility and the invisibility of extreme thinness—what many viewers do not know but can only *assume* is anorexia—that Sauvé cleverly exploits in his clothing design. For there, surprisingly, vanished is the notorious image of wafer-thin Kate Moss, whose hollowed eyes, sunken cheeks, and protruding bones are literally a fashion spectacle, one that, in the mid-1990s, became the face of the controversial "heroin chic" advertising campaign of designer Calvin Klein. In her place instead is an outline of a box filled with nothing, only empty numerical values. What is there is a kind of sardonic representation of a nutrition label for a food that cannot possibly exist, its caloric content being "zero." To read even the first part of the phrase—"nothing tastes"—next to this image is, thus, to throw into stark relief the virtual nonsense that these words convey. What does nothing taste like? And then, more elusively, how does skinny feel?

By opting not to include the spectacle that is essentially inseparable from the phrase, and whose meaning as a representation has largely become entangled with the "reality" of being anorexic, due in part to its adoption and circulation as "thin-spiration" by pro-ana communities, the T-shirt design provokes viewers to confront and challenge their own expectations.

Has the (presumed) anorexic, which the T-shirt seems so naturally to invoke, wasted away and succumbed to her death as so many predicted she would? Or, has she been returned to the realm of the imaginary, cast back into the ghostly presence that she, anyway, always already was? Can her absence reveal this stereotypical image of the anorexic body as a staged performance and construction as opposed to confirming its "real" presence? Can viewers engage with the different image on the T-shirt in less predictable ways and begin to explore alternative interpretive possibilities? High fashion's distorted narratives and idealized skeletal femininity aside, can we accept the possibility that the "body image" for which the anorexic strives might be derived from the sensations of the body rather than from alienating representations of "the body"?

In attempting to explore the embodied experience(s) of being anorexic, I have been inching closer to a thought, not quite about how representation and reality differ from one another, but about the ways in which art relates to the world. While it may be a common opinion that the purpose of art is to provoke reflection and awareness, to shift perspective, and to facilitate critical engagement with the world, my view on the subject veers in a different direction.

The way I see it, art is art. Art is not social justice, and neither is it social work. It is not the job of art to comment on matters pertaining to inequality, difference, human rights, and individual freedom, and it is not its responsibility, in instances where it does expose audiences to uncomfortable material, to present itself with a "trigger warning."

A declaration against eating disorders is not, therefore, something one should expect to see from the fashion industry ever, especially given the glamorous, emaciated supermodels who are known the world over as its face. And yet the public outcry over the T-shirt registers on some level the persistent wish that fashion could still be otherwise and that it might finally take a stand against the suicidal mission of anorexics. But what would that "art" look like? And, how can we be sure, in the enigmatical space of representation, which moves between presence and absence, appearance and invisibility, that the intended message would be "correctly" received?

If, as Sauvé seems to suggest, the public creates the message, in what sense might we possibly conceive of the new image as not repeating, or being susceptible to repeating, the very same problem? As I have endeavoured to explore here, there is the art object and there are the eyes that gaze upon it. In the end, while I cannot say for sure, I suspect that neither one is any more real or less impermanent than the other.

REFERENCES

Brumberg, J. (1989). *Fasting girls: A history of anorexia nervosa*. New York, NY: Random House.

Costin, C. (2007). *The eating disorder sourcebook: A comprehensive guide to the causes, treatments, and prevention of eating disorders*. New York, NY: McGraw-Hill.

Dziegielewski, S. (2014). *DSM-IV-TR in action* (2nd ed.). Hoboken, NJ: John Wiley & Sons.

Ferreday, D. (2011). Haunted bodies: Visual cultures of anorexia and size zero. *Borderlands*, *10*(2), 1–22.

Forani, J. (2014, June 24). Kate Moss "skinny" shirt axed by Hudson's Bay Company. *thestar.com*. Available at: www.thestar.com/news/gta/2014/06/24/kate_moss_skinny_shirt_axed_by_hudsons_bay_company.html

Hall, S. (1981). Notes on deconstructing the popular. In R. Samuel (Ed.), *People's history and socialist theory* (History Workshop series). London, England: Routledge & Kegan Paul.

MacSween, M. (1993). *Anorexic bodies: A feminist and sociological perspective*. London, England: Routledge.

C7

Dadaab Refugee Camp and the Story of School

Karen Meyer, Cynthia Nicol, Muhammad Hassan, Ahmed Hussein, Mohamed Bulle, Ali Hussein, Samson Nashon, Abdikhafar Hirsi Ali, Mohamud Olow, and Siyad Maalim

INTRODUCTION

The flight from Nairobi to Dadaab is relatively short. Heading east across Kenya, the landscape changes dramatically from subtropical to desert climate, from a capital city of over three million to the scattering of villages. Even more striking out the window is the abrupt sprawl of Dadaab refugee camps, spanning 50 square kilometres in red sand and currently home to over 350,000 people. From above, the congestion of modest makeshift structures and tent dwellings on the outskirts make Dadaab look more city than camp. Due to its long-term encampment situation since 1991, many say that it is more like prison than city for the displaced people who fled their homelands due to civil war and drought.

Windows to a Place

Two of us step off the UN plane into sand, red, resilient, but soft and thick enough to hold footprints. NGO greetings and official white vehicles are waiting for passengers next to the asphalt runway. The drivers know their vehicles intimately, following ruts pressed in the sand, proceeding full tilt to security checkpoints and NGO compounds around the complex of camps. Here again, the scenes from window seats in Hussein's UN vehicle are familiar but still foreign to us: white goats and unhitched donkeys; plastic litter; a wooden cart loaded down with thin bare branches, the boy in the driver seat commanding the donkey, his branches destined for structures and cooking fire; another UN vehicle passing from the other direction, kicking up sand that shrouds a woman walking, wrapped in black fabric and balancing a white container on her head; a market with modest metal-and-wood structures, cloth canopies, colourful fabrics hanging in clothesline fashion. The movement around, inside, and between the five camps, lays down dusty roads in the red sand. (Personal narrative by one of the authors.)

Displacement

Following on the heels of civil war in Somalia, as many as a million people fled its borders and 300,000 more died from war-triggered famine (Lewis, 2002). By 1991, Mogadishu, the central government, and the country's entire infrastructure had collapsed wherein schools, training facilities, and universities became casualties of war (Abdi, 1998). This tragic and urgent displacement of people seeking safe refuge led to the United Nations High Commissioner for Refugees (UNHCR), with the Kenyan government, establishing the first Dadaab refugee camps in Kenya, near the Somali border. Between October 1991 and June 1992 the UNHCR constructed three camps for 90,000 people.

Meanwhile international military and humanitarian efforts in Somalia were failing. By 1997, with no evidence of peace within Somalia, the Kenyan-Somali border was closed. However, refugees continued to arrive across the Kenyan border over the next decades, due to continued conflict and life-threatening drought. Dadaab wasn't meant to be so long term, or asylum for the overwhelming number of displaced people.

Despite two generations now born in Dadaab, the UNHCR still provides essential needs and life-sustaining support, and coordinates the camps' dozens of international NGO agencies and operational partners. As a consequence, Dadaab still functions inside "temporary" conditions. Resulting dependency on aid and limited, low-paying "incentive" jobs with agencies make life an unsettling, prescribed, yet impermanent existence. As if a place, home for the past 25 years, could be anything but enduring.

A Safer Place
Rewind to 2002. I'm 12 years old, fourth child of nine. Things have been deteriorating in Somalia my whole life. Daily shootings. Homicides everywhere. Ten-year-old soldiers carrying guns. It's hard for my parents to make ends meet. They fear we might get involved in undesirable activities. Warlords took my father's car. Now it's their military vehicle. My mother

lost her business—looted. She says we should go to the refugee camp in Kenya. A safer place. A chance at education. No civil war.

We board a convoy of jeeps and trucks. White with blue letters. UNHCR. Families start a two-day journey to Dadaab Refugee Camp. Makes me a refugee. Things are tough. But the peace overshadows adjustment after adjustment. No gunshots. My parents are comfortable with us playing with friends, not like in Somalia. I adapt to refugee life. Make new friends. I start school. Sometimes I go to school hungry. I learn English. Fall in love with football. My parents convince me it's a short-time struggle.

It takes 10 years. I finish primary and secondary school. Become a teacher in the camp. I earn a scholarship. Now I'm studying kinesiology in a first-class university in Canada. (Personal narrative by one of the authors.)

THE CALL TO EDUCATION

In 1993, UNHCR and relief agency CARE Kenya organized children of Dadaab into informal primary education, with no physical structures and UNESCO/ Somali curriculum. By 1996 some vocational secondary schools started. At that time, discussion began around a formal curriculum among the parent-teacher association (PTA), CARE Kenya, and UNHCR. A year later, debate ended with the decision to use the Kenyan National Curriculum, which consists of eight years of primary education and four years of secondary education, taught in English. The curriculum is exam oriented: the Kenyan Certificate for Primary Education (KCPE) and the Kenyan Certificate for Secondary Education (KCSE). Performance on the primary exam determines whether or not a child will secure a place in secondary school. Likewise, how a student performs on the KCSE determines the small number of university scholarship possibilities. The class of 2003 had the first secondary students to write the KCSE. Currently, there are 23 primary schools and seven secondary schools in Dadaab camps, which accommodate less than half the eligible school-age children, leaving 100,000 children out of school (UNHCR, 2014).

Buying Pencils

Sunrise in Dadaab is quite majestic. The morning sun is just peeking out, rays shining all over the shanties, forming morning shadows. It's time for children to go to school, for adults to take the goats out for their daylong rearing. I sit outside with my father. We take tea together and talk about my studies in Canada. It's been five years since I was last home to Dadaab.

I notice my four nieces coming through the gate and exchange pleasantries with my sister. My family lives near the primary school. Fatima, the youngest among the girls, lost her pencil. She asks for a pencil to write, and I take the girls to the shop on the edge of the blocks to buy them all pencils.

I remember my time as a primary pupil in the camp, and buying pencils. I remember the day I bought a pencil with my friend Ahmed Nasir. It was black with red stripes and cost us eight shillings. Each of us contributed four. In class, I wrote faster than Ahmed and could keep up with the teacher while he wrote on the blackboard. Every time the teacher made a mistake and rubbed out what he wrote, I erased the page in my notebook with the rubber at the back of the pencil. I gave the pencil to Ahmed Nasir to write his part while the teacher explained the writing on the board. It was more important to get the notes than listen to the explanation.

We later came up with the idea to break the pencil into two, sharpen it on both ends, and share the pencil's small rubber patch at the back. (Personal narrative by one of the authors.)

"We became the teachers of our own education"

The beginning and formidable task toward formal education in Dadaab was determining appropriate grade levels of the children. In 1997, only 10 students qualified for Grade 8 and writing the KCPE. Three years later, with many more children qualifying for secondary school, the UNHCR established the first secondary school and later two more secondary schools, one in each of the existing camps. Still, not all students who qualified for secondary school could be accommodated. Given the low possibility of graduating secondary school, in 2008 communities of parents demonstrated their agency and perseverance by establishing three additional community secondary schools, initially housed in primary classrooms. "They contributed their money by selling their [food] rations" (Marangu Njogu, NGO Director of Secondary Education, personal interview, November 2015).

The UNHCR hires teachers from within the camps. Local teachers play a critical role at the forefront of community efforts by reinforcing a community perspective that values education, social cohesion, and the importance of studying hard (Kirk & Winthrop, 2007). This means, however, that local teachers have no training; most have only recently completed their secondary education in the camp. The lack of teaching experience, large class sizes, exam-focused curriculum, and shortage of resources contribute to following lecture-dictation methods of teaching. One new teacher, fresh out of a Dadaaab camp secondary school, figuratively described his first day of teaching: "I looked like a lost goat in the jungle in the middle of a moonless night."

Distances (Found Poem)

Osman Abdullahi
boy child, born and raised
in the desert camp, refugee

dreams he will finish school
go home to Somali roots
serve his people with knowledge.

Dreams drive his distance
school days walking
in dust-bearing wind where

rowdy motorcycles
kick up sand scorched
footprints trapped, to and fro.

With child Fatima Noor
trekked long across borders
to the desert camp, refugee.

Now in darkness before prayer
she cooks her son's canjera,
subag, shai, and once more

the teacher

Osman Abdullahi walks daybreak
to school, white shirt spotless
navy blue trousers immaculate.

A curriculum: Shakespeare in refuge

AHMED *Form 4 student, storyteller*
JOHN (Mwalimu) *literature teacher, Hagadera Camp*
ABDI *Form 4 student, big fan of Shylock character in* The Merchant of Venice
HASSAN *Form 4 student who likes to make jokes in class*
SHYLOCK *moneylender character in* The Merchant of Venice

ACT I

Scene I

Classroom with tin roof

Ahmed [aside]: I remember the long journey of school almost ending. Today's the last day of Form 4 literature class. We need to finish reading *The Merchant of Venice* for the final exam in a couple of weeks. That's why there are big smiles and excitement on everyone's face.

John [excited, his guttural voice shaking the roof of the classroom]: Students, attention! Tomorrow I will bring a TV and DVD of *The Merchant of Venice*. We'll watch the whole play.

Abdi: Mwalimu, are we going to see Shylock? He's my favourite!

Hassan: No, dude, they're just actors, not the real characters. [Hassan and other students in the class laugh.]

Scene II

Next day, school grounds

Ahmed [aside]: It's a glorious afternoon, except for the scorching sun that hits the hot sandy ground. Students here are gathered under the shade to watch the play. This TV outside, connected to the long cord, is plugged into the only socket in the school.

Abdi [shouting from the back of the crowd, leaning on the tree]: Waaw! That is Shylock right there, speaking to Bassanio, I can tell. I know all his lines!

Hassan: Like I said, he's just an actor. Well, I think so …

[The play lasts for over an hour.]

Abdi: Can we watch the play again? [Heads nod throughout the crowd.]

John: No, I'm sorry. I promised to get the TV back to the UN compound after class.

Ahmed [aside]: Today is different. John used a teaching style rarely seen in Dadaab. We were watching "the real play being played."

ONGOING CHALLENGES

Establishing and maintaining schools in refugee camps is fraught with ongoing challenges, particularly funding constraints. Even in long-term refugee situations, education becomes ancillary to ongoing emergency services. Across the years, there can be a steady flow of new arrivals due to continual conflict, or other situations, such as drought, made more difficult by chronic insecurity. Any large influx puts added strain on the provision of basic services. In 2011, for example, 161,000 people sought refuge in Dadaab from severe drought in the region; over half were children and youth (Norwegian Refugee Council [NRC], 2012).

In emergency situations, relief agencies often view education as development rather than relief activity (i.e., saving lives). Organizations such as UNICEF and UNESCO, however, present strong arguments for emergency education. Firstly, refugee communities often put education for their children before immediate material needs. Education in emergency situations saves and sustains lives by offering physical, cognitive, and psychosocial protection when delivered in safe, neutral spaces, such as schools; restores routine and gives people hope for the future; serves as a "channel" for meeting other basic humanitarian needs and communicating messages for promoting safety and well-being (UNESCO, 2016).

When education is provided, there are more challenges—difficult school conditions and a large population of children who do not attend. The Norwegian Refugee Council reports such challenges in Dadaab schools as: overcrowded classrooms, scarce curriculum resources, untrained teachers (over 80%), and culture and language differences (NRC, 2012). Reasons for children and youth not attending school include: preference for religious education, inability to afford uniforms and materials, distance and safety getting to school, unfamiliar language, home chores, and low grades that do not meet the requirement for entry to secondary school. World University Service of Canada (WUSC) reports disparity between the challenges of boys and girls going to school, resulting in lower attendance and higher dropout rates for girls (WUSC, 2014).

In spite of the fact that education is the most underfunded sector in humanitarian assistance, advocacy and cooperation among the NGO agencies, the Dadaab community, its teachers, and the students themselves have created success in Dadaab schools. The establishment of community schools is one powerful example. Based on our research and experience, there is another critical and compelling but less known story that leads to student success—the students' own strategies for learning.

Inheritance

We used to share notes and we used to learn together. There's no electricity at night, so we used to go to the school for electricity. Also there's no library, so we used to form discussion groups and share our ideas and thoughts.... Then we help the guys who follow. It's like a train. If a student finished in 2003 and was using a certain method ... it's still being applied by his friend because it is something like an inheritance ... you give back to your friends. And I can say, students have a lot of resources within themselves in the refugee camps. (Personal narrative by one of the authors.)

TEACHER EDUCATION IN A REFUGEE CAMP

Dadaab's evolution of education persists with a groundbreaking project in higher education brought about by a consortium of NGOs and academic institutions in Canada and Kenya. The project seeks to improve the quality and accessibility of education for the large Dadaab camp community. Impetus came from Marangu Njogu, director of the organization responsible for running secondary schools in Dadaab. In 2009, he proposed a vision to the president of a Canadian university to provide teacher education and training for Dadaab teachers. Several interested faculty and administrators visited Dadaab that year. They concluded that a teacher-education program could improve education in the camp, providing children and youth with greater opportunities to complete secondary school and compete for scholarships. Securing large-scale funding and committed partnerships required several years and much patience on the part of an excited Dadaab community. In addition, tuition waivers and curriculum and program approvals through Kenyan and Canadian universities demanded much energy, time, and collaboration.

Both primary certificate and secondary diploma programs in teacher education began in 2014 with practicing teachers in Dadaab. This project would not be possible without the support of Kenyan and Canadian universities and funding from Global Affairs Canada.

Initial Visit to Dadaab

February 2009. We spent two nights in the camps, where the university team met all the stakeholders, including refugee community leaders, students, parents, teachers, [and] Kenyan administrators, as well as those in charge of security. We were interested in improving teaching and learning in Dadaab. The needs were overwhelming. I always thought education was "number one" because when I was growing up in Kenya, especially during the early years of independence, Kenya's first president, Jomo Kenyatta, used to say that the role of the state is to fight three enemies: ignorance, poverty, and disease. That order was very important, as education was the weapon to help us defeat [all] three enemies. To my surprise, I was told in the Dadaab camp that in the order of humanitarian needs, education was "number five" after security, food, health, and shelter. I became emotionally devastated! However, after careful thinking, I realized the list had to do with emergency situations. But, what gave me great hope was when I learned the refugee community had placed education of their children first! They denied themselves food rations to contribute toward construction of the community secondary schools for their children. (Personal narrative by one of the authors.)

Nineteen million people remain under controlled UNHCR care with refugee status hosted in challenging locations worldwide. Half are under the age of 18 (UNHCR, 2014).

REFERENCES

Abdi, A. (1998). Education in Somalia: History, destruction, and calls for reconstruction. *Comparative Education, 34*(3), 327–340.

Kirk, J., & Winthrop, R. (2007). Promoting quality education in refugee contexts: Supporting teacher development in northern Ethiopia. *International Review of Education, 53,* 715–723.

Lewis, I. M. (2002). *A modern history of the Somali.* Athens, OH: Ohio University Press.

Norwegian Refugee Council. (2012). *"Why are children not in school?" Multi-agency assessment of out-of-school children in Dadaab Refugee Camp, Kenya.* Available at: www.alnap.org/resource/11309

UNESCO. (2016). *"Education in emergencies: Preparedness, response and recovery." Crisis and transition responses, United Nations Educational, Scientific and Cultural Organization.* Available at: www.unesco.org/new/en/unesco/themes/pcpd/education-in-emergencies/

UNHCR. (2014). *Global trends 2014. United Nations High Commissioner for Refugees: The UN Refugee Agency.* Available at: www.unhcr.org/statistics/country/556725e69/unhcr-global-trends-2014.html

World University Service of Canada. (2014). *International Day of the Girl Child: Opening pathways for girl's education.* Available at: wusc.ca/en/story/international-day-girl-child-opening-pathways-girl's-education

INVOCATION

Re-memoring Residential Schools
through Multimodal Texts

Ingrid Johnston

The tragic story of Chanie Wenjack, the indigenous boy who died trying to walk home from a residential school in 1964, has been revived through Joseph Boyden's novella *Wenjack*, and Gord Downie and Jeff Lemire's graphic novel, music, and animated film *Secret Path*. Downie's fame as lead singer of The Tragically Hip, his struggle with brain cancer, and his determination to retrieve the legacy of residential schools have helped raise awareness of Chanie's story.

As teachers seeking to help students become more aware of past and present injustices against indigenous peoples, we can look to texts by indigenous authors. As J. K. Cone (2000) suggests, "The habit of reading not only opens a world of vicarious adventure to students; it also encourages them to weigh ideas, take informed stands, and think deeply" (p. 27). In a national study on social justice (Johnston, 2017), one teacher taught Richard Wagamese's novel *Indian Horse*, explaining, "It is hugely important that all Canadians know more about the history and legacy of residential schools. *Indian Horse* is plot driven, but it also has passages filled with beautiful imagery and rich symbolism." His Grade 12 students' responses to *Indian Horse* reflect the power of the text to engage them in re-imagining past abuses and the resilience of Wagamese's protagonist. One student commented, "I like how he put so much truth into it and how much history was behind it all," and another said, "I think it has history combined with strong imagination, mixed up with adversity." An immigrant to Canada explained, "When I came to Canada, I never knew there were schools like that. Then in school they just told you about Treaties … not how residential schools were. Now reading this book, it's kind of like you are experiencing it." While no one text can engage all students in thoughtful reflection on Canada's history of abuse against indigenous peoples, multimodal texts such as *Indian Horse*, *Wenjack*, and *Secret Lives* do offer possibilities for creating greater awareness and possible action for social justice.

REFERENCES

Cone, J. K. (2000). Appearing acts: Creating readers in a high school English class. In B. M. Brizuela, J. P. Stewart, R. G. Carrillo, & J. G. Berger (Eds.), *Acts of inquiry in qualitative research* (pp. 207–228). Cambridge, MA: Harvard Education.

Johnston, I. (2017, July). Revisiting the tragedy of an indigenous childhood through multimodal texts: Engaging Boyden's *Wenjack* and Lemire and Downie's *Secret Path*. Paper presented at the Congress of the International Research Society for Children's Literature. York University, Toronto, ON.

C8

The Melody of My Breathing: Toward the Poetics of Being[1]

Anar Rajabali

Poems are rough notations of the music we are.
(Rumi, as cited in Barks, 2003, p. 27)

I open this poetic essay with the philosopher-poet Rumi, who contemplates on both the nature of poetry and the nature of *being* human. I ruminate on his notion of poems as expressing an immediacy of a desire—this roughness he speaks of—to express and capture the rhythms of our lives in this space where identity is music, as in the sound of the wind on the surface of the ocean or the echoing resonances of a bird's calling. This place, where music becomes the "notation" and representation of the melody of experiencing experience, is where I know poetry as a perpetual "calling-into-being" (Corbin, 1983, p. 87), that is, of epiphanies as cyclical as the seasons.

As a painter's first brushstroke sets a colour into motion, I encounter the tones and hues of an endless hermeneutic circle in poetic seeing, each poetic turning a phenomenological place of heightened presence and possibility to the sea and spectrum of human emotions. Hazrat Inayat Khan (1994) writes of music in two-fold understandings: "We shall find that the beats of the pulse and the heart, the inhaling and exhaling of the breath, are all the work of rhythm" (p. 74). In rhythm that is both breath and then becomes sound—inside and outside—is where music is our primal and primary utterance. Moreover, as in the nature of our beings, the whole of nature is also breathing and becoming, moving, forming, and expressing life in line, in colour, in the rising and the falling, "and the signs of life given by this living beauty is Music" (p. 74). Hence, in this vision, to attune to the rhythms of beauty is to harmonize with creation and the Creator of this Music. And in this process of a poetic tuning in, I am discovering what I know as light, a profundity, as "behind all manifestations is the perfect spirit, the spirit of wisdom" (p. 73). In poetry I experience the very breath and breadth of creating, creation, and Creator.

As a poet, I am absorbing, drawing in to withdraw again into a source that keeps me held in this circle. Rumi speaks of poetry as this "rough notation," perhaps acknowledging the limitations of form that cannot truly encapsulate the boundless-ness that keeps one eternally moving in and out and through the realms of love *dwelling*. In poetry is where I touch both the human and the divine spheres, in this cross of horizontal and vertical, of material meeting spiritual. Poetry becomes a materialization of a spiritual enterprise (Corbin, 1983), where spirituality as Hazrat Inayat Khan (2012) conceptualizes is a "tuning of the heart" (p. 174). In this third space of experiencing both form and formlessness is "the site of a living pedagogy … of generative possibilities and hope" (Aoki, 2003/2005, p. 429). In my poetics of being is where newness comes, in a washing over and emerging in the veritable light of a poetic knowing (Bachelard, 1969). In this (re)generative space where metaphors hold and perpetually make meaning is a place to experience the very "plentitude of being" (Esmail, 1998, p. 72), in which the transcendental resonances give and echo. And it is the hope that my poems echo with others in some way to see a world anew. The melody of my own breathing into poems needs and desires others to evoke my words into being, and I visualize my own interpretive circle embracing those who will ride with me on the waves of its revealing.

My poems are a suprasensual semiotic spiritual chain of language connecting to the cosmos that is governed by a faith that opens and deepens the faculties of perception, where desire becomes "newness" becomes the knowledge becoming love. My poems are a living spirituality, a "theoria" (Lakhani, 2010), a way of en-gaging with/in the world (Leggo, 2004). Poetic seeing leads me to authentic ways of knowing myself and others, a way of seeing *being*. My art forms the expression of my faith where the discovery of knowledge is a responsibility toward pluralistic understandings. My traditional teachings (re)mind me to be eternally seeking as a social obligation to honour and nurture the full potentiality of all life. In poetry I am a soul-in-learning where "what we speak becomes the house we live in" (Hafez, as cited in Ladinsky, 1999, p. 281). In this homing, in language as this *house of being* (Heidegger, 1971), I am in relation, always in the middle of some *thing*.

In this contemplative pedagogy in action, I become "thought and soul embodied in the oneness of a lived moment" (Aoki, 1992/2005, p. 197). Ted Aoki's wisdom that we live and breathe curriculum reaffirms and gives me hope in (re)search that is revelatory where: *I become the music becoming me.* My epiphany is that poetry is the dance, is the whirling into this music. As Leonard Cohen (1984) sings out: "Lift me like an olive branch and be my homeward dove/Dance me to the end of love." And in a trinity of poetry, with a lyrically and vertically inspired vision, I hope to shed light on a question that sparks my search: *How does one dwell in the poetic I/eye?*

In my first dwelling, I am on Rathtrevor Beach[2] and I am seeking. I have come here to find a source of inspiration, to simply feel inspired again. And what transpired transformed my own Being into an "immanent realm" (Aoki, 1992/2005) of grace. This was a place of unfoldment, of a poetic order of things, of nature's revealing and unfurling to me and in me. In this unity of a sensuous symbiosis— of a calling and an answering—is where the landscape "responds to my emotions and calls forth feelings from me in return" (Abram, 1997, p. 33). In my writing, I contemplate how the poem falls into its own self. In this process of words moving comes what I can only call a hermeneutic humility toward a poem that fuels the desire of this pilgrim that feels and knows the inspiration, again.

Rathtrevor Beach

One summer morning
on Rathtrevor Beach
I go in search of poems
on the wings of desire
to discover
words that give music
to a longing for
lines
that will bloom
like rows of tulips
reaching
to the Sun
whose gentle gaze
warms its petals and keeps its face
vertical and musical
dancing to the rhythms of the
softness of the subtly sensuous wind

In the sand seeking
I pick up an empty shell

and cradle it in my hands
to then trace the veritable lines
that give the perfect pattern to its
being a shell
of lines I wish
to write
to Be
in the very flesh of language
echoing
the inner strings
of a heart
I find
somewhere
in the hollowness
of this shell which in its angelic beauty
decorates the sand
and as I lift it to the sky
it recalls
a butterfly

I then place its silent wings
In-between
the line of the water
and the sand's edge
to notice the lines of the butterfly shell
continuing
in the ocean's rhythmic calling
repeating unto itself
in rippling lines of
perpetual meditation—
One heart beating and repeating

And as I hearken
to the melody
of the ocean's
breathing
harmonizing with the wind
I begin to pray and follow

the pulsating lines to the horizon
onwards
to the sky
where for a moment
I envision my own hands
whirling
with the whispering clouds
vertically and musically
questing with unison to
the infinite line
that in its grace and givenness
gives to
a poet
her soul's true
lyrical
calling

On Rathtrevor Beach
I/eye
found
poetry.

The meeting of the sea's horizon and the infinite sky with the horizons of my own mind elevates the experience I have come to call the *lifting of the poet.* As my perception becomes meditation, I contemplate how the vertical dimensions of rising bring a harmony. Gaston Bachelard (1988) writes of poets obeying a unity of song, and it is in this space I see poetry descending to ascending to transcending. The wings of poetic expression have brought me to places that transform my soul. In my next dwelling, I cross over the Pacific Ocean to Jericho Beach in Vancouver, where my poetic I/eye hones in on three birds homing on a log. In my writing of this poem, in retrospect, I ruminate on why I did not describe the appearance or colour of the birds, and then I understand that in their aeriality, they are "the color of infinity" (Bachelard, 1988, p. 77). Jane Hirshfield (2007) asks: "Is there some quality in birds—the way their presence among us might be withdrawn at any moment, or the way that part of us follows them into the distance—that causes them to recur?" (p. 143). And I ask: *What does not distance us from the birds' journey?*

Three

I see three birds
perching
on a weathered log
crossing
into the line
of the low tide—
half onto the sand
and half into the waters
where now a trinity of birds
sit in one momentary stay
facing
the vastness
of the briny blue ocean
breathing

I know this
language of the birds
as the wind's embrace lifts me
forward
to something so familiar
in three birds
like three sisters
three years apart
of three lives
always in the possibility
of flight
to the west, to the north, and to the south
spaces in-between
of us
who once shared a single womb
wandering now afar
to come home, ever so often
like the birds where no words
are necessary
of a silence that gestures
and then speaks:
I know

I know
I know
I can almost hear them say
as they move together
> *Oh, how they show love*
> *how this will have to endure*

As one then takes her flight
not looking
behind anymore
to follow the single stroke
of a paint-brushed cloud
to her own
destiny disappearing
into the light
onwards
and then another,
leaving the other,
to follow with only her eyes
knowing she needs to stay
Here—

like my mother
who lost both sisters
and then sat with the empty bodies
she could not follow
with even her eyes
and
how I feel this pain now
of no returning
as I can almost hear the lone bird
whisper in the hollows
of my own heart
> Oh, please come home?

Maya Angelou (2010) writes, "Poetry is the human heart speaking in its own melody" (p. 15). And in the tones of poetic discourse as hues of human experiencing is where I contextualize poetry as akin to spiritual expression, that is, a (re)awakening to human *being* and standing in the very fullness of life. It is in this space where creativity knows no frontiers—as in the birds in my poem—in poetic purposing setting alight and reviving "the spiritual vision of imagination" (Lakhani, 2010, p. 228).

It is in this transitional space of learning where poetry reaches into vertical and musical realms to (re)turn onto the page, then nourishes the soul whose "language is at home in poetic imagery" (Moore, 2005, p. 10). As a teacher, poetry is a pathway for me to evoke and to invoke by creating the conditions for contemplative pedagogical encounters with learning that may linger beyond the classroom. Hence, the notion of (re)awakening (re)inspires and revives what already lies at the ontological core of being human, and what is also a place of perpetual renewal. It is in this strengthening that poetry—the reading and the writing of—may bring a crystallization of keen understandings. I resonate deeply with Aga Khan (2008), who writes in *Where Hope Takes Root* that "spirituality should not be a way of escaping from the world but actively engaging in it" (p. 129) toward living ethically, purposefully, and lovingly.

Cohen (1997) writes that what "our education and culture should be for is preparing the heart for that journey outside of the ribs" (p. 199). In my final offering, "Karim," there is a heart that beats in, out, and through the poem. The hermeneutic rhythm that I ride in writing this poem brings me to the shore of understanding that is not only at the conjuncture of the vertical and horizontal, but what I conceptualize as a river of swirling eddies. This poem journeys from present to past, returning to present, into a profundity where what remains is the heartbeat of all of my poetry, purely love.

And in "Karim" is where human love is then deepened into an understanding that could have only come through a relinquishing to the light of a poetic calling that filled me with utter surprise and wonder. In the melancholy of this poem is where I tuned into another being, reliving a history evoking itself through a poetic knowing that brings with it a rushing of grace. I am most human breathing into poems, *indwelling*. I am most human when I am brought into the abode of what lies beyond, reminding me somehow of both the vastness and smallness of who I am. And in attuning to the music of my own being comes the benevolence of knowing: "This being human is a guest house/Every morning, a new arrival/A joy, a depression ... some momentary awareness comes as an unexpected visitor" (Rumi, as cited in Barks, 1997, p. 109).

And in "Karim" I am the guest house, the poetess conduit that somehow brings him into an understanding. *What guides the pen then?*

It must be love

Here,

Is the heart.

Karim

I am reading Bakhtin[3]
His words spewed
Across my desk
Rendering another Sunday lost
In a dense sea of language

Karim is watching
Bugs Bunny cartoons
Rising laughter of a 45-year-old man
With the tender soul of a child
Innocent to a fault
Wanting of love

A young boy leaving Africa
With his uncle shot in the field
No clothes, no photographs, no returning
Only memories of a previous life
May endure

Not knowing ...

The snow that is Montreal
A young boy who looks
From the tiny plane window
To a white blanket
A dark face
A family displaced
And the rising angers of the house

His father loses his fingers
To a merciless machine
In a factory he despises
A once wealthy man now poor
In spirit

This same hand that used to
Beat the young boy
With sticks
For loving all new things
For wanting change
For music, for cartoons
The fingers never recovered
A relationship
Disjointed as the hand
Is

Now
He is wanting of love

He looks to me
With his cartoon heart beating
Outside of his chest

What's up, Doc?
Would you like some tea?
It may help you
Yes, I say, *yes*

Never being in love with him more
Than I am
Now

NOTES

1. I am inspired by Shams Tabrizi (n.d.) and his devotional song/qasida, "Dam Hama Dam Ali Ali," which translates to "The melody of my breathing is Ali, Ali." Available at: ismaili.net/qasidas/dam02.html

2. Rathtrevor Beach is in Parksville, British Columbia. At low tide, the ocean recedes a kilometre afar. One can then walk to what feels like the centre of the ocean.

3. I refer to Mikhail Bakhtin's (1986) work *Speech Genres and Other Late Essays.* I am inspired by his notion that "I live in a world of others' words" (p. 143).

REFERENCES

Abram, D. (1997). *The spell of the sensuous*. New York, NY: Vintage.

Angelou, M. (2010). Poetry is the human heart speaking in its own melody. *Learning Landscapes: Poetry and Education: Possibilities and Practices, 4*(1), 29–36. Available at: www.learninglandscapes.ca

Aoki, T. T. (1992/2005). Layered voices of teaching: The uncannily correct and the elusively true. In W. F. Pinar & R. L. Irwin (Eds.), *Curriculum in a new key: The collected works of Ted T. Aoki* (pp. 187–199). Mahwah, NJ: Erlbaum.

Aoki, T. T. (2003/2005). Locating living pedagogy in teacher "research": Five metonymic moments. In W. F. Pinar & R. L. Irwin (Eds.), *Curriculum in a new key: The collected works of Ted T. Aoki* (pp. 425–431). Mahwah, NJ: Erlbaum.

Bachelard, G. (1969). *The poetics of space*. (M. Jolas, Trans). Boston, MA: Beacon Press.

Bachelard, G. (1988). *Air and dreams: An essay on the imagination of movement*. (E. Farell & F. Farell, Trans.). Dallas, TX: The Dallas Institute.

Bakhtin, M. M. (1986). *Speech genres & other late essays*. (V. W. Mcgee, Trans). Austin, TX: University of Texas Press.

Barks, C. (1997). *The essential Rumi*. New York, NY: HarperCollins.

Barks, C. (2003). *Rumi: The book of love: Poems of ecstasy and longing*. New York, NY: HarperCollins.

Cohen, L. (1984). Dance me to the end of love. On *Various positions* [CD]. New York, NY: Columbia Records.

Cohen, L. (1997). The unbearable panic of being. In D. Ehrlich (Ed.), *Inside the music: Conversations with contemporary musicians about spirituality, creativity and consciousness* (pp. 190–201). Boston: MA: Shambhala Publications.

Corbin, H. (1983). *Cyclical time and Ismaili gnosis*. London, England: Kegan Paul International.

Esmail, A. (1998). *The poetics of religious experience: The Islamic context*. New York, NY: I. B. Tauris.

Heidegger, M. (1971). *Poetry, language and thought*. (A. Hofstadter, Trans.). New York, NY: Harper & Row.

Hirshfield, J. (1997). *Nine gates: Entering the mind of poetry*. New York, NY: HarperCollins.

Khan, A. (2008). *Where hope takes root*. Vancouver, BC: Douglas & McIntyre.

Khan, H. I. (1994). *The mysticism of music sound and word*. New Delhi, India: Motilal Banarsidass Publishers.

Khan, H. I. (2012). *The art of being and becoming*. New Lebanon, NY: Omega Publications.

Ladinsky, D. (1999). *The gift: Poems by Hafiz*. New York, NY: Penguin Putnam.

Lakhani, A. (2010). *The timeless relevance of traditional wisdom*. Bloomington, IN: World Wisdom.

Leggo, C. (2004). Living poetry: Five ruminations. *Language & Literacy*, 6(2). Available at: ejournals.library.ualberta.ca/index.php/langandlit/

Moore, T. (2005). Educating for the soul. In J. P. Miller, S. Karsten, D. Denton, D. Orr, & I. Kates (Eds.), *Holistic learning and spirituality in education* (pp. 9–15). Albany, NY: State University of New York Press.

Tabrizi, S. (n.d.). Dam Hama Dam Ali Ali. Available at: ismaili.net/qasidas/dam02.html

C9

Passing from Darkness into Light: A Daughter's Journey in Mourning

Sandra Filippelli

The act of grieving becomes a transformational process of reclaiming oneself when, after the death of a loved one, one sheds the past and embraces personal renewal. Nancy R. Hooyman and Betty J. Kramer (2006) state that throughout "the grief process, which entails searching for meaning, we need to learn how to live in this altered world" (p. 2). With mindfulness, we can recognize the impermanence of our pain, transform it through compassion and loving kindness, and shine it on other suffering beings. The impact of such an interior journey may be strongly felt by a writer who inhabits this liminal space between loss, recovery, and renewal and, thus, embarks on a path of creative exploration within herself and her community.

In my own writing about the cycle of death in my family over 47 years, I recall the loss of my brother and of my mother and father from cancer. I am climbing a Himalayan peak, where the view from the clouds spirals me into an investigative inquiry into the visceral yet mundane world of the *I* that I inhabit. Do I have the courage to tap into inner spaces that scare me and face them with love and patience, or will I retreat? As a Buddhist and a writer, I dwell in the liminal space between fear and love, aversion and patience, and it is this place that I must open for exploration.

In her article "We Compose Our Own Requiem: An Autoethnographic Study of Mourning," Yvonne Sliep (2012) embarks on a personal healing quest, to "walk [her] own journey" (p. 62), motivating her readers to engage in their own process. Her work reflects writing as a therapeutic autoethnographic act, with poetry an imagistic articulation of grief resonating within both private and public dialogical spaces. In poems mourning the sudden death of her son, Thomas, while working overseas, she articulates a profound sense of loss from the perspective of her home in South Africa and later in Taiwan, where his friends take her on a motorcycle tour of the places that marked his life. Sliep (2012) carries his ashes back to South Africa, then later goes to Namibia, where she begins to re-locate her lost self in the "vast empty spaces of the desert" (Sliep, 2012, p. 71). Then, "[n]ine months" into this "gestation" period, she shifts her focus to herself, and finally to both son and mother, in a "reconfiguration" (p. 81) of identity: "you and I, not just me" (p. 80). Three years later, she becomes aware of the non-separation of "time [and] space" (Sliep, 2012, p. 78), and, by the fourth year, her writing evolves to the word-specific art of haiku. Her Buddhist therapist friend encourages her to share her innovative view that "*we* have found a [new] way" (Sliep, 2012, p. 80), both her son and herself, of working through grief. She writes a letter to Thomas suggesting that "sharing this journey" (Sliep, 2012, p. 81) may open possibilities for other people. In composing her own requiem, she becomes an "'I-witness'" (Sliep, 2012, p. 83), broadening her experience by "[g]oing public" (p. 83) in the field of social science research, where mourning reflects "social phenomena" (p. 83).

Judy Tatelbaum and Dorothy Becvar maintain that "[g]rief is 'like a neighbor, who always lives next door, no matter where and how we lie, no matter how we try to move away'" (as cited in Hooyman & Kramer, 2006, p. 3). Hooyman and Kramer (2006) define grief as a derivative of "the Latin word *gravis*, meaning 'heavy'" (p. 16). The act of "[g]riev*ing* implies the movement from being injured or burdened to bearing or carrying on, making choices, and, ultimately, healing" (Hooyman & Kramer, 2006, p. 16). A process of insightful penetration of mind and body creates space for a shift toward self-determination and redefinition of the self. In the West, people are expected to "'get over it' ... and move on with life" (Hooyman & Kramer, 2006, p. 19), when they may still be emotionally attached to the deceased. Hooyman and Kramer (2006) state: "[E]ach of us must be permitted to struggle to come to terms with loss in a way that works for us. The journey of grieving is toward learning to accept and live with loss, not closure" (p. 8). While there may never be closure, with the right view, the survivor might release her pain and experience renewed awareness. Becvar asserts that "[p]aradoxically, when we lose someone we love, we may also lose our fear of death and whatever it represents, feeling a freedom that we once thought impossible" (as cited in Hooyman & Kramer, 2006, p. 5).

In 21 years of studying Tibetan Buddhism, I have seen how people maintain an organic view of death through acceptance of the impermanence of life and the inevitability of change. Conscientious practitioners may help the dying move on and also work through their own feelings of loss and bereavement by cultivating compassion, or *bodhichitta*. With the mind focused on the breath, clarity arises, inspiring the view to put others before themselves. A calm mind creates space for personal illumination of the absence of independence, or separateness, and the transformational process of renewal in letting go of the past. They can deconstruct Sliep's (2012) collective *we/I*, creating a more interdependent awareness of the impermanence that compassionately marks the passing of life and time.

> *Breathing in, I let go of darkness.*
> *Breathing out, I draw in light.*

At 24, I gave up hoping for the perfect life when my mother died of multiple myeloma, after a four-and-a-half year illness, at a time when I could have been exploring life and love. Twelve years earlier, my brother Ken, five years my senior, had died in a motorcycle accident on his 17th birthday. Haunted by the image of him flying over the handlebars of his new Triumph 500, I carried on in the role of companion/daughter while my mother's illness ate away her bone marrow. During my final undergraduate years, I occupied the delicate position of ancillary caregiver in a triad consisting of my mother, father, and me. Still craving parental presence, I lingered within a liminal space between my parents and my yearning for independence and achievement. A retired competitive swimmer, I had passed through the dark years of high school following my brother's death swimming 10 or more kilometres a day until I started university, the bleak period of my mother's illness. It was as if I had crawled out of one black hole and fallen into another.

> *Auburn hairballs on the bathroom floor,*
> *my mother's head the dome of a bald eagle,*
> *an image fit for a minted coin,*
> *food for talk, a vent for tears.*

Thirty years after my mother's death, my father passed away peacefully following a seven-year bout with prostate cancer. A caring daughter, I stayed by him while he maintained a joyful outlook on life, meticulously collating on Excel spreadsheets postage-stamp meter marks he had cut off envelopes collected from his many friends. Our weekly trips to Safeway were most memorable. He would hook his cane onto the cart, holding it for support, while I walked behind, ready to lift him up by the waist whenever his knees collapsed. "Time for cappuccino," he would say as we sat in silence, aware of the inevitable finality of these trips. I wondered what I would do without him to phone every evening and spill out my day.

Father

My father sips a cappuccino,[1]
eyes the tomato vines, snaking
tendrils, tangled like the tumours
invading his brain. Remembers
pots of pasta on the stove,
meatballs browning in a skillet,
the shiver of the curtains on still nights,
an old country aunt's augury
of life and death.

His eyes track through thoughts, memories
of a life now faint whispers
ringing in his ears:
forgotten lectures he gave on fair play,
strolls through Bocchigliero and Cosenza
a walkabout down under with a vibrant wife,
a rosary gracing
his mother's neck.

I pour more milk into his mug, draw
a heart with my spoon. He taps my hand,
his finger bony, smiles, sighs, sleeps,
face drawn, calm, slips
into the earth, an embryo.

I endeavoured to help him as a compassion practice, expressing my gratitude for the life he had given me. Some evenings, after a long day of teaching, I would drop into bed early. Other times, I helped him make his mother's signature meatballs and spaghetti, a way for him to connect and make peace with his roots while the cancer ravaged his body. It was as if we had transported ourselves back to Italy to inhale the land and the sea.

Like Sliep (2012), I "walk my own journey" (p. 62) through mourning. As an Anglo-Italian Canadian, I too feel the resonant echo of the relocation and subsequent dislocation of my ancestors. My Italian and Irish Catholic grandmothers inhabit my bone marrow with my long-deceased mother and the Asian Buddhist teacher who has entered my life. I wonder to what extent I have shaped my own identity and found a home within myself while painting a picture of it through poetry, drama, and prose. I question whether I inhabit this world as *I/me* or a composite of my ancestors and the Asian cultures I have immersed myself in. More likely, however, I now dwell in liminal space as a re-forming individual. A Caucasian woman crossing Asian lines, I traverse the ancestral path without having borne children to inherit my disappearing family line. My children are my students, and my offspring arise from my creative process, a mirror of my experience to others. I turn to writing poetic language of love and self-discovery to document this process of inquiry of a woman inhabiting a third space, a bridge between displacement and harmony.

Darlene McCown and Betty Davies maintain that for pre-teenage children "making the transition to concrete thought, the event and cause of a sibling's death may create confusion, anxiety and fear about their own safety" (as cited in Hooyman & Kramer, 2006, p. 102). No doubt, I have unconsciously been afflicted by this phenomenon; I do know that I was overcome by emotion when, upon clearing out our family boxes, including Ken's four-decade-old trunk, a myriad of memories flooded out. His burgundy-black, red-white, and red-blue Speedos, worn lifeguarding and swim training, had remained surprisingly intact, as had a picture of him standing with a backstroke medal around his neck. While his motorcycle helmet appeared to have shrunk in storage, the shell of his pet tortoise, hibernated in the basement over our last long Montreal winter, had not deteriorated at all. Hooyman and Kramer (2006) point to the "intensified feelings of guilt and hopelessness" felt by "survivors" (p. 57) of a sudden, violent death in the family. Rummaging through my brother's trunk opened as many wounds as it provided closure for, yet I could feel his protection once again, particularly the memory that he had not picked me up from school just prior to his accident.

My feelings shifted, when I opened my mother's boxes and mounds of her copiously written letters fell out onto the floor. Had she been a frustrated writer, scribbling pages of anecdotes for her friends and family, or for herself? Had I not become a mother because I had lost a mother who lost her own mother? As the descendant of British/Irish and Italian grandparents who had laboured to establish families in Canada, I wondered if, like other second-generation Canadians, I could harbour feelings of immigrant displacement as my great-grandmother had.

Archangela

Archangela inhabits her New World abode, a field of burnt²
earth sprouting tomato vines, carrots, pepper and basil,
key ingredients of a successful marriage to Pepino,
wisp of a man not five feet tall. A dusty little girl grips

the pocket of his blanched denim overalls, tugs the folds
of Archangela's long skirt, her lips parted as if speaking, only
there is no sound, just a parched, yellow photograph.
Testament to a family's planting under mountain
sky, feet gripping the earth of a land
they barely know, hands still submerged
in an old country garden.
A mother, squat and stout,
her belly swollen,
a picture framed,
stranger in an alien time.
~ 1905

In my engagement of heart/mind inquiry, I turn to mindfulness. Jon Kabat-Zinn (2013) advises that one must "drop in on [oneself], to live more in the present moment, to stop at times and simply *be* rather than getting caught up in endless doing while forgetting who is doing all the doing, and why" (p. xxxi). The aim is to stay in the present moment where "you don't have to *do* anything other than to pay attention and stay awake and aware" (Kabat-Zinn, 2013, p. xxxi). Through focus on the breath, I free my busy mind, creating a space for serenity and creativity. Cultivating a spacious mind requires discipline and resting in brief moments of mental quiescence throughout the day.

Breathing out, I release pain
breathing in, I allow peace,
let go of separation,
embrace the interdependence of all beings,
animate and inanimate.

Rock meets fish in riverbed,
turbulent waters cascade into still pools,
earth and sky dissolve into silence.

In his article "Lifewriting: A Poet's Cautionary Tale," Carl Leggo (2010) espouses poetic inquiry as an energetic, innovative method to question and understand our lives, ethics, and politics while designating our place in home and community. Stories, Margaret Atwood asserts, carry us into the dark and out through the light to enhanced understanding (Leggo, 2010, p. 68). Leggo maintains that the danger of lifewriting lies in too much introspection into the nature of the *I*, yet sees hope in personal renewal. He boldly writes a poem about his father to capture the feeling of a perturbing event that occurred by "naming [then] declaiming" it (Leggo, 2010, p. 71) as a means of absolution. In the act of "declaiming," he reclaims his father and himself. Like Leggo, I strive to first name then "declaim" (Leggo, 2010, p. 77) my place of trauma in order to reclaim inner peace and a happy, compassionate life.

During the time of the Buddha, a distraught mother, whose child had died, searched for the elixir to restore his life. Finally, she took the body to the Buddha, who told her to "'bring back a mustard seed from any house in which there [had] never been a death'" (Sogyal Rinpoche, 1992, p. 28). The woman returned empty-handed and said, "'Grief made me blind and I thought that only I had suffered at the hands of death'" (Sogyal Rinpoche, 1992, p. 28). She asked the Buddha to tell her "'the truth ... of what death is, what might lie behind and beyond death, and what in [her], if anything, [would] not die'" (Sogyal Rinpoche, 1992, p. 29). The Buddha told her there was one immutable "'law in the universe ... that all things change, and that all things are impermanent'" (Sogyal Rinpoche, 1992, p. 29).

I/eyes I/eyes I/eyes, mother's hazel
pupils inlaid in whiteness, her mother's I/eyes inside
her/mother, her/mother, the mother/mother line
I/daughter mirror of my/mother.

This "difficult knowledge" (Britzman & Pitt, 2004, p. 354) is expressed by Donald Winnicott, who

distinguishes between a past traumatic event and the devastating effects of fear toward an experience that happened in the past but that, due to the immaturity of the ego, remains unintegrated *as experience*. He formulates a paradox to identify the qualities of this non-experience: "The patient needs to 'remember' this but it is not possible to remember something that has not yet happened, and this thing of the past has not happened yet because the patient was not there for it to happen to." (as cited in Britzman & Pitt, 2004, p. 364)

How can a child have the awareness to deal with trauma, or a mother accept the reality of a dead child she has borne and cradled? It may take a lifetime, or never, to integrate the trauma "*as experience*" (as cited in Britzman & Pitt, 2004, p. 364).

As a reminder of impermanence, Sogyal Rinpoche (1992) asserts that "[i]n the Buddhist approach, life and death are seen as one whole, where death is the beginning of another chapter of life. Death is a mirror in which the entire meaning of life is reflected" (p. 11). I take note as the faces of my loved ones pass in front of me. My mother catches my eye; she reminds me to straighten my hair. My teacher models grace and fortitude, her gait steady, eyes kind. I am not to ruminate but to accept everything that comes and goes.

Therese Rando claims "we are grievers a thousand times over in our lives" (as cited in Hooyman & Kramer, 2006, p. 3). If the end of every day represents the death of time, we could continuously mourn our loss, but instead we should watch the passing of the sun and moon with delight. Through Buddhism, I find a dialogical space for compassionate wishes that all beings will be relieved of suffering. Because the cultivation of quiescence and compassion, or *bodhichitta*, is a lifetime endeavour, I strive to practice patience, the *bodhissatva* path.

> *Breathing in, I see the thought.*
> *Breathing out, I let it go,*
> *rest in compassion.*

With prolonged effort, my compassion will grow in the manner of ivy, a member of the "botanical family of radicants, which develop their roots as they advance, unlike the radicals, whose development is determined by their being anchored in a particular soil" (Irwin & O'Donoghue, 2012, p. 232). An evolving radicant and aspiring *bodhissatva*, I find myself "opening to the other" (Irwin & O'Donoghue, 2012, p. 232) in a dialogical space of love and compassion, inner healing and transformation. Through mindfulness and writing, I strive to transform my grief into a heart/mind healing of *bodhichitta*. The renowned teaching of remembering the kindness of one's mother (Bstan-'dzin-rgya-mtsho, Dalai Lama XIV, 2005, p. 52) inspires me.

> *Mother, you were so kind,*
> *you bore me, nursed me, cradled me*
> *when I cried, fed me, clothed me,*
> *yet I did not recognize your kindness.*
> *Even when you lay rasping on your hospital*
> *bed, I still wished you would not leave.*

I, your daughter, send your compassion
back to you, turn my eye to a panhandler, wish
him happiness, smile at my enemy, send
the love of the great mother to him, to a friend,
to all sentient beings, the great compassion.

We must accept the reality of death and suffering and embrace happiness. As Carl Leggo (2011) asserts, "I think we can learn to live with delight, to love delight, if we are willing to acknowledge the possibility that, like light, delight is all around us and in us" (p. 78). Through a poetics of love, we can transform ourselves and the world.

NOTES

1. First appearance in *EVENT* magazine. North American serial print rights and limited, non-exclusive digital rights to this poem are held by *EVENT* magazine under the title "Guiseppe Lorenzo." Filippelli, S. (2017). Guiseppe Lorenzo. *EVENT, 46*(1), 47.

2. First appearance in *EVENT* magazine. North American serial print rights and limited, non-exclusive digital rights to this poem are held by *EVENT* magazine under the title "Archangela." Filippelli, S. (2017). Archangela. *EVENT, 46*(1), 46.

REFERENCES

Britzman, D. P., & Pitt, A. J. (2004). Pedagogy and clinical knowledge: Some psychoanalytic observations on losing and refinding significance. *JAC, 24*(2), 353–374. Available at: www.jaconlinejournal.com/archives/vol24.2/britzman-pedagogy.pdf

Bstan-'dzin-rgya-mtsho, Dalai Lama XIV. (2005). *How to expand love: Widening the circle of loving relationships*. (J. Hopkins, Ed. & Trans.). New York, NY: Atria Books.

Hooyman, N. R., & Kramer, B. J. (2006). *Living through loss: Interventions across the life span*. New York, NY: Columbia University Press.

Irwin, R. L., & O'Donoghue, D. (2012). Encountering pedagogy through relational art practices. *International Journal of Art & Design Education, 31*(3), 221–236. doi: 10.1111/j.1476-8070.2012.01760

Kabat-Zinn, J. (2013). *Full catastrophe living: Using the wisdom of your body and mind to face stress, pain, and illness*. New York, NY: Bantam.

Leggo, C. (2010). Lifewriting: A poet's cautionary tale. *LEARNing Landscapes: Poetry and Education: Possibilities and Practices, 4*(1), 67–84.

Leggo, C. (2011). A heartful pedagogy of care: A grandfather's perambulations. In J. A. Kentel (Ed.), *Educating the young: The ethics of care* (pp. 61–83). New York, NY: Peter Lang.

Sliep, Y. (2012). We compose our own requiem: An autoethnographic study of mourning. *Creative Approaches to Research, 5*(2), 60–85.

Sogyal Rinpoche. (1992). *The Tibetan book of living and dying.* (P. Gaffney & A. Harvey, Eds.). San Francisco, CA: Harper.

INVOCATION

A Narrative Template for Making Room and Vitalizing English-Speaking Quebec

Paul Zanazanian

As a history educationalist by profession, I am engaged in a social-justice quest for bringing about positive change for a misunderstood and unusual minority in Quebec. I am faced with a challenging puzzle that I am determined to solve in a democratic and win-win manner for all parties involved. How can room be made for the province's English-speaking minority in the teaching of school history, and by the same token help strengthen its weakening vitality? How can one integrate this historic community's presence and contributions into the workings of the province's official history program, while simultaneously respecting the Francophone majority's collective story that underlies the narrative framework and content-matter destined for all Quebec students? The heightened level of language and identity politics in the province makes contesting the state's official history very difficult to achieve. As a solution, I present a workable narrative template on English-speaking Quebec's realities and experiences as a pedagogical tool for making room and vitalizing the community through the teaching of school history. This postcard illustrates an initial attempt at how I envision to do so—one that is based on empirical data on community leaders' historical memory of English-speaking Quebec's past. Deriving my legitimacy from official government recommendations, the template, or schematic-like script, is intended to be conducive to fostering a positive sense of Self and living together with Francophones. It works as a springboard for helping English-speaking students produce personalized narratives of belonging, but in a way that counters the dangers of closed-mindedness and indoctrination. Having students employ historical-thinking concepts serves to help them develop well-informed and well-reasoned histories, while learning about the workings of historical consciousness and narrative for knowing and acting in time assists them in taking critical distance from their knowledge claims and accounting for their claimed perspectives.

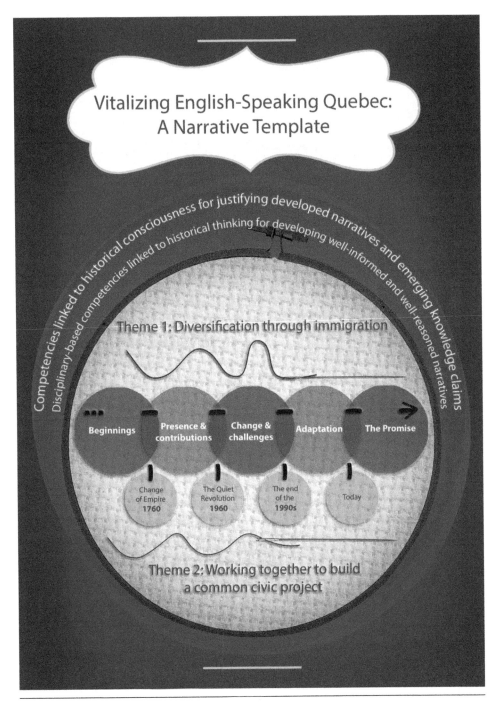

Paul Zanazanian (2016). *Vitalizing English-speaking Quebec: A narrative template.* Graphic diagram

C10

Provoking the (Not So?) Hidden Curriculum of Busy with a Feminist Ethic of Joy

Sarah Bonsor Kurki, Lindsay Herriot, and Meghan French-Smith

The sharing of joy, whether physical, emotional, psychic, or intellectual, forms a bridge between the sharers which can be the basis for understanding much of what is not shared between them, and lessens the threat of their difference.
(Audre Lorde, 2007, p. 56)

INTRODUCTION

In an environment of schooling where, for many students, being seen as being busy equals better and being the busiest equals best, we are choosing to do "it" differently. By intentionally searching out joyful practices and spaces, we find welcome alternatives to the compulsory, performative stress of formal education, a phenomenon with distinctly gendered manifestations. This personal and provocative research deliberately unsettles the hidden curriculum's relentless expectation that for a learner/scholar to be successful they must adhere to an unspoken enactment of ongoing accomplishment and excessive competition. As an act of feminist research, conducted and presented through *métissage*, we were guided by the question, "How, when, and where do we find and/or choose joy in formal and hidden curricula?" We highlight how, by intentionally searching out joyful practices and spaces, we as young women learners/scholars found welcome alternatives to the obligatory, intense anxieties of formal education. In a neoliberal socio-political climate where women's "leaning in" is presented as the only, and often best, solution to professional and academic gender equity (Sandberg, 2013; Strober, 2014), there exists a hidden curriculum in which women need to be seen as the busiest in order to justify their place in academics. It is this curriculum of "busy" that we disrupt.

MÉTISSAGE AS A PATH TO JOY

We, Lindsay and Sarah, began our exploration for joy as two doctoral candidates at different universities. We invited Meghan, a high-school student and research participant in Lindsay's PhD study, to join us after discovering her own struggles within academia mirrored much of what we were experiencing in our post-secondary settings. It soon became clear that we had multiple perspectives and voices that needed to be expressed and included in our research. Métissage provided a process by which we could share our experiences and create one narrative, while simultaneously honouring our own individual stories. Métissage is the weaving of stories from participants that "retains the integrity and distinctiveness of the individual texts/voices and at the same time creates a new text, one that illuminates the braided, polysemic, and relational character of our lives, experiences, and memories, as well as the interconnections among the personal and the public realm" (Chambers, Hasebe-Ludt, Donald, Hurren, Leggo, & Oberg, 2008, p. 142).

Our métissage was written following three themes that organize the work: Strand 1: Performative Busy-ness; Strand 2: Agency/Courage/Authenticity; Strand 3: Joyfulness in Academia. A performance element of métissage allows the audience to become engaged with the polyphonic nature of the narrative. As such, we invite our readers to consider the following questions as they read the text:

- What emotions do our stories invite?
- With what do you connect?
- Where do you find joy in your academic experiences?

PROVOKING THE (NOT SO?) HIDDEN CURRICULUM OF BUSY WITH A FEMINIST ETHIC OF JOY

Strand 1: Performative Busy-ness

Lindsay: When I think about performative busy-ness, I understand it as being about status, dominance, and shaming others. It doesn't work without an audience, so in that sense, it's relational. But rather than nurturing *connection* with the other, it's about *dominating* the other. Neoliberalism, with its constant demands to do more with less, seems to facilitate this performative busy-ness. We are pitted against each other for ever-diminishing resources, grants, jobs, and even A+ grades, competing for who can be seen as the most overworked, and therefore the most worthy.

In addition to neoliberalism, performative busy-ness is further fuelled by other systems of hierarchical inequality, such as patriarchy and white supremacy. Toxic competition intensifies for young women (who are rarely taken seriously), and can manifest in mansplaining, whitewashing, and other tactics that diminish, or undermine. We are less likely to feel that we are legitimate, that we *belong*, so we are under even more pressure to perform the part perfectly—an academic iteration of the respectability politics that black feminists have been calling out for decades.

Performative busy-ness is strictly policed. We police each other, we police ourselves.

Sarah:

- COMPETITION—THE OPPOSITE OF JOY?
- Up: ahead, winning, lead, happy, positive, GOOD
- Down: depressed, dejected, despondent, sad, low, BAD
- What about when UP is BAD?
- MEASURE UP

"What did you get?" A familiar phrase from elementary school, and perhaps it even carried over into high school. "What did you get?" the mind whispers.

But did you know you'll hear this in graduate school too? "What did you get?"

As our papers are handed out these words are silent but I think we are all wondering them. "What did you get?"

Despite all the acknowledgements of being accepted to a PhD program and having my intelligence confirmed because I am a doctoral student, I am still searching for external confirmation that I should be here. "What did you get?" That I am smart enough and good enough to be here. "What did you get?" So, as the papers are flipped open and the comments read, I try to sneak looks at their grades, hoping to see minuses beside As or curves of Bs, hoping that my pointy A will STAND UP to the rest. "What did you get?"

Meghan: In high school, competition is a constant. Whether it is with others or ourselves. I saw this in Grade 9 after joining the Venture program. There were a few factors to me not feeling successful in that environment, such as social stress and not being prepared for what the program and the people in it create: competition. This competition starts with an obsession with marks. In Grade 8 my worst class was math but I still got on the honour roll. It was a major confidence booster but it shouldn't be. Combined with big numbers and everyone around me telling me that I was *so* smart I developed a complex. I unconsciously became dependent on others to judge my intelligence; I can't be the only one who feels that way. One friend of mine was brought to tears at the thought of her parents seeing her report card. If we get a mark less than we hoped or come away from an exam with a feeling of dread we are immediately disappointed because we don't come up to the level we want to be. This happened to me after a math provincial that I knew went badly. I was 15 and I was so stressed about what I got that I was a sobbing mess. When my mom said to me that these exams didn't define me, I later told this to my friend and she said: "I wish I had your mom."

Provocation: Performative busy-ness is not only the antithesis of a feminist ethic of joy, it smothers, inhibits, and otherwise discourages a feminist ethic of joy from taking root.

Competition for young women in academia is not just "I want to win," but "I want to be better and be what I am supposed to be: put together." We fight against ourselves and try to conform to the idea of being a perfect "lady" instead of embracing our human-ness and finding who we are.

Strand 2: Agency/Courage/Authenticity

Lindsay: Choosing joy is indeed a *choice*. But that said, it's really only available as a choice when one has decent self-worth, and confidence as a learner, and as a scholar. And like all choices, it is constrained by the systemic oppressions that regulate all of our choices, such as colonialism, ableism, sexism, heteronormativity, racism, et cetera.

Meghan: I have just left the International Baccalaureate (IB) program for the "regular" stream, a program for high-school students looking to challenge themselves toward success. I am trying to make a more conscious effort to ... how do I say this? ... not care? As in marks and how well I do on tests, the phrase "as long as I do my best and pass" comes to mind. I made my last year of public education as simple and stress-free as I could. There isn't one class that I dread, except gym, but I am managing. I am still figuring out why I am doing better. Is it because the IB environment wasn't for me? The teachers? My peers? Am I so incredibly condescending toward my new peers because I don't see them as smart as my IB peers? It could be all of the above; in fact, it probably is.

Sarah: AUTHENTICITY = PhD COMPLETION

Just before beginning my PhD I was struggling with the decision to begin at all. I had recently completed my master's degree, and although I enjoyed the challenges that it brought and the sense of accomplishment I gained when I finished it, it was hard, tiring work. However, as I stared down the four-plus years of effort on a topic that I hadn't really narrowed down yet—how I could possibly sign up? As an elementary teacher who used to rearrange the desks in her classroom every three to four weeks, the thought of committing to one topic for that long was beyond my experience!

Choosing to opt out of performing busy-ness is not without consequences. In my lived experiences of having occasionally chosen joyfulness over busy-ness, I've felt shame, embarrassment, and self-doubt. I've felt stupid, frivolous, and like I don't belong. There's a price to pay for joy, and it costs more for some than for others (often correlated with how many ways someone is politically and socially marginalized). It simply can't be done in all times or contexts. The price is too high, the retaliation too vicious.

Meghan: The consequences of leaving IB are losing the subject matter I actually find interesting, so in order to make up for that I have to find it outside of school. I analyze movies and television and I read feminist books. I actively participate in my Queer Straight Alliance, of which I am president. To get out my feelings I write poetry about not fitting in and how annoying five years of school can be. With my confidence growing and with coming out of my shell, I take bigger chances, like singing for a school play, and I'm actually starting to enjoy speaking in front of people. I've learned to breathe through my nerves and make sure to take more self-care. I am learning to not take these last five years as seriously as some do, in order to keep a practical perspective on life and my future.

Lindsay: Choosing joy sometimes feels more like a desperate act of self-preservation than like a mere choice. Being literally schooled in performing stress, and therefore unhappiness, can sometimes consume me. I'm not a good scholar when that happens, and moreover, I'm not a good human. Similar to how becoming educated—whatever that might mean—is surely more than mastering a written curriculum on a high-stakes test, there must be more to being a robust student or scholar than being constantly busy/stressed/overworked. How then, under a climate of neoliberalism, patriarchy, and white supremacy, can we intervene? How can this hidden curriculum be *provoked*?

Sarah: It was then I realized that if I wanted to complete this challenge I needed to feel *authentic* in this work. It would have to be about something that was more than a fleeting inkling or flash-in-the-pan idea. Somehow, I needed to create a research project that brought together my feminism, my knowledge of adolescents, critical literacies, and ... me. Sure—my supervisor had possible projects which I could easily join, and yes—she would have been thrilled to have me work alongside her research, but deep down I knew that if I wanted to get to the end of this degree, I needed a personal connection that would feed my passion over the long term. I had two long-standing interests—photography and fibre arts. Although fibre arts did put up a good fight (and having a supervisor who knows how to knit made the decision even trickier), it was the opportunity to combine critical visual literacies and photography with my feminist lens on female youths' text engagement that eventually won.

Strand 3: Joyfulness in Academia

Lindsay: Joyfulness is, in part, constrained by Rousseau's mind-body dualism. By this I mean that because joy is an emotion, and emotion is often irreducibly female, joy can therefore be understood as frivolous, soft, unstable, unnecessary, not-as-good-as. Because of this, my choosing joy is always grounded in my feminism, in my rejection of sexism and a gender binary.

Meghan: I have yet to find joyfulness in academia; joy is something I have to find in other areas that aren't directly related to school. High school is a big giant hoop with a bunch of little ones in it, so learning what I find interesting is something I have to be patient with. I am looking forward to college, where I hope to find like-minded people. Leaving public education will hopefully bring me new freedom and avenues for finding joy in learning. I like learning but the confines of my current learning environment stop me from being joyful. How can I be joyful when I don't even want to be there? I have to look at what I am passionate about and find it on my own; this is how I find joy. But what is joy? I don't know what joy *is* in learning to be honest. Between Grade 5 and Grade 7 I was homeschooled. During that time I did the things I wanted to do, like read books about Amelia Earhart and Gandhi. I got to have singing lessons and manage my time independently. Those three years brought me confidence in my intelligence that was not based on what others thought but on how I felt about myself—at the end of my homeschooling experience I could say that I *was* smart. During high school I have needed to find moments and savour them, like my Grade 8 spelling bee, and the first essay that I was actually proud of doing. Joyfulness takes work to find and as cliché as it is, I have to try to be *positive* in order to find it.

Lindsay: There is pluralism in joyfulness, there must be. Part of my own joy is recognizing that others find joy in different forms, and that that's okay. In my lived experience, joyfulness in academia is a delicious struggle. It's sitting in a moment of uncomfortable vulnerability, at the edge of the zone of proximal development, sussing through a problem, fermenting in the questions. It's not knowing the answer, but knowing I'm close. It's imbued with gratefulness that I am doing this, and not some other work, at 9:30 on a Thursday morning. It's relational—it's sharing an article or news story that connects to a colleague's research, giving strength-based feedback, collaborating on something meaningful. It's also relational with participants and students—approaching them with genuine care, finding opportunities for them, sharing space, soaking in their stories, their feelings. It's that agonizing, sumptuous frustration of being tantalizingly close to making sense of a difficult problem, asking a new question, finding an answer. In short, it's vulnerability, openness, and care.

Sarah: January 14, 2015

Hey Lindz,

I'm having trouble writing, and I don't think it's just because I am getting a cold (although that is a reason that my mood is the colour of the sky at the moment—monotone grey!!!). I am having a hard time finding that excitement and joy that I was struck with when we spoke in the summer about applying to this conference. I've lost it and I feel lost.

At the time, I felt a driving force, pushing me to figure out how to put this project together. Words spilled out of me and my mind raced with ideas, possibilities, and ways in which we could approach joyfulness. I was in lust with the prospect of how our adventure could unfold! Remember that day in June when I called with the invitation for you to join me in this joyous journey? I was thinking faster than I could talk and I was talking faster than I could write! To this day, I don't know what some of the scribbles are. My excitement turned into learning when I realized that our combined ideas and commitment to this project were, in fact, an example of joy within the academy. It was very meta. Our work about our work became the work! The joyful spirit we shared fed my thoughts and our letters helped me channel the rush. We moved from tossing around notions to sketching plans as to how to proceed. The connection between us was fostered in our co-joy-ned (co-joined—get it? ha ha!) document—in which we offered suggestions for each other's work and updated each other on our own. The moral support and unexpected connections were just what we each needed then, and perhaps that's what I'm searching for now.

In this letter, I'm throwing out my net hoping to catch some little remnant of what we had going before because I've lost it now ... except that I haven't really, because in the 20 minutes I've spent writing this letter and reviewing our notes, unbeknownst to me at first, I again have come to see that the work about which I'm writing is the work I am doing! Somehow, out of nowhere, it happened again. That little flicker of an idea, where this went from being an email to a narrative within the métissage. It's magic. But more importantly, it's empowering and inspiring and ... it's joyful.

Joyfully yours,

Sarah

Provocation: All these characteristics—emotion-based, relational, easing into vulnerability—make joy an inherently feminist practice for me. The fact that it's so closely intertwined with the feminine helps me to understand why it's not taken seriously, why it doesn't count, why it's taboo.

IMPLICATIONS AND IMAGINATIONS

By deliberately choosing joyful experiences of learning, teaching, and research, we rebuke this not-so-hidden gendered curriculum of "busy," and its pervasive effects on young women's full participation in formal education. Using métissage allowed our often contradictory experiences to be braided together and created one simple but essential narrative: the joy of learning, which is in fact the joy of vulnerability. In weaving a feminist ethic of joy into curricular conversations, we open the door for a new appreciation of knowledge and learning, an appreciation that has been stifled by the current learning climate of competition and stress. What does this mean then, for written curriculum? For hidden curriculum? What are the provocations, big and small, that can be brought about in our respective institutions, our teaching, our research, and our publishing? We like to imagine what we could do, as scholars, learners, teachers, and leaders if we could infuse even a little bit of this joy in our work.

REFERENCES

Chambers, C., Hasebe-Ludt, E., Donald, D., Hurren, W., Leggo, C., & Oberg, A. (2008). Métissage: A research praxis. In J. K. Knowles & A. L. Cole (Eds.), *Handbook of the arts in qualitative research* (pp. 141–154). Los Angeles, CA: Sage.

Lorde, A. (2007). *Sister outsider: Essays and speeches.* Berkeley, CA: Crossing Press.

Sandberg, S. (2013). *Lean in: Women, work and the will to lead*. New York, NY: Knopf.

Strober, M. H. (2014). Lean in: Women, work, and the will to lead. *Feminist Economics, 20*(2), 149–150. doi:10.1080/13545701.2014.900569

INVOCATION

leaf spinning

Susan Walsh

suspended by a
spider-like thread a leaf spins
and spins in the breeze

May we turn toward one another and the world:
strengthen our intention to love well together.

Susan Walsh (2016). *leaf spinning*. Halifax, Nova Scotia. Text and digital Miksang photograph

Contributors

Wisam Kh. Abdul-Jabbar is a doctoral candidate and a sessional instructor at the University of Alberta. He holds master's degrees in English from the University of Baghdad, in Humanities from California State University, and in English Literature in Canada from Lakehead University. He has taught in Iraq, Libya, and Canada. His areas of research interest are postcolonial theory, diaspora, critical pedagogy, and Anglophone Arab literature. His articles have appeared in *Critical Discourse Studies, Changing English, Teachers and Teaching: Theory and Practice*, and the *Journal of Commonwealth Literature*.

Veena Balsawer is a doctoral candidate at the Faculty of Education, University of Ottawa, in the Culture, Society, and Literacies stream. She works as Children's Storyteller and Programmer at the Ottawa Public Library. Her research interests are narrative inquiry, autoethnography, multimodal literacies, children's literature, found/generated poetry, drama, and storytelling. Her PhD thesis is a métissage of Indo-Canadian women's stories as they navigate their hyphe-nated curriculum of life with/in the liminal spaces that are both home and not-home.

Stephanie J. Bartlett is an educator with the Calgary Board of Education and the University of Calgary who seeks to blend her pedagogy with her personal outlook on life. The result is an ecology that fosters creativity and questioning, with a love for community and the natural world. Stephanie is inspired by the ancestry in the field of curriculum studies and enjoys sharing her research and classroom practice with others.

Sarah Bonsor Kurki is a sessional instructor in the Department of Curriculum Studies at the University of Victoria. Sarah's research interests include critical literacies, visual literacies, and feminist methodologies. Her current research explores the visual literacies of adolescent girls' photographic practices using arts-based and feminist methodologies. Sarah is the director of membership with the Canadian Association for the Study of Women and Education (CASWE).

Sandra Chang-Kredl is an assistant professor in the Department of Education at Concordia University, specializing in Early Childhood Education. Her research profile revolves around teacher identity, children's popular culture, memory work, curriculum studies, film theory, and cultural studies. She has recently published in

Reflective Practice, Teacher and Teacher Education, Children's Literature in Education, Continuum: Journal of Media and Cultural Studies, Early Education and Development, and *Teachers and Teaching: Theory and Practice.*

Cindy Clarke is a doctoral candidate at the University of Saskatchewan living in Saskatoon. Cindy is a narrative inquirer who uses poetic expression in research to explore curriculum making and identity making on the edges of community.

Diane Conrad is an associate professor at the University of Alberta. Through participatory arts-based methods, her research engages youth who experience struggles in relation to mainstream society, including many aboriginal youth, to explore and analyze their lived experiences. Her current study, *Researching the Education of Aboriginal Students: A Youth Exchange through Arts & Technology: Stories of Culture, Identity, Community & Place,* is a curriculum exploration with three aboriginal schools in Alberta and the Northwest Territories.

Kent den Heyer is an associate professor in the Department of Secondary Education, University of Alberta. He has published and presented research internationally on student and teacher interpretations of the conditions necessary for social change, psychoanalytic approaches to anti-racist education, curriculum theory, teacher education, historical consciousness, and thinking education through the philosophical lens of Alain Badiou. He presently serves as editor of the journal *Canadian Social Studies.*

Margaret Louise Dobson received a PhD from McGill University in 2015. Prior to returning to her alma mater to explore the intuitive hunches gleaned from a career in education, she taught high school French and English and held leadership roles in Ontario and Quebec schools. Based on her research on identity, she sees the role of education (to lead forth being/thinking/*who*) as critical to the reinvigoration of the meaning and purpose of schooling (to train in doing/knowing/*what*).

Dwayne Donald is a descendant of the *amiskwaciwiyiniwak* and the Papaschase Cree and is an associate professor in the Faculty of Education at the University of Alberta. His work focuses on ways in which indigenous philosophies can expand and enhance our understandings of curriculum and pedagogy.

Claudia Eppert is associate professor in the Department of Secondary Education at the University of Alberta. Her research focuses on the complexities of witnessing social and environmental suffering through literature and the arts, and possibilities for transformation. She is co-editor of *Between Hope and Despair: Pedagogy and the Remembrance of Historical Trauma* and *Cross-Cultural Studies in Curriculum: Eastern Thought, Educational Insights.*

Lisa Farley is an associate professor in the Faculty of Education at York University in Toronto. Her research examines the history of psychoanalysis and theories of childhood to investigate the uneven qualities of development and meaning making as these relate to contexts of social conflict. Her work appears in *Psychoanalysis, Culture & Society, The Journal of the American Psychoanalytic Association, American Imago, Psychoanalysis and History, History and Memory, Curriculum Inquiry,* and *Pedagogy, Culture & Society.*

Sandra Filippelli is a doctoral student in Arts-Based Research in the Department of Language and Literacy Education at the University of British Columbia. Sandra holds an MFA in Creative Writing and an MA in English. She has published creative and academic writing in several periodicals, produced her plays, and taught ESL for 30 years. Sandra researches poetic inquiry, a/r/tography, art education, visual literacy, Buddhism, grief theory, mindfulness, compassion, and happiness.

Rita Forte is a doctoral student in Education at the University of Ottawa with a concentration in Society, Culture, and Literacies. Her focus is on peace education, cosmopolitanism, and the interrelationships between/within curriculum and governance.

Meghan French-Smith is currently studying English and Women's Studies at Langara College in Vancouver.

Yoriko Gillard is a doctoral student in the Department of Language and Literacy Education at the University of British Columbia. Her research is about how human trust is enhanced by creative commitments and acts. She is raising questions about life through her prominent artwork series called *Kizuna (Bond)*, which is accompanied by her poetry *Liminal Space*. Her work *Kizuna (2013)* won the UBC student art-based research award from the Peter Wall Institute for Advanced Studies in 2013.

Peter P. Grimmett is a professor and recent Head of the Department of Curriculum and Pedagogy in the Faculty of Education at the University of British Columbia. His most recent (2012) book, *Teacher Certification and the Professional Status of*

Teaching in North America: The New Battleground for Public Education, locates recent developments in teacher certification in North America within a broader, international policy context characterized as hegemonic neoliberalism wherein economic rationalism has begun to trump professional judgment.

John J. Guiney Yallop is a parent, a partner, and a poet. He is also an associate professor at Acadia University, where he thinks, talks, and writes about creativity and literacy in teaching, learning, and research. John's most recent poetry collection, *OUT of Place*, explores growing up gay in a Catholic community and subsequently teaching as an out gay educator. John lives in Wolfville, Nova Scotia, with his partner and daughter, and their pets.

Mary J. Harrison holds a PhD in Language, Culture and Teaching from the Faculty of Education at York University, where her studies were supported by a SSHRC Doctoral Fellowship. In her dissertation, *Thinking Through the (M)Other: Reading Women's Memoirs of Learning*, Mary argues that psychoanalytic concepts of maternal loss animate women's experiences of thinking and language. Mary is a curriculum consultant at Fanshawe College in London, Ontario.

Erika Hasebe-Ludt is a professor in the Faculty of Education at the University of Lethbridge. She teaches and researches in the areas of multiple literacies, life writing, and literary métissage, in the context of Canadian and transnational curriculum studies. Her co-authored and co-edited publications include *Life Writing and Literary Métissage as an Ethos for Our Times*; *A Heart of Wisdom: Life Writing as Empathetic Inquiry*; and *Contemplating Curriculum: Genealogies/Times/Places*.

Tamar Haytayan is a photographer based in Vancouver, by way of Lebanon, England, and Armenia. Her experiences have shaped her photography, with which she creates nostalgic and emotive captures. Tamar consistently works on her various projects and has had many exhibitions and publications in Europe and North America.

Joel Heng Hartse is a lecturer in the Faculty of Education at Simon Fraser University. Before completing his PhD in Teaching English as a Second Language at the University of British Columbia, he taught in the US and China. His work has appeared in the *Journal of Second Language Writing*, *Asian Englishes*, and *Composition Studies*.

Lindsay Herriot is a recent doctoral graduate of the Department of Educational Policy Studies at the University of Alberta. Lindsay's research interests include

LGBTQ youth, educational policy, and citizenship education. Lindsay is also the program director for the Canadian Association for the Study of Women in Education (CASWE).

Bruce G. Hill lives in North Vancouver with his partner, Ricki Reine. He attended the University of British Columbia (BA) and the University of Victoria (MEd). From 1971 to 2005, he taught in several school districts, including stints as a substitute teacher, classroom teacher, community school coordinator, PE teacher, and support teacher. He retired in 2005. In his free time, he does a little gardening, reads curriculum theory, and writes essays.

Alyson Hoy holds a PhD in Curriculum and Instruction from the University of British Columbia. Working at the intersection of memoir writing and queer and feminist theories of feeling and embodiment, her writing weaves the poetic and the autobiographical to explore themes of intimacy, emergent queer identities, sex and sexuality, trauma, eating disorders, and self-harm. Her current project is a book proposal of her doctoral dissertation on queer memoir. She lives and works in Vancouver.

Wanda Hurren grew up on the prairies, and now lives and works on the traditional lands of the Salish and Straits Salish peoples, in Victoria, British Columbia. She is a professor of Curriculum Studies at the University of Victoria and her *auto/bio/geo/ carto/graphical* non-fiction, photographs, and poetry have been published in several anthologies and journals. Wanda's current mapwork project explores intricate meanderings connecting people, places, and bodies of water on the prairies.

Derek Hutchinson is a doctoral candidate at the University of Kansas. Derek explores curriculum making and identity making around gender and sexuality and the role of place in experience through narrative inquiry.

Diana B. Ihnatovych is a doctoral student in Cross-Faculty Inquiry in Education at the University of British Columbia. Her diverse academic career in music combined with her passion for nature, sustainable living, and wellness led her to pursue interdisciplinary research in music and sustainability. Her primary research question is: How will the integration of music into elementary environmental education enhance the process of learning about nature?

Rita L. Irwin is a professor of Art Education and Curriculum Studies at the University of British Columbia. While her research interests include arts teacher education, artists-in-residence, and socio-cultural issues, she is best known for her work in expanding how we might imagine and conduct arts practice-based research methodologies through collaborative and community-based collectives.

David W. Jardine is a retired professor of education. His most recent books include *In Praise of Radiant Beings: A Retrospective Path through Education, Buddhism and Ecology* (2016) and, with Jackie Seidel, *The Ecological Heart of Teaching: Radical Tales of Refuge and Renewal for Classrooms and Communities* (2016).

Ingrid Johnston is a professor emerita of English Education and Curriculum Studies in the Department of Secondary Education at the University of Alberta. Her research and teaching interests focus on postcolonial literary theories and pedagogies, Canadian literature, curriculum development, and teacher education for diversity. She has published numerous refereed articles and has authored and edited four books, with another co-edited book in press with Canadian Scholars.

RM Kennedy is a faculty member in the Department of Liberal Studies, Centennial College, in Toronto. His work draws on psychoanalysis and continental philosophy to highlight the emotional and ethical dimensions of making relationships across differences, particularly in contexts of social and environmental breakdown. His published work appears in *Psychoanalysis, Culture & Society, Curriculum Inquiry,* and *Ethics and Education.*

Sheena Koops has taught within Saskatchewan private, band, public, and community schools for over 20 years. She has a master's degree in Curriculum and Instruction from the University of Regina. In 2015 she was shortlisted for the Governor General Award for History Teaching thanks to her passion for Treaty Walks (www.treatywalks.blogspot.ca). Sheena is the author of the work of fiction *Voice of the Valley* (2006, Orca Books). The Koops have raised three daughters—Victoria, Moira, and Arwen—in the heart of Treaty Four Territory, Fort Qu'Appelle, Saskatchewan.

Mandy Krahn is a doctoral candidate in the Faculty of Education at the University of Alberta, specializing in curriculum studies. Her research draws upon wisdom traditions while focusing on the pedagogical implications of children's understandings of well-being. She is also completing advanced studies in Art Therapy, working with children through art as a way to connect with their inner life.

Carl Leggo is a poet and professor at the University of British Columbia. His research interests include: life writing, a/r/tography, narrative inquiry, poetic inquiry, creative writing, and arts-based research. His books include: *Growing up Perpendicular on the Side of a Hill*; *Come-by-Chance*; *Teaching to Wonder: Responding to Poetry in the Secondary Classroom*; *Life Writing and Literary Métissage as an Ethos for Our Times* (co-authored with Erika Hasebe-Ludt and Cynthia Chambers); and *Sailing in a Concrete Boat*.

Amélie Lemieux is a doctoral candidate in Literacy and Curriculum at McGill University. She researches youth's aesthetic meaning making and reading reception of literary works in classroom settings. She has been awarded the Tim Casgrain Prize for research excellence in literacy studies by the Canadian Foundation for Economic Education. Her original research contributions to language and literacy studies have been recognized by the Social Sciences and Humanities Research Council of Canada, the Quebec Culture and Society Research Council, and the Language and Literacy Researchers of Canada.

David Lewkowich is an assistant professor in the Department of Secondary Education at the University of Alberta. His research interests include: reading experience, young adult literature, visual response, psychoanalytic theory, the emotional life of education, and the representation of adolescence in comics and graphic novels.

Patricia Liu Baergen completed her Master of Education at the University of Ottawa. Currently, she is a doctoral candidate in the Department of Curriculum & Pedagogy at the University of British Columbia. Her research interests include curriculum studies, theorizing pedagogy, and educational philosophy. She lives in Vancouver.

Rebecca Lloyd is an associate professor in the Faculty of Education at the University of Ottawa. She promotes interdisciplinary thinking in her Function2Flow.ca framed research as well as her teaching within the Comprehensive School Health teacher education cohort (uottawa-comprehensive-school-health.ca/). She has chaired several conferences (IHSRC, PHE Canada, and the PHETE SIG within CSSE), been invited to speak at international conferences (IPLA, Japanese Society of Sport Education), and lives her curricular and phenomenological theorizing through competitive salsa dance.

Mitchell McLarnon is a doctoral student and sessional lecturer at McGill University. Currently serving as the Chairperson of the Graduate Committee of the Canadian Association of Curriculum Studies, Mitchell has worked as a lecturer at the University of Edinburgh and has held research contracts at DAL, UPEI, and McGill. He also sits on the editorial board of *Pathways: The Ontario Journal of Outdoor Education*. His research interests include: social justice in environmental education, arts-based educational research methodologies, and multiliteracies.

Anna Mendoza earned a BA in English and Creative Writing from Bryn Mawr College and an MA in TESL at the University of British Columbia. Having taught English for Academic Purposes for eight years, she intends to research the socio-cultural aspects of academic writing during her PhD. She presented "From Teaching Disciplinary Writing to Cultivating Disciplinary Identities: An Alternative Syllabus for a Freshman EAP Writing Course" at the 2015 Provoking Curriculum Studies Conference.

Karen Meyer, Cynthia Nicol, Muhammad Hassan, Ahmed Hussein, Mohamed Bulle, Ali Hussein, Samson Nashon, Abdikhafar Hirsi Ali, Mohamud Olow, and Siyad Maalim: Seven members of the research team grew up in the Dadaab camp, became teachers in secondary schools there, and are currently studying on scholarships in Canadian universities. Three of the team have taught secondary teachers in the camp within a Teacher Education Diploma Program and are curriculum researchers in a Canadian university.

Saeed Nazari is a doctoral student in the Department of Curriculum and Pedagogy at the University of British Columbia. He has been teaching English in Vancouver and Iran for over 15 years. Saeed is interested in theorizing curriculum, learner-centred education, inter-faith dialogue, and ideology in curriculum.

Robert C. Nellis is a past co-president of the Canadian Association for Curriculum Studies and continuous faculty member in the Red Deer College School of Education. His PhD thesis received a 2008 CACS Dissertation Award, and he is the author of *Haunting Inquiry: Classic NFB Documentary, Jacques Derrida, and the Curricular Otherwise* (Sense, 2009). Recent work explores place, home, and trespass; more-than-human encounters; and life writing.

Soudeh Oladi received her PhD from the University of New Brunswick. In her doctoral research, Soudeh explores how the Deleuzian nomadology is permeated with values that can destabilize the instrumentalist paradigm in education. By examining the concept of nomadic potential in the works of Freire and Rumi and positioning it within an educational context, Soudeh draws attention to how unleashing the nomadic potential in learners empowers them to envision a world where authentic change is possible.

Erin L. Quinn is an educator with the Calgary Board of Education and believes, above all, that the purpose of education is for learners (teachers included!) to think, wonder, and discover together.

Anar Rajabali is a doctoral candidate in Language and Literacy Education at the University of British Columbia. As a poet, Anar is intrigued by the kinship between poetic discourse and spiritual expression. As an English educator, Anar's work embraces the role that poetry can play in inviting the contemplative into the classroom. Her research promotes how aesthetic encounters can foster spiritual literacy in pedagogical practices.

Shauna Rak is an artist, researcher, teacher, and currently a doctoral student at McGill University, in the Department of Integrated Studies in Education. Her research focuses on intergenerational family stories, multi-sensory learning, and the complexities of teaching difficult knowledge through versatile creative approaches that include storytelling, visual art, performance, and multi-media technology.

Pauline Sameshima is a Canada Research Chair in Arts Integrated Studies at Lakehead University in Thunder Bay, Ontario. She curates the Lakehead Research Education Galleries. Pauline's interdisciplinary projects integrate multi-modal ekphrastic translations of data to catalyze experiential learning and provoke new dialogues.

Jackie Seidel is an associate professor at the University of Calgary. She loves fiction, poetry, beekeeping, and walking by the Bow River. She recently edited (with David Jardine) *The Ecological Heart of Teaching: Radical Tales of Refuge and Renewal for Classrooms and Community* (2016). This book emerged from years of writing in community with teachers, attempting to compose ourselves together, in joy and sorrow, in this place and time in which we find ourselves.

Anita Sinner is an associate professor in the Department of Art Education at Concordia University, Montreal. Her interests include theoretical perspective in the visual arts; arts research methods, including life writing and a/r/tography; international art education; curriculum development; teacher education; and community art education.

Hans Smits is retired from the University of Calgary but is continuing to teach courses in curriculum studies, ethics, and philosophy of teaching and doing occasional writing and research, as well as trying to improve his wood-working skills.

Celeste Snowber is a dancer, poet, and educator who is an associate professor in the Faculty of Education at Simon Fraser University. She is the author of *Embodied Prayer*, many essays, and a collection of poetry, *Wild Tourist*. Her most recent book is *Embodied Inquiry: Writing, Living and Being Through the Body*. She is also the Artist in Residence in the UBC Botanical Garden, where she creates performances of dance and poetry.

Kyle Stooshnov is a doctoral student in the Department of Language and Literacy Education at the University of British Columbia, researching virtual reality and narrative inquiry. He teaches multimodality and classroom discourse for UBC's Bachelor of Education program. He has presented at numerous international conferences on Shakespeare's plays and virtual reality.

Samira Thomas is a doctoral candidate at the University of British Columbia in the Department of Curriculum and Pedagogy in the Faculty of Education. Her research focus is on intimate dialogue and its relationship to the curriculum of cosmopolitanism. She currently serves as the Academic Director of the Sparks Academies in Afghanistan.

Katie Tremblay-Beaton is a doctoral student at the University of Toronto, Ontario Institute for Studies in Education (OISE). Her research interests involve student experience in beginning band, non-traditional instructional techniques, and the process of musical inquiry. She also teaches in an Ontario public school and has experience teaching music from Kindergarten to Grade 8. Outside of school, Katie enjoys playing in pit orchestras with local musical theatre companies.

Shirley Turner is a doctoral student at Simon Fraser University. She works with at-risk youth in an alternate school in Vancouver using a permaculture garden as her main teaching resource for sustainability coursework. She also teaches Iyengar yoga and is deeply interested in how we make sense of the world through our embodied experience of place rooted in growing our own food as a path for extending our relationality with the earth.

Susan Walsh is a professor in the Faculty of Education at Mount Saint Vincent University. Her research process involves contemplation, innovative forms of writing, and various arts practices. Her publications appear in journals such as *Qualitative Inquiry* and *Qualitative Studies in Education*. Her new book, *Contemplative and Artful Openings: Researching Women and Teaching*, is forthcoming from Routledge. Susan also co-edited *Arts-Based and Contemplative Practices in Research and Teaching: Honoring Presence*.

Boyd White is an associate professor in the Department of Integrated Studies in Education, Faculty of Education, McGill University. Originally a studio-art instructor, his teaching and research interests are in the areas of philosophy and art education, particularly on the topics of aesthetics, art interpretation, meaning making, and values.

Sean Wiebe is an associate professor of education at the University of Prince Edward Island in Charlottetown. For the last four years he has been the principal investigator for the Digital Economy Research Team, investigating connections between new literacies and the digital economy.

Elizabeth Yeoman is a professor of Education at Memorial University. Her scholarly work is about language, culture, history, and memory. Her poetry, essays, and travel writing have appeared in literary journals and media including the *Globe and Mail*, W Network, and CBC Radio. She is currently working with Innu environmental and cultural activist Elizabeth Penashue on a SSHRC-funded book and cross-media curriculum materials based on Penashue's diaries.

Kelly Young is a professor at Trent University's School of Education and Professional Learning, where she teaches English curriculum methods, curriculum theory, and foundational courses. Her areas of research include language and literacy, curriculum theorizing, leadership in eco-justice environmental education, writing pedagogies, and arts-based research. She is co-editor of *Contemporary Studies in Canadian Curriculum: Principles, Portraits, & Practices* (2011).

Paul Zanazanian is an assistant professor in the Department of Integrated Studies in Education at McGill University. His research examines the workings of historical consciousness in individuals' means of knowing and acting when constructing social reality for purposes of living life. Seeking to go beyond linking historical sense making to issues of identity, he is currently investigating how individuals and groups use historical knowledge to bring about social change.

Index

a/r/topography, 88, 92
Abdul-Jabbar, Wisam Kh., 47–54
Abowitz, Kathleen, 99
Abram, David, 208
academia
  academic landscape, 187–188
  joyfulness in, 297–299
accommodation, 55
Acknowledging my Elders (Turner), 219
Adams, Douglas, 68
aesthetic experience, 99
aesthetics, 98–107, 164
afterwardness of thinking, 228
"The Age of Oil" (Ihnatovych), 28
agency, 295–297
  community agency, 35–46
  and the social contract, 175–182
Alexander, Thomas, 98, 100–101, 105
algorithms, 175–182
Ali, Abdikhafar Hirsi, 257–265
Alrawi, Karim, 66
analysis, 176
Angelou, Maya, 274
anorexia, 251–256
anthropocene, 113
Aoki, Douglas, 178
Aoki, Ted, 141–150, 200, 201, 203–204, 269–270
Apple, Michael W., 167
'Arabi, Ibn, 89
Arcadia (Stoppard), 67–68
"Archangela" (Filippelli), 284–285
Arendt, Hannah, 183, 230–231
Arnold, Janice, 119
art
  artful portable library spaces, 35–46
  eros, and aesthetics, 98–107
  Holocaust, role in art education, 114–122
  and the hungering body, 250–256
  as reflective-self, 235–237
Ashton, David, 179–180
assimilation, 51
attentive listening, 27–33
attunement, 203–206
Atwood, Margaret, 70, 285
Auerbach, Erich, 67, 71
authenticity, 295–297
awareness, 101–105

Bachelard, Gaston, 272
Baergen, Patricia Liu, 141–150
balance, 202
Balsawer, Veena, 159–163
band-aids, 155–156
Bartlett, Stephanie, 200–206
Basso, Keith, 188
The Bay, 250
Beal, Bob, 3–4
Becvar, Dorothy, 281
being, 268–279
belonging/not belonging, 159–161
Berry, Wendell, 208, 224
Biesta, Gert, 177
bilingualism, 63–64
Bitter Milk (Grumet), 228–229
Blue Eyes Remembering Toward Anti-Racist Pedagogy
  (Koops), 2
bodhichitta, 287
bodhissatva, 287
bonding, 44
Book of Sands (Alrawi), 66
the border, 56–57
Boyden, Joseph, 266
Brass, Keitha, 3–4
bridging, 44
Britzman, Deborah, 230, 231, 286
Brown, Phillip, 179–180
Buber, Martin, 99
Bulle, Mohamed, 257–265
Burch, Kerry, 100
busy, 292–300
"But where are you really from?" (Balsawer),
  159–161
"Buying Pencils," 259–260

Caputo, John, 55
CARE Kenya, 259
Cat's Eye (Atwood), 70
Chambers, Cynthia, 78, 81
Chang-Kredl, Sandra, 152–158
chora, 47–54
Clarke, Cindy, 186–198
Clearing the Plains (Daschuk), 7
common culture, 231
community, 130
community agency, 35–46

community mapping, 18–19
CompPsy, 179
Cone, J.K., 266
Conrad, Diane, 18–19
Cook, Mike, 5
Corbin, Henry, 133
cosmopolitanism, 58–64
courage, 295–297
Crease, Robert, 68, 73
cross-culturalism, 59
cultural mythologies, 81–83
currere, 19, 21–24, 26, 80, 91, 166–167, 176, 181, 224
"Currere: Toward Reconceptualization" (Pinar), 166
curriculum
    action *vs.* acquiescence, 229
    art. *See* art
    of busy, 292–300
    character of contemporary curriculum studies,
        78–84
    and *currere,* 80
    curriculum-as-lived, 26, 144–145, 201, 205
    curriculum-as-plan, 141–143, 147, 201, 203, 205
    essence of curriculum, 145
    imaginal curriculum, 133–138
    instrumentalism of curriculum-as-plan, 141–143
    is-ness of curriculum-as-lived, 144–145, 147
    legitimized knowledge, 167
    music. *See* music
    as nocturne, 183
    reconceptualist approach, 81
    and religion, 165–173
    rhizomatic curriculum, 131–139
    of tension, 200–206
    thinking, and spaces, 164
    of travel writing, 56–65
    windswept curriculum, 77

Dadaab refugee camp, 257–265
Dancing in the dirt (Turner), 212
Daniel's Story (Matas), 117
Dark Reading Matter (Fforde), 69
darkness, 183–184
Daschuk, James, 7
Davies, Betty, 284
death, 280–289
Deleuze, Gilles, 131
den Heyer, Kent, 151
Derrida, James, 55
detention, 249
deviance, geography of, 192–197
Dewey, John, 100
The Diary of Anne Frank, 117

Dictator (Harris), 72
difficult knowledge, 226–232, 286
displaced truths, 152–158
displacement, 258–259
"Distances (Found Poem)," 261
Dobson, Margaret Louise, 108–112
Dodge, Arnold, 178
Doll, William, 200, 203
Dolloff, Lori, 22
Donald, Dwayne, 18–19
Downie, Gord, 266
Driftnet Abstraction (Robins), 85, 86
Dunant, Henry, 60
duoethnography, 165–173
Dussaud, François, 58
dwelling in-between, 146–148
"Dwelling" (Turner), 209

Early Riser (Fforde), 69
early-years teachers, 152–158
the earth, listening to, 27–33
earthquakes, 96–97, 234–235
eating disorders, 250–256
Eaton, Marcia Muelder, 99
ecological nature of language, 78–84
Edison, Thomas, 90
Edmonton map, 18–19
educational research. *See* research
Einstein, Albert, 70
emergency education, 263
empowerment, 136
enlightenment, 134–138
Eppert, Claudia, 34
eros, and aesthetics, 98–107
events of identification, 81–83

famine, 258
fana (nothingness), 137
Farley, Lisa, 77
fashion, and the hungering body, 250–256
"Father" (Filippelli), 283
feminist ethic of joy, 292–300
Ferreday, Debra, 254
Fesperman, Dan, 101, 105
Fforde, Jasper, 69–70
figurative language, 207
Filippelli, Sandra, 280–289
Fillmore, Lily Wong, 48
Finnegans Wake (Joyce), 71–72
First Among Sequels (Fforde), 69
first-language attrition, 47–54
The flower clock (Forte), 62

Foddy, Margaret, 236
Ford, Henry, 90
Forte, Rita, 56–65
Francophones, 290
French-Smith, Meghan, 292–300

Gadamer, Hans-Georg, 201, 202
gardens, 60–62
gender, and education, 226–232
generosity, 174
Geneva, 57–65
The Geography of Childhood (Nabhan and Trimble),
   79
geography of deviance, 192–197
Gibson, William, 66
The Gift of Death, The Work of Mourning (Derrida), 55
Gillard, Yoriko, 233–248
Global Affairs Canada, 264
globalization, 59
Goldhaber, Alfred, 68, 73
Great East Japan Earthquake, 234–235
Great Hanshin-Awaji Earthquake, 234–235
Greene, Maxine, 89, 122
grieving, 280–289
Grimmett, Peter P., 96–97
Grisham, Dana, 181
Grumet, Madeleine, 80, 166, 228–229, 230, 231

Harris, Robert, 72
Harrison, Mary J., 226–232
Hartse, Joel Heng, 165–173
Harvest owl (Turner), 222
Hassan, Muhammad, 257–265
Haytayan, Tamar, 199
Heidegger, Martin, 141–150
Herriot, Lindsay, 292–300
Hill, Bruce G., 123–129
Hillman, James, 224
Hirsch, Sivane, 118
Hirshfield, Jane, 272
Hitchhiker's Guide to the Galaxy (Adams), 68
Hoagland, Sarah, 154
Holocaust, 114–122, 123–129
home/not home, 159–161
Hooyman, Nancy R., 280, 281, 284
Hoy, Alyson, 250–256
Hudson's Bay Company, 250
Hull, Kathleen, 100
human being, valuing the, 178–180
human variant, controlling for, 177–178
the hungering body, 250–256
Hurren, Wanda, 164

Hussein, Ahmed, 257–265
Hussein, Ali, 257–265
Hutchinson, Derek, 186–198
hy-phens, 159–163

I-Thou concept, 99, 101, 105
identity
   events of identification, 81–83
   and the imaginal curriculum, 136–137
   Jewish identity, 114–122, 123–129
   nomadic identity, 131
   teacher identity, and music curriculum, 20–25
ideology, 165–173
Ihnatovych, Diana B., 27–33
imaginal curriculum, 133–138
imagination, 89–90, 93, 133–134, 137
impersonal pedagogical conventions, 228
in-between, 146–148
Indian Horse (Wagamese), 266
indigenous peoples
   indigenous authors, 266
   music and, 29–30
   place and, 29–30
"Inheritance," 264
"Initial Visit to Dadaab," 264–265
instrumentalist education system, 141–143
Intimate Dialogue, 88–95
intraconnection, 34
is-ness of curriculum-as-lived, 144–145, 147
Islamic doctrine, and love, 89

Japan, 234–235
Japanese Canadian community, 235–236
Jardine, David, 200, 224–225
Jewish identity, 114–122, 123–129
Johnston, Ingrid, 266
Joyce, James, 71–72
joyfulness, 292–300
justice, 135

Kabat-Zinn, Jon, 285
kalam, 89
Kalbach, Madeline A., 52
Kanu, Yatta, 52
"Karim" (Rajabali), 275, 276–277
Kasagan, Terence, 4
Kennedy, R.M., 77
Kenya, 257–265
Khan, Aga, 275
Khan, Hazrat Inayat, 268, 269
Kizuna, 233–248
"Kizuna: Bond" (Gillard), 237–240

Kizuna digital photographs (Gillard), 237–247
Klein, Calvin, 255
knowledge economy, 179–180
"Knowledge is Power, Understanding is Liberation" (Turner), 214–215
Kobe, Japan, 234–235
Kokoro no Kea, 235
Koops, Sheena, 2–10
Kouritzin, Sandra, 48
Krahn, Mandy, 18–19
Kramer, Betty J., 280, 281, 284
Kristeva, Julia, 47–51
Kurki, Sarah Bonsor, 292–300

language
    ecological nature of language, 78–84
    figurative language, 207
    first-language attrition, 47–54
    language acquisition, 47–54
    metaphorical nature of language, 78–84
    poetry, and *being* of language, 146
Last Dragonslayer (Fforde), 69
Lauder, Hugh, 179–180
leaf spinning (Walsh), 301
Leggo, Carl, 191, 285–286, 288
legitimized knowledge, 167
Lemieux, Amélie, 35–46
Lemire, Jeff, 266
L'Engle, Madeleine, 70
Lewis Powell (a.k.a. Payne) in holding cell (Gardner), 104
Lewkowich, David, 140
liberating-constraint method, 81–82
library spaces, 35–46
"Lifewriting: A Poet's Cautionary Tale" (Leggo), 285
liminal third space, 159–163
listening to the earth, 27–33
literacies movement, 180
Little Free Library, 35–46
living with generosity, 174
Lloyd, Rebecca, 26
The Lord of the Rings (Tolkien), 70–71
loss of first language, 47–54
love, 55, 77, 88–95, 136, 174, 224–225
Lugones, Maria, 186
Luhrmann, Bazz, 55

Maalim, Siyad, 257–265
madness, 96
magpies, 151
Mandel, Emily St. John, 66
maps, 18–19

March of the Living, 120
Maslow's hierarchy of needs, 126
McAndrew, Marie, 118
McCown, Darlene, 284
McGill University, 35–46
McLarnon, Mitchell, 35–46
meaning making, 23–24
Mendoza, Anna, 11–17
Merleau-Ponty, Maurice, 207
metaphorical nature of language, 78–84
"The Method of Currere" (Pinar), 166
métissage, 174, 292–293
Meyer, Karen, 257–265
Mimesis: The Representation of Reality in Western Literature (Auerbach), 67
mindfulness, 285
Minkowski, Hermann, 70
miyowicehtowin, 4–7
modernity, 175–182
Moore, Ronald, 99
Morris, Alexander, 3
Moss, Kate, 250, 251
motivational displacements, 154–155
mourning, 280–289
multicultural citizenship, 57–59
multimodal texts, 266
museums, 60
music
    currere, 21–24
    melody of experiencing experience, 268–269
    songs of indigenous peoples, 29–30
    songwriting, 2–4
    soundscape, 31
    teacher identity, 20–25
"Music of the Forest" (Ihnatovych), 29
musicking, 23
"My Liminal Place" (Gillard), 233

Nabhan, Gary, 79, 80–81
Narrative as Virtual Reality 2 (Ryan), 67
narrative inquiry, 187
Nashon, Samson, 257–265
nature, and sound, 31
Nazari, Saeed, 165–173
Nellis, Robert, 55
neoliberal discourse, 133
Neruda, Pablo, 183–184
Nēhiyaw-itwēwina, 4–7
Nicol, Cynthia, 257–265
Nijinsky (Numeier), 96
Ninno, Domenico, 178–179
nocturne, 183

Noddings, Nel, 154
nomadic identity, 131
Norwegian Refugee Council, 263
Number the Stars (Lowry), 117–118
Nursery Crimes (Fforde), 69

Obama, Barack, 175, 178
Ohama, Linda, 235
oil, 28–30
Oladi, Soudeh, 131–139
Olow, Mohamud, 257–265
"Opening" (Turner), 215–217
openness, 174
Orzel, Chad, 71
Ozeki, Ruth, 70

Pahl, Kate, 43
parents, 229–230
Pasqua, Chief Ben, 3–4
pedagogical anxiety, 230
pedagogical rhythm, 34
pedagogical role model, 231
performative busy-ness, 293–295
The Peripheral (Gibson), 66
The Petrified (Forte), 61
Piaget, Jean, 55
Pigott, Brooke S., 52
pimâcihowin, 4–7
Pinar, William F., 80, 166, 176
pipe, 3
Pitt, Alice, 230, 231, 286
place, 29–30, 78, 186–198
placelessness, 131
Plato, 34, 49–50, 100
playfulness in research, 186–198
pluralism, 99
poetry
    Aoki's poetic style of theorizing, 141–150
    and *being* of language, 146
    as calling-into-being, 268
    and grief, 280–281
    poetic dwelling, 148–149
    poetic inquiry, 82–83, 201
    poetic thinking, 145–146
    poetics of being, 268–279
    practicality of poetry, 11–17
    See also specific poems
Poitras, Alma, 5–7
Poitras, Delma, 5–6
portable library spaces, 35–46
*Possible Worlds, Artificial Intelligence, and Narrative
    Theory* (Ryan), 67

Powell, Lewis, 103
"The Practicality of Poetry" (Mendoza), 11–17
prayer, 89
process-oriented learning, 208–209
programming, 179
progression, 176
Proust, Marcel, 71
Provoking Curriculum Studies Conference, 2, 66,
    188

Quantum Moment, 68, 73
quantumeracy reading list, 66–76
Quebec
    English-speaking Quebec, 290–291
    Quebec education system, 114–115, 118–119
"The Question Concerning Technology"
    (Heidegger), 143–144
"The Question Holds the Lantern" (Dobson),
    108–112
questioning, 143–144
Quinn, Erin L., 200–206

Rajabali, Anar, 268–279
Rak, Elka, 123–129
Rak, Shauna, 114–122
Rando, Therese, 287
"Rathtrevor Beach" (Rajabali), 270–272
reading
    quantumeracy reading list, 66–76
    reading list, 67–68
reciprocity, 44
reconceptualist approach, 81
recursive function, 179
reflection, 200–201
reflexive reflection, 200–201
refugee communities, 257–265
regression, 176
relational approach, 208
religion, 165–173
research, 177–178
    academic landscape, 187–188
    multiple stories of research, 188
    playfulness in research, 186–198
    research politics, 178
    vulnerability in research, 186–198
residential schools, 266
"Responsive Reciprocity" (Turner), 218
reteaching, 224
Revolution in Poetic Language (Kristeva), 47, 48–49
rhizomatic curriculum, 131–139
rhythm, 34
Richardson, Laurel, 187, 201

Rinpoche, Sogyal, 287
Romeo + Juliet (Luhrmann), 55
root metaphors, 79
Rosenblatt, Louise, 67, 68
Rumi, 131–139, 268, 269
Ryan, Marie-Laure, 67

"A Safer Place," 258–259
Sameshima, Pauline, 85–86
Schafer, R. Murray, 28–29
second-generation youth, 47–54
Secret Path (Downie and Lemire), 266
"Seeds of Memory" (Young), 82–83
Seidel, Jackie, 113, 200
self-identification, 101–105
sensus communis, 202–203
Shade of Grey (Fforde), 69
"Shakespeare in refuge," 262
shared knowledge, 35–46
shariah, 89
Shusterman, Richard, 99
Silverberg, Ruth, 178
singing Treaty education, 6–8
Sinner, Anita, 174
"Siren's Ghost Net" (Sameshima and Wiebe), 85–86
Slaughterhouse Five (Vonnegut Jr.), 70
Sliep, Yvonne, 280–281, 282
Smith, David, 200
Smith, Stephen, 26
Smits, Hans, 183–184
Snowher, Celeste, 199
social contract, 175–182
social imaginary, 175–176
Somalia, 258
songs of indigenous peoples, 29–30
songwriting, 2–4
soundscape, 31
spaces, and thinking, 164
spirit, 90–91
St. Pierre, 201
Station Eleven (Mandel), 66
STEM subjects, 68, 72
Still Dancing: My Bubby's Story (Rak), 123–129
Stooshnov, Kyle, 66–76
Stoppard, Tom, 67–68
Strangers to Ourselves (Kristeva), 48
strangler fig phenomenon, 96
stream-of-consciousness, 71
Stretching into each other (Turner), 215, 217
Stretching into myself (Turner), 213
"Structural Correspondence" (Turner), 210–211
Sufism, 89, 138

sustainability, 43–44
"Sustenance" (Turner), 212
Swanger, David, 105
Switzerland, 59–64
synthesis, 176

A Tale for the Time Being (Ozeki), 70
Tapestry of creation (Turner), 210
Tatelbaum, Judy, 281
tattoos, 116
Taylor, Charles, 175–176, 177, 179
teacher identity, and music curriculum, 20–25
technology, 143–144
tension, curriculum of, 200–206
theorizing as poetic dwelling, 141–150
"The Thinker as Poet: *Aus der Erfahrung des Denkens*" (Heidegger), 146
The Thinker (Rodin), 101–102, 105
thinking, and spaces, 164
third space, 159–163
Thøgersen, Ulla, 100
Thomas, Samira, 88–95
"Three" (Rajabali), 273–274
Thursday Next series (Fforde), 69–70
Tibetan Buddhism, 281–282
Tillich, Paul, 100
Time Quintet (L'Engle), 70–71
Tipping Point: The Age of the Oil Sands (Suzuki), 27
To enchanted lands that the story (of school) does not tell (Lewkowich), 140
To the Lighthouse (Woolf), 71
Tohoku region, Japan, 234–247
Tolkien, J.R.R., 70–71
"A Topography for Canadian Curriculum Theory" (Chambers), 78
topos, 78, 80–81, 83
Totaro, Paolo, 178–179
Toward a Poor Curriculum (Pinar and Grumet), 166
transitional spaces, 152–158
travel writing, 56–65
Treaty awareness, 3
Treaty Education, 2
Treaty Four Gathering, 7–8
Treaty Law School, 7
Treaty Walking, 2–4
Tremblay-Beaton, Katie, 20–25
Trimble, Stephen, 79, 80–81
trust, 236
tsunami, 234
Turner, Shirley, 207–223
Twitter, 227, 229
Tyler, Ralph, 142

UNESCO, 263
United Nations, 63
United Nations High Commissioner for Refugees
    (UNHCR), 258, 259, 260–261, 265
urgency, 224

"Viscera" (Snowher and Haytayan), 199
Vonnegut Jr., Kurt, 70
vulnerability in research, 186–198

Wagamese, Richard, 266
"Waking Up the Rake" (Turner), 219–221
walking, 2–4
Walsh, Susan, 301
"We Compose Our Own Requiem" (Sliep), 280–281
We state, 105–106
Wenjack (Boyden), 266
"What Are Poets For?" (Heidegger), 144
Where Hope Takes Root (Khan), 275
White, Boyd, 98–107
Wiebe, Sean, 85–86, 175–182
Williamson, Ben, 178
wind, 77
"Windows to a Place," 257–258
Winnicott, Donald, 286
witaskewin, 4–7
Wolsey, Thomas, 181
Woolf, Virginia, 71
World University Service of Canada, 263
writing
    liberating-constraint method, 81–82
    as method of inquiry, 201
    poetry inquiry, 82–83
    stream-of-consciousness, 71
    as therapeutic autoethnographic act, 280–281
    writing activities, 81–83
    See also poetry

Yallop, John J. Guiney, 130
Yamagishi, Toshio, 236
Yeoman, Elizabeth, 249
yogic philosophical approach, 208
Young, Kelly, 78–84
young children, 152–158

Zanazanian, Paul, 290–291